THROUGH THE EYES OF THE WORLD'S FIGHTER ACES

THROUGH THE EYES OF THE WORLD'S FIGHTER ACES

The Greatest Fighter Pilot's
of
World War Two

Robert Jackson

Pen & Sword
AVIATION

First published in Great Britain in 2007 by
Pen & Sword Aviation
an imprint of
Pen & Sword Books Ltd
47 Church Street, Barnsley, South Yorkshire S70 2AS

ISBN 978 1 84415 421 0

A CIP catalogue record for this book is
available from the British Library

Typeset in Palatino by
Phoenix Typesetting, Auldgirth, Dumfriesshire

Printed and bound in England by
Biddles Ltd, Kings Lynn

Pen & Sword Books Ltd incorporates the Imprints of Pen & Sword Aviation, Pen
& Sword Maritime, Pen & Sword Military, Wharncliffe Local History,
Pen & Sword Select, Pen & Sword Military Classics and Leo Cooper.

For a complete list of Pen & Sword titles please contact
PEN & SWORD BOOKS LIMITED
47 Church Street, Barnsley, South Yorkshire, S70 2AS, England
E-mail: enquiries@pen-and-sword.co.uk
Website: www.pen-and-sword.co.uk

Contents

Author's Note

When I was at school in the late 1940s and 1950s, many of the men whose names appear in this book – men who, in fact, had mostly been born only twenty years before those of my generation – were my boyhood heroes. Over the years that followed, in a career that was to encompass both flying and writing, I was privileged to meet many of them, and I think the last occasion on which so many aces could be found in one place was at the Battle of Britain 50th Anniversary Seminar, which was held at the RAF Staff College, Bracknell, in 1990, and which I was also privileged to attend.

Now, sadly, as I write this in the summer of 2006, almost all of them are gone. This book is a tribute to them all, of whatever nationality, who fought in every theatre during the Second World War. I have tried to present this work as a history of the world-wide air war as seen through the eyes of the men who fought it. It is the last book of this kind I shall ever write, for as I wrote it I felt an infinite sadness, such as never before, at the huge loss of so many young lives all those years ago, and at the madness that brought it all about.

I hope I have done their memory justice.

Robert Jackson, Darlington, County Durham, June 2006.

The Publishers have included several wartime photographs that cannot be reproduced to our usual high standards. It was felt that they were of sufficient interest to the reader to be included.

CHAPTER ONE

Destiny Can Wait: Poland, September 1939

It was a beautiful morning. Five thousand feet below the vibrating wings of the nine fighters the silver snake of the Vistula wound its way through the September colours of the Polish countryside, finally disappearing under a thin curtain of blue haze that shimmered over the horizon.

The fighters, gull-winged PZL P-11Cs of No. 142 Squadron, Polish Air Force, were fighting hard to gain altitude, their noses pointing towards the north-east. From the cockpit of his Jedenastka, as the little aircraft was known, Lieutenant Stanislaw Skalski scanned the horizon over to the left; the treacherous quarter of the sky from which the formations of the *Luftwaffe* came to unload their deadly cargoes on Polish targets, their guardian Messerschmitts roving everywhere to challenge Poland's pitifully outclassed fighter defences.

Skalski still found it hard to grasp that his country had been at war for twenty-four hours. He was still dazed by the sudden fury of the German attack the day before, in the early hours of 1 September 1939. Both he and his fellow pilots had known that war was inevitable, but now it had come it seemed unreal.

Slightly ahead of Skalski's aircraft and to the right, the Jedenastka flown by his squadron commander, Major Lesniewski, rose and fell gently on the currents of air, its red and white insignia and the distinctive wild-duck marking of 142 Squadron standing

1

out boldly against its drab camouflage. It could have been just another pre-war training flight; any moment now, thought Skalski, they would emerge from the nightmare and return to base for a meal.

It was then that he saw the enemy: a cluster of black dots, sliding low across the Vistula away to port. Opening the throttle, Skalski brought his P-11 alongside Lesniewski's aircraft and waggled his wings, pointing at the enemy formation. The squadron commander waved in acknowledgement and winged over into a dive, followed by the other eight fighters. The wind screamed past Skalski's open cockpit as the Jedenastka gathered speed, plummeting down towards what could now be recognized as slim, twin-engined Dornier 17 bombers; seven of them, holding a tight arrowhead formation.

With eyes only for the leading bomber, Skalski levelled out and sped towards it head-on, crouching low in the cockpit as tracer flickered past from the Dornier's nose gun. The Pole forced himself to hold the fighter steady as the distance between the two aircraft narrowed with terrifying speed, holding his fire until the bulk of the Dornier filled the sky ahead. A gentle pressure on the trigger, and a stream of bullets from the Jedenastka's twin 7.7mm machine guns tore into the enemy bomber at point-blank range. At the last moment, Skalski rolled the little fighter over on its back and pulled on the stick, passing inverted under the bomber. Pulling the P-11 up in a steep climbing turn, he looked back in time to see the Dornier nose-dive into a field and erupt in a tremendous explosion as its bomb load went off.

Pushing the throttle open, Skalski came up behind a second Dornier, closing in to fifty yards and firing in short bursts. Suddenly, a jet of flame burst from the Dornier's starboard engine. Skalski fired again, and this time the bomber's 'glasshouse' cockpit shattered into fragments. The stricken aircraft went into a steep climb, hung poised for an instant, and then spun into the ground.

Climbing, Skalski looked around. The remaining Dorniers had jettisoned their bombs and were heading flat out for the border. There was no sign of the other Polish fighters. Later, when he landed, Skalski learned that the rest of the squadron had attacked a second formation of nine Dorniers, shooting down five of them. With Skalski's two, that made seven – and all the Polish fighters had returned safely to base. Nevertheless, their victory did little to boost the Polish pilots' morale. For every German aircraft they

Stanislaw Skalski,
pictured later in the
war in the cockpit of a
Mustang fighter. He
was then a wing
commander in the
RAF, commanding
No. 317 Squadron.
(Polish Ministry of
Information)

destroyed there seemed to be ten more to take its place, and each pilot was grimly aware that if the Dorniers had been escorted by Messerschmitts, the outdated P-11s would have been massacred.

When, shortly after 0400 on 1 September 1939, it was reported that German reconnaissance aircraft were flying over Polish territory, the news came as no surprise to the Polish General Staff. The political unrest of the previous months had given the Poles ample warning of Germany's intention to invade, and plans to resist the invasion had already been in force for several weeks. On 29 August all Polish operational squadrons had been moved from their peacetime bases to specially-prepared secret airfields. But the defensive preparations came too late. Because of high-level confusion and the belief of the Polish High Command that a major European war was unlikely to begin before 1941 or 1942, plans for the expansion and modernisation of the Polish Air Force had been delayed time and again, with the result that when Poland finally went to war it was without modern aircraft or reserves and with critical shortages of spares, fuel and ammunition.

The last pre-war expansion scheme had been approved by the Polish government in 1936 – to be put into effect in 1941. It envisaged a total of seventy-eight operational squadrons with 642 first-line aircraft and 100 per cent reserves. The force was to consist of fifteen interceptor squadrons, each with ten fighters; ten twin-engined heavy fighter squadrons with ten aircraft each; fourteen light bomber-reconnaissance squadrons, each with ten aircraft; twenty-one bomber squadrons, each with six aircraft; and eighteen army co-operation squadrons, each with seven aircraft.

Home-produced combat aircraft were to be the mainstay of the force; new types as good as any in the world. They were to include 300 Jastrzab (Hawk) fighters, 300 P-46 Sum (Swordfish) bombers, 180 P-37 Los (Elk) medium bombers, 200 LWS-3 Mewa (Gull) army co-operation aircraft, a number of twin-engined Wilk (Wolf) heavy fighters and dive-bombers, and some 200 training aircraft. Then came the blow; the government announced cuts in the military budget, and the whole expansion scheme was placed in peril. Air Force Commander General Rayski resigned, and his post was taken over by General Kalkus – who promptly cancelled the order

The PZL P.24, seen here in Romanian markings, was basically an export version of the P.11, fitted with a Gnome-Rhone engine instead of a Bristol Mercury. (Source unknown)

for the 300 Jastrzebs on the grounds that the prototypes had proved to be badly underpowered, and ordered more P-11s to make up for the deficiency.

During 1939, the maximum normal monthly output of the Polish aircraft industry was 160 machines; with careful planning and shift-work, the figure could have been doubled at any time. Yet right up to the outbreak of war Poland's newest and largest factory –PZL WP-2 at Mielec, which was capable of producing 450 aircraft a year – employed only a skeleton staff engaged on completing a handful of Los bombers transferred from another factory. Incredibly, combat aircraft were still being exported at a time when the Polish Air Force was desperate for new machines.

At the end of August 1939, the Polish Air Force possessed some 436 operational aircraft and a personnel strength of 15,000 men. In the spring of that year, the first-line units had been reorganised around a combat nucleus consisting of a pursuit and a bomber brigade under the direct command of the C-in-C of the Polish armed forces, the remainder being split up among the six army regions. The Pursuit Brigade – whose main task was the defence of Warsaw – was equipped with four squadrons of P-11C fighters and one squadron of even older P-7As; eight more P-11C and two more P-7A squadrons served with the Army Air Force. The Bomber Brigade operated four and a half squadrons of Los bombers – a total of thirty-six aircraft – and five squadrons of Karas (Carp) light bombers. In the event of a German invasion, plans had been laid to rush British and French squadrons to Poland's aid; apart from helping indirectly by bombing targets in Germany, the RAF was to send 100 Fairey Battle light bombers and a squadron of Hawker Hurricane fighters to Polish bases, and the French planned to send five bomber squadrons.

But the expected help never arrived; the terrifying swiftness of the German *Blitzkrieg* put paid to all hope of that.

By midnight on 31 August, all Polish operational units were in place on their new bases. They were only just in time. At 0345 on 1 September, fifteen minutes before the German armies rolled into Poland, three Junkers Ju 87 Stuka dive-bombers of III Gruppe, *Stukageschwader* 1 (III StG 1) crossed the Vistula and bombed the railway line and demolition cables near the bridge at Dirschau, paving the way for the capture of this vital river crossing by an army task force. By 0500, flying over thick fog, four bomber groups had been committed to the battle; they were joined by two more in the course of the morning. All told, some 900 bombers and a similar number of fighters and army co-operation aircraft stood ready for the assault on Poland, but because of the adverse weather it was left to a relative handful of units to spearhead the attack.

The all-out assault on Warsaw, originally scheduled for 1 September, had to be postponed; dense cloud hung 600 feet over the Polish capital and visibility was reduced to less than 800 yards. And of the *Luftwaffe* bombers that did manage to get airborne, only a few succeeded in attacking their assigned targets. The weather cleared a little in the afternoon, and the main *Luftwaffe* attacks were directed against Polish troop concentrations, which included cavalry. The Stukas and the Henschel 123 ground-attack biplanes tore the Polish formations to shreds. After two hours of concentrated attacks by ninety German aircraft, the Polish cavalry Brigade had virtually ceased to exist.

It was in the late afternoon that the onslaught began in earnest, with all twenty bomber groups of *Luftflotte* 1 engaged in heavy attacks on airfields – mostly the Polish Air Force's peacetime airfields, now devoid of aircraft – ammunition dumps, railway and factory installations, anti-aircraft defences and the Baltic ports. Then, at 1700, three groups of Heinkel He 111s from Wunsdorf,

The Junkers Ju 87 Stuka dive-bomber led the air assault on Poland.
(Bundesarchiv)

The Messerschmitt Bf 110 'Destroyer' saw much action over Poland,
where it s heavy firepower proved damaging. (Bundesarchiv)

Delmenhorst and Langenhagen in northern Germany droned over
the frontier. Their target was Warsaw.

This time, the Polish Air Force was ready for them. So far, apart
from a few scattered combats by small units – such as the action of
No. 142 Squadron – the Poles had not met the *Luftwaffe* in strength.
But now, as the Heinkels and their escort of Messerschmitt 110
fighters approached Warsaw, two squadrons of the Pursuit
Brigade, Nos 111 ands 112, were already patrolling the capital. In
all, there were twenty-two Polish fighters to take on a hundred
German aircraft.

Led by Captain Sidorowicz, the eleven Jedenastkas of No. 111
'Kosciuszko' Squadron plummeted towards the bombers while the
fighters of No. 112 under Colonel Pawlikowski took on the fighter
escort. The Messerschmitt 110s of I/*Lehrgeschwader* 1, under the
command of Captain Fritz Schleif, spotted the Poles coming and
turned to meet them. A brief air battle ensued in which five P-11s
were shot down. The Germans lost two Heinkels and a Bf 110; the
remaining German bombers flew serenely on as though the one-
sided fight had never taken place, unloaded their bombs and
turned for home.

Ninety minutes later, Nos 111 and 112 Squadrons were in action
again against a second wave of bombers. Two Heinkels went

down, one of them under the guns of Captain Sidorowicz, who was himself wounded in the battle. But four more P-11s never returned to base. In just two air fights, the two Polish squadrons had lost fifty per cent of their aircraft. Altogether, the fighters of the Polish Pursuit Brigade claimed fourteen German aircraft destroyed on that day, but their own losses had been disastrous. Then the fog came down again, providing a respite for Warsaw and the exhausted Polish pilots.

The following morning dawned bright and clear, and began with an attack on a trio of airfields near Deblin by eighty-eight Heinkels of *Kampfgeschwader* 4. The hangars and runways were destroyed and a number of aircraft, mostly trainers, were left in flames after a series of strafing attacks by Messerschmitt 110s of *Zerstörergeschwader* (Destroyer Wing) 76. The Messerschmitts, however, did not haver things all their own way. In a sortie later that day, the pilots of ZG 76, patrolling over Lodz, became involved in a battle with Polish fighters. Two P-11s were shot down, but the Germans lost three 110s.

Then, suddenly, it was the turn of the Polish Bomber Brigade. Towards noon on 2 September, eighteen Karas aircraft of Nos 64 and 65 Squadrons attacked concentrations of German armour on the northern front. They inflicted heavy casualties, but severe light flak and the Messerschmitts sent seven of the Polish bombers crashing in flames, and three of those that returned to base were so badly damaged that they crashed on landing.

The Polish fighters fared a little better the next day, when they destroyed a number of German army cooperation aircraft in the Lodz sector. The day after, however, found the Messerschmitt 109s of JG 2 providing cover for the observation machines, and in the course of two air battles the the 109s, led by Lieutenant von Roon, destroyed eleven P-11s.

Meanwhile, the Bomber Brigade's four Los squadrons, as yet untouched by the German air attacks, had been bombed-up and fuelled on their airfields in readiness for a retaliatory bombing raid on Königsberg, in East Prussia. Throughout the first three days of the war, the aircrews waited in bitter frustration for the order to go. It never came. It was not until 4 September that Poland's most modern bomber saw combat, attacking German armour advancing on the central front.

The first Los attacks were a complete success. The bombers swept down on the 1st and 4th Panzer Divisions, pushing ahead of the Tenth Army, and released their bombs at low level with devastating effect. The two divisions lost twenty-eight per cent of their strength, and were thrown into temporary confusion when a second attack was made by twenty-eight Karas bombers from Nos 21, 22 and 55 Squadrons. Between 2 and 5 September the Bomber Brigade mounted nine major attacks from airfields between Radom and the river Bug against German armour and supply columns, but no fighter cover was available and the bombers suffered crippling losses.

Meanwhile, the dwindling numbers of Polish fighters battled on valiantly. During the first six days of the fighting the pursuit squadrons attached to the field armies claimed the destruction of sixty-three German aircraft, many of them army cooperation types. But with the breakdown of the supply system and the critical shortage of fuel, ammunition and replacement aircraft, the air force components were gradually withdrawn to the south to reinforce the hard-hit Pursuit Brigade in the Warsaw sector. Only one fighter unit, the Poznan Squadron, remained with the army to the end.

The Pursuit Brigade, fighting in the skies over Warsaw during the first week of September, destroyed forty-two enemy aircraft for the loss of thirty-seven of its own machines. Then, on the seventh, the remnants of the brigade were withdrawn from the Warsaw area to be reorganised. They never returned to the defence of the capital. Crippled by the lack of essential supplies and spares, the brigade ceased to exist as an effective fighting force, and between 7 and 17 September it accounted for only three enemy aircraft, at the same time losing seventeen more fighters.

The turning point of the war came on 8 September. On that day several Polish divisions were surrounded near Radom and shattered by Stuka attacks, while the 4th Panzer Division reached the outer defensive perimeter of the capital, Warsaw. In the air the Polish situation was desperate, with more and more aircraft being put out of action by the lack of spare parts and the shortage of fuel. Only the bomber brigade was still able to operate in any strength, owing to the fact that its main supply base at Deblin was still functioning. Nevertheless, attrition was high and the last major mission by Polish bombers was flown on 12 September. Scattered attacks were made after that date by aircraft operating in twos and threes, but they were of little significance.

Then, on 17 September, came a new development. Nine Soviet fighter-bombers swept down on a Polish airfield near Buczacz, strafing installations and the handful of aircraft that remained. In accordance with the secret agreement between Germany and the Soviet Union, an agreement that involved the partition of Poland between the two powers, Russian troops and armour came flooding into the country from the east.

On the following day, what was left of the Polish Air Force was evacuated to Romania. Among the aircraft that got away were thirty-nine Los and fifteen Karas bombers; ironically, they were pressed into service with the Romanian Air Force and later fought on the side of Germany during the invasion of Russia. Thirty-eight fighters of the Pursuit Brigade, many of them damaged and only just airworthy, were also evacuated.

During the entire campaign, the Polish fighters claimed the destruction of 126 aircraft. The Bomber Brigade claimed seven more and dropped a total of 350,000 lb of bombs, but the Polish Air Force had lost eighty-three per cent of its aircraft and thirty per cent of its aircrews.

There was one last act still to be played in the Polish tragedy. On four occasions between 18 and 24 September, *Luftwaffe* aircraft dropped leaflets over Warsaw, calling on the strongly-fortified Polish garrison to surrender. The Poles did not reply; the 100,000 troops in the besieged city dug themselves in still further and awaited the onslaught, many still expecting that Britain and France would come to their aid by launching an attack on Germany.

At eight o'clock in the morning of 25 September, wave after wave of bombers and dive-bombers began the systematic destruction of Warsaw. By noon an immense pall of smoke hung over the Polish capital, rising to a height of 10,000 feet and spreading out in a great banner across the countryside. And the assault continued; for hour after hour, 400 bombers of *Lufflotten* 1 and 2 dropped 500 tons of high explosive on the city, pounding street after street in smoking rubble.

Early the next morning, stunned by the ferocity of the attack, the garrison and what remained of the civilian population emerged from their shelters and surveyed the devastation around them. Heavy fighting was still in progress around the besieged city and German attacks were being held up everywhere, but faced with a continued massive onslaught from the air it was useless to resist. That same day, the garrison offered to surrender, and the capitulation was signed on 27 September.

The Polish fighter pilots who had escaped to Romania now

turned their faces towards France and Britain, in whose service they would ultimately fly and fight again. Many of the men like Stanislaw Skalski, would earn high rank and enormous prestige. As a symbol of their country's enslavement, the Polish eagle that was their flying badge would now bear a silver chain. The motto they adopted was 'Destiny Can Wait.'

CHAPTER TWO

RAF *v* Luftwaffe:
First Contacts

I t was the afternoon of 4 September, 1939, and the Second World War was four hours old. On the *Luftwaffe* airfield at Nordholz, guarding the approaches to the big German naval base at Wilhelmshaven, a sudden alert sent the pilots of 2 *Staffel*, *Jagdgeschwader* 77 – II/JG77 – racing for their Messerschmitt 109s. RAF bombers were attempting to attack warships moored off Wilhelmshaven, including the battlecruisers *Scharnhorst* and *Gneisenau*.

Climbing at full throttle over the anchorage, Sergeant Alfred Held sighted a twin-engined bomber heading for the cover of a bank of cloud. It was a Vickers Wellington. Held closed in, braving heavy fire from the Wellington's rear gun turret, and fired at the bomber in short, accurate bursts. The bomber began to stream petrol vapour, which quickly ignited, and went down in flames. Alfred Held's victim, which belonged to No. 9 Squadron, RAF Bomber Command, was the first RAF aircraft to fall to a *Luftwaffe* fighter pilot in the Second World War.

On 16 October, it was the *Luftwaffe*'s turn to venture into British territory for the first time. At 1300 hours, a force of Ju 88 bombers of 1 *Staffel*, *Kampfgeschwader* 30 (I/KG 30) took off from Westerland, on the island of Sylt, with orders to attack British warships – primarily the battlecruiser HMS *Hood* – at Rosyth, in the Firth of Forth. The Ju 88s flew in loose formation as they

The Vickers Wellington was robust and could absorb a huge amount of battle damage, but it went to war without self-sealing fuel tanks, which led to horrendous casualties. (Roger Hartley)

approached the target area seventy-five minutes later; their crews were confident that they would not encounter much fighter opposition, for German intelligence had indicated that the RAF had only a handful of obsolescent Gloster Gladiator biplane fighters in Scotland.

In fact, intelligence was wrong. RAF Fighter Command had two squadrons of Spitfires in Scotland, No. 602 at Drem in East Lothian and 603 at Turnhouse, near Edinburgh, while the Hurricanes of No. 607 Squadron were across the border at Acklington in Northumberland.

Sections of both Spitfire squadrons were 'scrambled' to intercept the raiders. The first to make contact with the enemy was Blue Section of No. 602 Squadron led by Flight Lieutenant George Pinkerton. Climbing to 10,000 feet with orders to patrol Turnhouse, The pilots sighted nine Ju 88s dive-bombing the warships off Rosyth and gave chase, latching on to the leading bomber as it pulled out of its dive and raced away over the water towards May

Germany's 'wonder bomber', the Junkers Ju 88. Its high speed made it a difficult target. (Bundesarchiv)

Island. The Junkers, flown by I/KG 30's commanding officer, Captain Helmut Pohle, was attacked by each of the three Spitfires in turn. The burst of fire killed Pohle's flight engineer and rear gunner and mortally wounded his navigator. First one engine failed as bullets tore into it, then the other.

Pohle spotted a trawler and turned towards it, using all his strength to keep the Junkers airborne. Then the bomber ploughed into the sea and he lost consciousness. The crew of the nearby trawler made no attempt to rescue the German airmen. Pohle and his badly injured navigator, who died the next day, were picked up by a Royal Navy destroyer; the pilot collapsed on its deck and regained consciousness five days later in Port Edwards Hospital.

Meanwhile, Red Section of No. 603 Squadron led by Squadron Leader E.H. Stevens, had pursued a twin-engined bomber north of Dalkeith. The aircraft was a Heinkel He 111 of *Kampfgeschwader* 26, its task to cause a diversion and also to observe the results of the Ju 88s' attack. Another section of No. 603 Squadron lead by Flight Lieutenant Pat Gifford, also joined the chase, and between them they sent the Heinkel down into the sea off Port Seton. Three crew members were picked up shocked but unhurt; the fourth was dead.

The CO of No. 602 Squadron, Squadron Leader Douglas Farquhar, and two of his pilots, Flight Lieutenant A.V.R. 'Sandy' Johnstone and Flying Officer Ferguson, had landed after an earlier

Spitfires in the sun. Early Fighter Command tactics involved tight
formation flying, which was quite useless in combat. (RAF)

and fruitless patrol a few minutes before the enemy bombers
appeared over the Firth. They now took off again and joined the
battle, in time to catch a Ju 88 heading east at 2000 feet off
Aberdour. Joined by two Spitfires of No. 603 Squadron, they made
repeated attacks on the Junkers and sent it down into the sea. None
of the crew escaped.

One of the pilots in George Pinkerton's section on this first day
of action for Fighter Command was Flying Officer Archie Mc-
Kellar. A diminutive man, only five feet four inches tall, McKellar
was born in Paisley in 1912 and had two childhood ambitions: to
become a plasterer and to learn to fly. Overcoming all manner of
famility objections, he achieved both. In 1936 he joined No. 602
(City of Glasgow) Squadron, Auxiliary Air Force – having already
gained his pilot's licence at the Scottish Flying Club – and was
called up for active service at the outbreak of war.

On 29 November 1939, Red Section of No. 602 Squadron,
including McKellar, was scrambled to intercept two Heinkels, one
circling on reconnaissance over Rosyth, the other over Dalkeith.
McKellar, guided by anti-aircraft fire, was the first to sight the
second Heinkel, and drew ahead of the rest of his section. Diving
into the attack, he opened fire from 200 yards, giving the bomber

two bursts. The first struck the Heinkel's wing root and killed its dorsal gunner, the second riddled its tail surfaces. McKellar drew away to make another firing pass, but was beaten to it by three Spitfires of No 603 Squadron, whose fire hit the bomber's starboard wing and cockpit area. The Heinkel crash-landed in a field at Kidlaw, near Haddington, with both gunners dead and the pilot wounded. Only the navigator was unhurt. It was the first enemy aircraft to fall on the British mainland in the 1939-45 war.

Four days before Christmas, McKellar was one of several pilots who were scrambled to intercept a formation of suspect aircraft approaching the Scottish coast. Over the Firth of Forth they sighted six twin-engined bombers with twin tail fins slipping in and out of cloud. Identifying them as Dornier Do 17s, the Spitfire pilots attacked and shot two of them down. But the bombers were not Dorniers; they were Handley Page Hampdens, returning from a raid on Sylt and, because of a bad navigational error, making landfall much too far to the south. They had been heading for RAF Lossiemouth, and their crews had mistaken the Firth of Forth for the Moray Firth. It was not the last time that such a tragedy would occur in the course of the war.

Although the two Auxiliary squadrons in Scotland had several skirmishes with the enemy in the winter months of 1939-40, results were mostly inconclusive, but on 13 January 1940, No. 602 Squadron, assisted by the Hurricanes of No. 111 Squadron from Acklington, shot a Heinkel into the sea off Carnoustie.

The majority of 'kills' so far had been shared between several pilots, although Squadron Leader Farquhar had been given the credit for the Junkers destroyed on 16 October. Farquhar's next chance came on 9 February, 1940, when, accompanied by Flying Officer A.M. Grant on a patrol over the mouth of the Firth of Forth, he was vectored (steered) by ground control to intercept an enemy aircraft some 20 miles out to sea. The enemy turned out to be a Heinkel 111, which dived into cloud as Farquhar attacked. The Spitfire pilot followed into the murk while Grant circled, waiting to catch the Heinkel in case it feinted back, but Farquhar caught up with it in a clear patch and opened fire, hitting it in one engine. The Heinkel turned in towards the coast and made a wheels-up landing near North Berwick. Three of its crew escaped unhurt, but Farquhar's machine-gun fire had seriously wounded the dorsal gunner, who died later in hospital.

Farquhar was in action again on 22 February. Together with

Flying Officer George Proudman, he attacked a Heinkel 111 at 1150 hours, his fire wounding the German dorsal gunner in both legs and putting the bomber's engines out of action. The enemy pilot turned in over the coast and made a skilful crash-landing at Coldinham, near St Abbs Head in Berwickshire. Farquhar, circling overhead, saw the crew scramble clear, assisting the injured gunner, and realised that they were about to set fire to their more or less intact aircraft, so he decided to land alongside and stop them. Unfortunately, the Spitfire hit a patch of mud as it rolled down the field and turned over on its back.

Farquher was unhurt, but hung helplessly upside down in his straps until the Heinkel's crew, seeing his predicament, ran across and helped him out of it – having first set light to the nose section of their bomber. Farquhar, seeing some armed Local Defence Volunteers approaching, advised the German crew to surrender to them, which they did. Farquhar collected their Luger pistols, and was promptly arrested by the LDV men, who took him for one of the enemy. He extricated himself from this fresh embarrassment by delving into his pocket and producing an Inland Revenue tax return form, which he had received that morning!

On 13 March 1940, Farquhar, with three victories to his credit, was promoted to wing commander and given command of RAF Martlesham Heath in Suffolk, a fighter station. He continued to fly in combat occasionally, and in November 1940, at the tail-end of the Battle of Britain, he shared in the destruction of two Junkers Ju 87 Stukas. Later in the war, he became Wing Leader of the Hornchurch Wing, flying a number of fighter sweeps over occupied France.

Few of the pilots who fought in those early skirmishes with the *Luftwaffe* went on to become aces by destroying five or more enemy aircraft. For example, of thirty-nine pilots who fought with No. 602 Squadron during the Battle of Britain, from July to October 1940, thirteen were killed or injured, and seven more lost their lives later in the war.

There were, of course, exceptions. Flight Lieutenant Robert Findlay Boyd, one of the 'original' auxiliaries, ended his war in the Far East with twelve victories, some of them Japanese, and retired as a group captain with a DSO, DFC and Bar; Sandy Johnstone, later to become an air vice-marshal, shot down at least six enemy aircraft; and Sergeant Andrew McDowall later became a wing commander with seventeen victories, going on to command the

RAF's first jet fighter squadron in 1944 and afterwards joining Rolls-Royce as a Service test pilot.

While the Auxiliary Air Force pilots were skirmishing with the *Luftwaffe* over Scotland in the closing weeks of 1939, the German fighter pilots were reaping their own harvest against RAF bomber command on the other side of the North Sea. On 3 December, twenty-four Vickers Wellington bombers of Nos 38, 115 and 149 Squadrons took off from their bases at Marham, Norfolk and Mildenhall, Suffolk to attack German warships off Heligoland in daylight. The Wellingtons ran through heavy anti-aircraft fire as they made their approach and two of them were hit, though not seriously. A few moments later the bombers were attacked from astern by Messerschmitt 109s and 110s. These attacks were in-effective and at least one of the fighters was damaged. The Wellingtons bombed from 8000 feet, but although some of their bombs fell in the target area no hits were registered on the warships. All the aircraft returned safely to base.

This operation seemed to justify the belief that a tight bomber formation was sufficient defence against fighter attacks in daylight. The Messerschmitt pilots had seemed wary of facing the Wellingtons' rear armament of four 0.303 calibre machine guns at a range closer than 400 yards, and although one straggling bomber had been attacked simultaneously by four fighters it had fought its way clear without having sustained a single hit. Bomber Command was sufficiently encouraged by the result of the 3 December raid to try again.

The opportunity came on 14 December, when it was reported that the cruisers *Nürnberg* and *Leipzig* had been torpedoed by a British submarine and were limping back to the Jade Estuary, badly damaged. Twelve Wellingtons of No. 99 Squadron set out from Newmarket to attack them. The weather was bad, and by the time the Dutch coast was sighted the Wellingtons were forced to fly at 600 feet or less in order to stay below the overcast. The pilots had been ordered not to attack unless they could bomb from at least 2000 feet; they nevertheless continued on course in the hope that the cloud would lift.

By this time they were coming under heavy and continuous fire from warships and armed merchantmen lying in the approaches to the estuary. At this low altitude the bombers presented excellent targets and several were hit. Suddenly, the flak died waway as enemy fighters came speeding up. They were the Messerschmitt

Messerschmitt Bf 109s. The 'Bf' appellation is an abbreviation of
Bayerische Motorenwerke, or Bavarian Aircraft Factories. The *Luftwaffe*
never used it, referring to the aircraft simply as the Me 109.
(Bundesarchiv)

109s of II/JG 27, led by Major Harry von Bülow, and this time the
pilots showed no hesitation in pressing home their attacks to point-
blank range. The Wellingtons' gunners accounted for one Bf 109,
which was seen to crash in flames, but the fighters destroyed five
bombers in a matter of minutes. A sixth Wellington crashed on
landing at Newmarket.

Despite the unfortunate outcome of this raid, another attack on
the German fleet was planned for 18 December. Twenty-four
Wellingtons of Nos 9, 37 and 149 Squadrons, loaded with 500 lb
semi-armour-piercing bombs, set out to attack any shipping
located in the Schillig Roads, Wilhelmshaven and the Jade Estuary.
The minimum bombing altitude was to be 10,000 feet, and crews
were instructed that if no worthwhile targets could be found, the
aircraft were to return with their bombs still on board.

About two-thirds of the way over the North Sea, two aircraft
dropped out with engine trouble. The remainder pressed on in
brilliant, cloudless weather, making a detour around Heligoland to
avoid the anti-aircraft batteries there and turning in towards
Wilhelmshaven from the north.

The first German fighters to intercept the bomber force were six
Messerschmitt 109s of 10/JG 26 from Jever, led by First Lieutenant

Johannes 'Macki' Steinhoff went on to become one of the highest-scoring German fighter pilots, with 176 victories, He was terribly burned in the crash of an Me 262 jet fighter in the closing weeks of the war, but survived. (Bundesarchiv)

Johannes 'Macki' Steinhoff. The 26-year-old pilot had originally joined the German Navy in 1934, but had transferred to the *Luftwaffe* in 1936. His leadership talents were such that, only three days later, he had risen to the position of group commander.

Steinhoff and his wingman, Corporal Hailmayr, each made two beam attacks on individual Wellingtons. Both bombers fell in flames. For 'Macki' Steinhoff, it was the first success on a road that would end, 167 victories and five and a half years later, in the blazing wreckage of a Messerschmitt 262 jet fighter – remarkably, he surviveed the accident, although he suffered terrible disfigurement.

After their first kills, the Bf 109s sheered off as the bombers flew at 13,000 feet through the heavy flak of the Wilhelmshaven defences. The Wellingtons crossed the naval base without dropping any bombs, then turned and crossed it again, still without bombing, before heading away towards the north-west. By this time, the Bf 109s of 10/JG 26 had been joined by the twin-engined Bf 110s of Zerstörergeschwader ZG 76 and the 109s of JG 77, and the combined force of fighters now fell on the Wellington formation as it passed to the north of the island of Wangerooge.

One of the pilots who entered the battle at this juncture was Lieutenant Helmut Lent, flying a Bf 110 of ZG 76. Sighting a pair of Wellingtons near Borkum Island, he attacked from the beam and then astern, killing the rear gunner. With the latter dead the bomber was defenceless against attacks from behind, and Lent continued to fire at it from close range until its engines began to stream smoke. It crash-landed on Borkum, and only one of its six-man crew got out alive. Lent went after the other bomber and made a determined attack on it, again from astern. Both its engines caught fire and it went down, breaking up on impact with the sea. Like Steinhoff, Lent had begun to climb a ladder of fame which would bring him 110 victories, mostly against the RAF's night bombers.

On this grim December day twelve Wellingtons failed to return, an appalling loss that highlighted the folly of sending bombers deep into enemy territory in broad daylight without fighter escort. After December 1939, RAF Bomber Command's policy was to operate increasingly under cover of darkness, while later in the war the Americans were to adhere to the theory that bomber formations with heavy defensive armament were capable of making successful daylight penetration attacks. They, too, would learn the hard way.

CHAPTER THREE

Phoney War

For the aircrews who faced each other on the Western Front in the autumn and winter of 1939, the term 'Phoney War' was a misnomer. From the very first week of the war, Allied and German fighters skirmished over the Maginot Line on an almost daily basis, except when the state of the weather precluded such meetings, and each side did its best to shoot down the other's reconnaissance aircraft. The consequences of sending unescorted bombers and reconnaissance aircraft had also been brought home to the RAF in France, where Fairey Battle light-bombers engaged in this kind of activity had suffered terrible losses. On 20 September 1939, for example, two out of three Battles of No. 88 Squadron were shot down by Bf 109s over Aachen. Then, on the last day of the month, five Battles of No. 150 Squadron were sent out to make a reconnaissance of the Saarbrücken area. They had just penetrated enemy territory when they were attacked by eight Bf 109s, and four of the Battles were shot down in as many minutes. After that, the Battles of the RAF's Advanced Air Striking Force in France were withdrawn from daylight operations.

At the outbreak of war in September 1939 the RAF had six fighter squadrons in France. Two of them, both equipped with Hawker Hurricanes – No. 1 at Vassincourt and No. 73 at Norrent-Fontes – had the task of assuring protection for the Battles of the Advanced Air Striking Force, while Nos 85 and 87 Squadrons, also equipped with Hurricanes, were deployed in support of the British Expeditionary Force's Air Component, together with Nos 607 and

Fairey Battle light-bombers of No. 88 Squadron accompanied by Curtiss Hawk 75As of GC I/5, 1939. (IWM)

615, which were equipped with Gloster Gladiator biplanes.

On 30 October 1939, a Dornier Do 17 reconnaissance aircraft flew directly over No. 1 Squadron's base at Vassincourt. It was intercepted and destroyed near Sauvigny by Pilot Officer P.W.O. 'Boy' Mould, who thus became the first RAF pilot to destroy an enemy aircraft on the Continent in World War Two. (The first enemy aircraft to be destroyed by the RAF over France in WW2 was actually claimed by Sergeant F. Letchford, the gunner in a Fairey Battle – the sole survivor of the three attacked by Bf 109s over Aachen on 20 September.)

Mould was later to lose his life on 1 October 1941, while commanding No. 185 Squadron in Malta. His Hurricane was hit by an Italian Macchi C.202 fighter; Mould baled out and came down in the sea, but he was never found.

On 2 November, a pair of Hurricane pilots of No. 87 Squadron, based at Merville, shot down a Heinkel He 111 at Staple; three of the crew were taken prisoner. No. 73 Squadron, which had now moved up to Rouvres, gained its first victory on 8 November 1939. At 1000 that morning, after a fifteen-minute battle that ended with a dive from 26,000 feet to ground level, a Hurricane pilot watched the Dornier 17 he had been chasing dive into the ground. The pilot was a young New Zealand Flying Officer named James Edgar Kain – 'Cobber' Kain, whose personality and prowess in the cockpit of a

A Dornier Do 17 reconnaissance aircraft brought down by RAF fighters over France, 1939. (ECP Armées)

fighter were to capture the imagination of the British and French public during the months to come. Kain, who was twenty-one when war broke out, had joined the RAF in 1937. He had already learned to fly in New Zealand. He gained his second victory, another Dornier 17, on 23 November 1939, just before the onset of bad weather severely curtailed flying in France for several weeks. It was 3 March 1940 before he once more got to serious grips with the enemy.

November 1939 was a hectic month for the French fighter pilots, too. On the day 'Cobber' Kain gained his first victory, the Germans lost a second Dornier, shot down over Hanviller by the Curtiss Hawks of Groupe de Chasse (GC) II/5.

In an attempt to counter the threat of the fast Dornier 17 intruders, seven fighter defence-sectors were set up in mid-November within the Northern and Eastern Zones of Air Operations. On the day this system came into being – 21 November – Sergeant Sales, a pilot of GC II/5 with three confirmed victories, destroyed a Do 17 of long-range reconnaissance unit 3(F)22 over Eischeville. At about the same time, two Bf 109s were shot down in flames over Saverne by six Curtiss Hawks of GC II/4.

The next day, the French fighters flew their biggest number of sorties so far – 203 – and claimed a Do 17 probably destroyed by the Morane 406s of GC III/2 over Cambrai, a Heinkel 111

HM King George VI inspecting units of the BEF Air Component in
France, late 1939. Picture shows Hurricanes of No. 85 Squadron and
Gladiators of 615. (IWM)

destroyed near Thorout in Belgium by Curtiss Hawks of I/4 and
Hurricanes of the Air Component, and a Do 17 shot down over
Mooswald by four Morane 406s of GC II/7. The French lost one
fighter, a Curtiss Hawk of GC II/4, shot down at Phalsbourg by a
Bf 109 flown by First Lieutnenant Helmuth Wick of 3/JG 2. In the
course of the day the French captured a Bf 109 virtually intact
when, having suffered battle damage, it landed on Strasbourg-
Neuhof airfield. Two more 109s of the same unit (JG 51) were shot
down by Allied anti-aircraft fire, while two more 109s were forced
to make emergency landings behind their own lines after a fight
with six Morane 406s of GC I/3.

All in all, 22 November had been a hectic day, and the 23rd
followed the same pattern. This time, French and British fighters
joined forces to claim several victories. It was a bright, clear day,
and from early morning plots came in indicating enemy air activity
throughout the seven Allied fighter defence-sectors. No. 1
Squadron destroyed two Dorniers during the morning, and shortly
after midday three Hurricanes combined with Curtiss Hawks of

GC II/5 to shoot down a Heinkel of I/KG 53 over Macker. No. 73 Squadron also claimed two Dorniers (one of them 'Cobber' Kain's), and shared a third that had been damaged by French pilots of GC I/5. Two more Dorniers were shot down by GC II/3 and Cotebrune and Brassy-sur-Meuse, bringing the day's total tally to eight. One Hurricane of No. 1 Squadron had its engine knocked out by machine gun fire from a Dornier and had to make a forced landing, although the pilot was unhurt; a second suffered damage to its fin and rudder when a Curtiss clipped it with a wingtip while the fighters were attacking the He 111 near Metz.

December was a dull month by comparison, with bad weather severely restricting air activity on both sides. Reconnaissance aircraft, however, took advantage of the occasional break to slip across the lines, and on 20 December a Potez 63 of Groupe de Reconnaissance (GR) I/33 carrying out a photo-recce mission between Mainz and Frankfurt was shot down by flak after being damaged by enemy fighters. The crew of three baled out. The next day, a dozen Messerschmitts attacked half as many Moranes of GC II/7, escorting a Potez 63 over the front line, and in the course of a ten-minute battle the French pilots claimed two kills and one probable for the loss of one of their own number.

The Potez 63 reconnaissance aircraft suffered fearsome losses in the fighting over France, and had to be heavily escorted. This example bears Vichy French markings and was pictured over North Africa in 1942.
(ECP Armées)

The New Year brought with it a spell of clearer weather, and with it an early success for the French fighters. On 3 January they flew 107 sorties, and pilots of GC II/7 claimed a Bf 109 destroyed and a second Bf 109 probably destroyed, together with a Dornier 17. A week later, on the 10th, fifteen Curtiss Hawks of GC II/5 destroyed two more 109s; a third Messerschmitt caught fire in the middle of the dogfight for no apparent reason and crashed near Kurtzenhausen. The pilot, *Oberfeldwebel* Balka, was seriously hurt when he struck the tail unit on baling out. A fourth 109 was destroyed that day by the gunner of a Potez 63 of GR II/55, but the French aircraft was itself shot down by five more 109s of I/JG 54.

The next day – apart from the destruction of two Dornier 17s by pilots of GC I/5 – was characterised by a remarkable event. That morning, a Messerschmitt 108 Taifun communications aircraft carrying a Major Reinberger, a liaison officer with *Luftflotte* 2, to a conference in Cologne took off from Munster in poor visibility and set course south-westwards. However, the Bf 108's pilot soon became lost in the murk, and a strong easterly wind carried the little machine across the Rhine without either of the occupants realising it. Then the engine failed and the pilot had to make a forced landing, bringing the aircraft to rest more or less intact in a field.

The crew learned from a farmer that they had come down in Belgium, not far from Malines. It was a serious error, for in his briefcase Reinberger carried nothing less than the German operational plans for the coming offensive on the western front. Reinberger and his pilot were arrested before they had a chance to burn the papers, which were duly turned over to the Belgian authorities. The documents were examined by Belgian, British, Dutch and French intelligence experts – who came to the conclusion that the whole thing was an elaborate hoax and that the Messerschmitt 108 had deliberately landed on Belgian territory. So nothing was done, and the steps that might have averted catastrophe five months later were never taken.

Meanwhile, the war in the air went on. On 13 January 1940, two Curtiss Hawks of GC I/4 became involved in an epic chase after their pilots, Capitaine Barbier and Sergent Lemare, sighted a contrail over the coast at Gravelines. At its head was a Dornier 17, making for England at over 30,000 feet. The two French pilots shadowed the Dornier as it flew in a lazy curve over the English coast and turned out to sea once more. Still they followed it, reluctant to destroy it over the Channel; if the Dornier went down into the sea their victory might not be confirmed. So they waited until it was over land once more, then closed in and poured their ammunition into it. The Dornier went down in flames and exploded near Hondschoote.

It was in January 1940 that one Frenchman began to establish a reputation as a first-rate fighter pilot. He was Edmond Marin la Meslée, who flew Curtiss Hawks with GC I/5. One of his early air battles is described in his own words:

I was on patrol with my wing-man, Sous-Lieutenant Rey, at 8000 metres when I suddenly spotted a splendid Dornier 17, heading for Belgium about 200 metres below us and two kilo-metres away. I warned my wingman, then placed the sun at my back and attacked from astern. The German machine-gunner opened fire when I was about 400 metres away . . . I manoeuvred to throw him off his aim, closing all the time, and opened fire at 200 metres. I gave him several bursts, closing right in until I was obliged to break off and let my wingman have his turn. The German gunner was firing at me all the time, but his bullets went wide. I could see my own bullets hitting the Dornier's fuselage and engines, and some debris struck my aircraft.

The Dornier flew straight on, and I came in for a second attack. More debris hit my aircraft, and oil spattered my wind-screen. I thought that I had been hit and broke away, but just as Rey was preparing to fire the Dornier went into a vertical dive. He must have been hit pretty badly, because he was losing fuel and his engines were belching smoke. Rey fired in the dive, broke away, and I took over. The Dornier levelled out at 2000 metres, then went into a dive once more and turned towards the frontier. We took it in turns to fire at him, not giving him a moment's respite. The German gunner was still firing and it seemed likely that the Dornier might escape, because we were very close to the border. I remember shouting words of encouragement to my wingman. We were now very close to the ground, so close in face that I had to break off an attack. A moment later, I had the immense satis-faction of seeing the Dornier make a belly landing in a field. On returning to base I learned that he had come down only one kilometre from the frontier; the crew had been taken

Edmond Marin la Meslée, one of France's finest fighter pilots, was killed tragically close to the end of the war in Europe. (ECP Armées)

prisoner, and only one of them was wounded. My aircraft was unscathed, although my wingman's had been hit five times.

After the Battle of France, Marin la Meslée escaped to North Africa with the other surviving pilots and eventually took command of GC I/5. In August 1944 this unit, equipped now with Republic P-47 Thunderbolts, took part in the invasion of southern France. On 4 February 1945, while carrying out a ground attack mission against enemy ground forces near Colmar, Edmond Marin la Meslée was shot down by flak and killed.

The 'Phoney War' period also witnessed the rise of Germany's leading air aces, many of whom had fought in the Spanish Civil War, where they had gained their early victories. Some had added to their scores during the brief campaign in Poland. The highest-scoring German pilot of the Polish campaign, and the first German ace of World War Two, was *Hauptmann* Hannes Gentzen, who scored seven victories in a Bf 109; but one pilot had already gained twice that many kills during the air fighting in Spain.

His name was Werner Mölders, who in Spain had commanded the 3rd Staffel of *Jagdgruppe* J88 (III/J88). In July 1938 this unit received its first Messerschmitt Bf 109C-1 fighters, and it was while flying one of these aircraft that Mölders fought his first air combat. While carrying out a patrol over the Northern Front, the pilots of III/J88 encountered a strong formation of Russian-built Polikarpov I-16 fighters. Mölders soon got on the tail of one of them, but was over-excited and opened fire while the range was still much too great. The I-16 escaped, but a few seconds later Mölders attacked another. This time there was no mistake; the enemy fighter burst into flames and crashed after Mölders opened fire at point-blank range.

By the time Mölders' tour of duty ended in Spain in Otober 1938 he had destroyed fourteen enemy aircraft, making him the top-scoring German pilot in the Civil War. More important than that was the experience he gained in the science of air fighting, experience that was put to good use on his return to Germany. Together with other leading German pilots who had served in Spain, Mölders later virtually rewrote the *Luftwaffe*'s manual of fighter tactics, helping to devise the combat formations which, a few months later, were to prove far superior to any employed by the German Air Force's opponents.

The outbreak of the Second World War in September 1939 found Mölders in command of III/JG 53, and it was not long before the unit was in action. On 20 September, six Curtiss Hawks of GC II/5 were escorting a reconnaissance aircraft over the front line when the top flight of three fighters was attacked by four Bf 109s, led by Mölders. The Frenchmen broke away, but they were too late.

Mölders got on the tail of a Curtiss and sent it down on fire; the pilot baled out. In the air battle that followed a second Curtiss went down, while the French pilots accounted for a 109.

The next day, three Messerschmitts led by Mölders pounced on a luckless Potez 63 reconnaissance aircraft over Altheim. A very gallant French pilot in a Morane 406 fighter came to the Potez' rescue, but he was too late and the

Known as 'Daddy' to his fellow pilots, Werner Mölders was an outstanding tactician. (Bundesarchiv)

Messerschmitts attacked him in turn. Mölders allowed his wingmen to get in the first bursts, then he closed in and gave the Morane the coup de grace. The French pilot baled out, but his parachute failed to open.

At the end of January the weather clamped down once more, remaining virtually solid throughout February. The wiser unit commanders, realising that the tempo of air operations would be stepped up considerably with the spring weather, took advantage of the respite to send as many of their personnel as possible on home leave.

They returned, at the beginning of March, in time to take part in some of the most hectic air battles of the war so far. Once again, it was the French who scored the first victories of the month, two Dornier 17s being destroyed within minutes of each other by pilots of GC II/7 and III/6. Later, six Moranes were attacked by twelve Bf 109s of I/JG 53 while escorting a reconnaissance aircraft over Saarbrücken and one of the French pilots was mortally wounded, although he managed to bring down his aircraft safely in friendly territory. A second French pilot was wounded the next day in a scrap over Metz between the Moranes of GC II/3 and the 109s of Werner Mölders' III/JG 53.

On 2 March it was the RAF's turn to score. Two Hurricane pilots of No. 1 Squadron shot down a Dornier, but one of them – Flying Officer Mitchell – was subsequently killed while trying to make a forced landing after the Dornier's bullets had knocked out his engine. The next day, the RAF pilots had their revenge when they shot down a Heinkel 111 in no-man's land. The German crew were seen to escape.

The pilots of No. 73 Squadron were also active on 3 March. At 1300, Flying Officer Kain and a sergeant pilot were patrolling the front line at 20,000 feet after escorting a Potez 63 when they sighted anti-aircraft bursts over Thionvelle and flew towards them. A minute later Kain spotted seven He 111s some 5000 feet higher up and at once gave chase, gradually leaving the other Hurricane behind. Suddenly, as he gained on the Heinkels, Kain heard a warning shout from his number two; they were being shadowed by six Bf 109s. Kain looked round, just in time to see a 109 blazing away at him. Cannon shells struck the Hurricane's fuselage and then the 109 was past and diving away. Almost at once Kain was attacked by a second 109, which also scored hits on his aircraft. This time, Kain was ready for the enemy fighter as it overshot; he gave it three short bursts and it went down, trailing black smoke.

Kain, who by this time was well inside Germany, began a turn towards the Allied lines, only to be hit by a third Messerschmitt. The Hurricane's engine stopped with a loud bang and smoke filled the cockpit. Unable to see his compass, Kain pointed the nose of his aircraft in what he hoped was the direction of Metz and trimmed the Hurricane for a long glide, turning his oxygen full on in order to breathe. A few minutes later, by which time flames were breaking through into the cockpit, he crossed the front line and made a perfect emergency landing on a French airfield. Kain was awarded the Distinguished Flying Cross for this action. A few days later he brought his score to five enemy aircraft destroyed, so becoming the first RAF 'ace' of World War Two.

Kain's 109 was No. 73 Squadron's eleventh victory. The unit had seen more action than No. 1 Squadron, primarily because its base at Rouvres was on one of the main routes followed by the German reconnaissance aircraft on their way into France. On 9 March, however, No. 1 Squadron came back into the limelight with another 'first' – a Messerschmitt 110. Three Hurricanes sighted

Flying Officer James Edgar 'Cobber' Kain, the New Zealander who became the RAF's first air ace of World War Two, seen in the cockpit of his Hurricane. (IWM)

nine Bf 110s north of Metz, isolated one and shot it down. It was No. 1 Squadron's second enemy fighter that day; earlier, a Bf 109 was shot down by Flying Officer Paul Richey, but this aircraft went down in enemy territory and was not confirmed from the ground.

No. 1 Squadron had a brush with the 109s again on 29 March, when three Hurricanes were attacked over Bouzonville by a mixed group of nine 109s and 110s. A 109 was shot down at Apach and a 110 north-west of Bitche; one Hurricane pilot was killed while making an emergency landing at Brienne-le-Chateau.

For the French fighters, March ended with a tragedy. On the last day of the month, eleven Morane 406s of GC III/7 were patrolling the Morhange area between 20,000 and 25,000 feet in four separate, widely-spaced flights when they were attacked by twenty Messerschmitt 109s. In less than five minutes, two of the Moranes were shot down in flames, a third crashed out of control, two more were written off after making forced landings and two received such severe battle damage that, although they returned to base, they were classed as irreparable.

Enemy activity continued to be devoted mainly to reconnaissance during the early days of April, although packs of fighters patrolled the front line and became increasingly aggressive. Sometimes, two or three squadrons of Messerschmitt 110s carried out a sweep over French territory as far as Metz of Nancy. The Bf 110s usually stayed up very high and only engaged in combat when pressed by Allied fighters. It appeared that the *Luftwaffe* was experimenting with new battle formations and offensive tactics, a sure sign that something big was in the offing.

It was: on 9 April, 1940, the Germans struck with numbing speed. Their objective was not France, as everyone had expected, but Norway.

CHAPTER FOUR

Battle over the Fjords

On 9 April 1940, the day that German forces invaded Norway, the tiny Royal Norwegian Air Force possessed only one fighter squadron. Based at Fornebu airfield, and charged with the defence of Oslo, it was equipped with nine Gloster Gladiators, supplied by Britain a couple of years earlier. The handful of Norwegian pilots fought valiantly and succeeded in destroying a number of enemy aircraft. With the exception of one pilot who was badly wounded, the rest survived the encounters and would have gone on fighting to the last, had not their airfields and aircraft been destroyed by German bombing.

In RAF service, the Gladiator had been mostly replaced – except overseas – by Hurricanes and Spitfires, but one unit of RAF Fighter Command was still using it; this was No. 263 Squadron, which had re-formed at Filton, near Bristol, on October 1939. On 24 April 1940, eighteen Gladiators of this squadron flew from the aircraft carrier HMS *Glorious* to land on the frozen surface of Lake Lesjaskog. This was about forty miles from Andalsnes, where a British infantry brigade had landed five days earlier. A second British brigade and and three battalions of French Chasseurs had also been landed at Namsos, farther north, the idea being that these forces would advance jointly to recapture the German-held port of Trondheim. The Gladiators were to provide the necessary fighter support.

Conditions at Lesjaskog were appalling. Working in sub-zero temperatures, a handful of airmen worked all night to refuel and

34

The Gloster Gladiator biplane fighter bore the brunt of the RAF's air campaign in Norway. (Jim Rosser)

rearm the Gladiators; even then, when they checked the aircraft at daybreak they found that the carburettors and control surfaces were frozen solid. Two Gladiators were made airworthy by 0500, and these took off to patrol the lake. They had not been airborne long when their pilots sighted a Heinkel 115 reconnaissance seaplane, which they attacked and shot down. Under cover of the diversion, a Heinkel 111 flew across the lake unopposed and dropped a stick of bombs, but without causing any damage.

The Gladiators flew in support of the ground forces throughout the morning of 26 April, often taking off while the lake was under attack. No. 263 Squadron suffered its first loss at 1100 when a Gladiator was destroyed on the ground by a low-flying Heinkel; its pilot, Sergeant Forrest, had just stepped clear of his aircraft. In the space of an hour, nine more Gladiators were destroyed, all on the ground, in exchange fore one Heinkel 111 shot down by Flight Lieutenant Randolph Mills. At noon, an intruding Heinkel 111 was attacked by a section of Gladiators led by Pilot Officer Sidney McNamara; the bomber went into a spin and crashed on the edge of the lake.

Early in the afternoon, the surviving Gladiators shot down

another Heinkel and badly damaged its companion, which limped away trailing smoke. Not long afterwards, Squadron Leader John Donaldson and Flight Lieutenant Mills caught a Heinkel near Andalsnes and shot it down into a ravine. That evening, Mills became involved in a running fight with half a dozen Junkers Ju 88s. His ammunition ran out, followed by his fuel, and he had to make a forced landing. He had just finished surveying the bullet holes in the battle-worn Gladiator's fuselage and wings when two Heinkels flew over at low level and destroyed it with machine-gun fire.

When darkness fell, the surface of Lake Lesjaskog was pitted and torn by countless bomb craters. Only four Gladiators were left now, and these were evacuated to Andalsnes. This small force was further depleted on the morning of 27 April, when Pilot Officer Michael Craig-Adams took off on a reconnaissance sortie. He had been flying for about ten minutes when the Gladiator's Mercury engine seized. The pilot baled out and made his way safely back to Andalsnes.

It was the end. Later in the day the last fuel stocks ran out, and the next day the squadron personnel received orders to destroy their remaining aircraft. That evening they embarked on the cargo vessel *Delius*, and after running the gauntlet of several dive-bombing attacks off the Norwegian coast, they reached Scapa Flow naval base in the Orkneys on 1 May without further incident.

On 14 May, No. 263 Squadron, now re-equipped with Gladiator Mk IIs, once more sailed for Norway aboard HMS *Glorious*. This time, the aircraft were to fly from the carrier to a landing ground at Bardufoss, near Narvik, from where they were to provide air support for the Allied forces' second Norwegian expedition. It was 21 May before the carrier reached her flying-off station, and the first two sections of Gladiators, each led by a Fairey Swordfish of the Fleet Air Arm, took off from her flight deck in sleet. With the weather deteriorating, one section returned to the carrier and landed-on safely; the other, lost in fog and snow, crashed headlong into a mountainside at Soreisa. The Swordfish crew was killed, as was one of the Gladiator pilots, Pilot Officer Richards; the other, Flight Lieutenant Mills, was badly injured.

An advance force of eight Gladiators eventually reached Bardufoss on 22 May, and went into action immediately. On that day, No. 263 Squadron suffered its first aircrew loss in action when Pilot Officer Craig-Adams failed to return. His body was found in the wreckage of his aircraft, which lay close to that of a Heinkel 111. The opinion was that the two had collided during an air combat. The remaining Gladiators arrived the next day, making a total of fourteen airworthy aircraft, and soon after their arrival Sergeant Basil Whall shot down a Heinkel 111; however, his own aircraft ran out of fuel and he was forced to bale out.

On the morning of 24 April, four Messerschmitt 110s strafed the squadron's airfield. They were met with very accurate anti-aircraft fire, and after making a couple of firing passes they drew off to a safe distance and circled watchfully. Pilot Officer Francis Grant-Ede took off and attacked the enemy formation single-handed, and after a brief exchange of fire the Messerschmitts dived away and disappeared.

Grant-Ede was airborne again that afternoon. With Flying Officer William Riley, he came upon a lone Heinkel 111 flying at 500 feet over Bardufoss. He fired a burst from close astern, killing the rear gunner, then half-rolled away. Riley attacked in turn, putting the Heinkel's starboard engine out of action, then a third Gladiator, flown by Flight Lieutenant Caesar Hull, dropped into the fight and riddled the bomber's port motor. The bomber slewed round in a diving turn and crash-landed near Salanger, its crew being taken prisoner.

The next day, while on patrol, Grant-Ede encountered a big four-engined Junkers Ju 90 transport at 15,000 feet north of Harstadt. He closed in, firing two bursts at short range, and the aircraft went down into the sea off Dyroy Island. Grant-Ede caught a second Ju 90 on a subsequent sortie, killing the transport's mid-upper gunner and putting all four engines out of action with accurate burst of fire from close range. The aircraft crashed in flames on Finnoen Island, south of Narvik. A third Ju 90 was shot down that evening near Harstadt by Pilot Officer Phillip Purdy and Sergeant Herbert Kitchener.

The following day, 26 May, saw No. 263 Squadron engaged in some bitter air fighting. During one of the first sorties of the day, Flight Lieutenant Alvin Williams and Sergeant George Milligan destroyed a Junkers 88 over Skaanland, and a little later in the day a section of three Gladiators flown by Caesar Hull, Lieutenant Tony Lydekker, RN, and Pilot Officer Jack Falkson deployed to the airstrip at Bodo, near the front line. Soon after their arrival, Hull attacked Heinkel 111 over Saltefjord and set one of its engines on fire, and immediately afterwards he sighted a Junkers Ju 52 transport flying in formation with another Heinkel. The latter turned away, and Hull shot the Junkers down in flames.

Hull turned to intercept two more Heinkels, which eluded him, but then he sighted a pair of Ju 52s heading for a cloud bank. He attacked one of them, using the last of the ammunition in his wing guns, and shot it down. Almost at once, he sighted another He 111 below him and dived to attack it. Only his nose machine-gun was working, but he succeeded in damaging the enemy bomber, which departed with smoke trailing from one engine. Hull had barely sufficient fuel to regain Bodo, where he landed at dusk.

Meanwhile, back at Bardufoss, it had been a hectic day for the rest of No. 263 Squadron. Some vicious fighting had taken place over Harstadt when Pilot Officers Purdy and Michael Bentley attacked six Dornier 17s and shot down one each, subsequently driving off the others. On a later patrol over Harstadt, Flying Officer Riley and Pilot Officer Parnall came upon a formation of Heinkel 111s which they attacked. Two Heinkels went down in flames, but Riley was wounded in the neck and hands.

On this day, the Gladiators were joined at Bardufoss by fifteen Hawker Hurricanes of No. 46 Squadron under the command of Squadron Leader Kenneth Cross. These aircraft had, in fact, accompanied No. 263 Squadron on its first expedition to Norway aboard HMS *Glorious*, but had been unable to fly off because their intended landing ground at Skaanland had not been ready. Eighteen Hurricanes were actually flown off the carrier on 26 May, with Skaanland as their destination, but the first three to land nosed over in soft ground and so the rest were diverted to Bardufoss. The Hurricanes scored their first success on 28 May, when Pilot Officer McGregor destroyed a Ju 88 over Tjelbotn, and later that day a section of Hurricanes surprised two Dornier Do 26 seaplanes on the water at Rombaksfjord, disembarking troops, and destroyed both of them.

Meanwhile, on 27 May, Bodo airstrip and the adjacent town had been heavily bombed and strafed by Ju 87 Stukas and Messerschmitt 110s. Hull and Lydekker took off to intercept, each shooting down a Ju 87, but Hull was attacked by a Bf 110 and forced down in the hills, wounded in the head and knee by cannon shell splinters. He was evacuated to England two days later Lydekker was also wounded in the neck and shoulder, and – unable to land at Bodo because of the prowling Messerschmitts – he flew his aircraft to Bardufoss, where he crash-landed.

General Claude Auchinleck , later
to distinguish himself in the
Western Desert, commanded the
Allied Expeditionary Force in
Norway. (IWM)

The *Luftwaffe* made few
sorties into No. 263 Squadron's
sector during the next five days,
and the exhausted pilots and
ground crews were able to
snatch a few hours' well-earned
rest. The only successful combat
took place on 28 May, when
Flight Lieutenant Williams
caught a Heinkel 111 attacking
shipping in Ofotfjord and drove
it off with both engines pouring
smoke. During this week of comparative respite, the squadron flew
about thirty sorties against ground targets, one of which was the
German Army Headquarters at Hundalen.

The end in Norway, however, was fast approaching. On 3
June, General Claude Auchinleck, commanding the Allied
Expeditionary Force, gave orders for evacuation and, as soon as its
reconnaissance aircraft detected what was happening, the
Luftwaffe renewed its heavy air attacks on both shipping and
ground forces in the area of Narvik, the principal port of evacuation. Narvik was to have been covered by the Hurricanes of No. 46
Squadron, but owing to the unserviceability of Skaanland the
pilots found themselves at a disadvantage, for Bardufoss was a
considerable distance away and the time that could be spent over
Narvik was consequently short. Nevertheless, the Hurricane pilots
did what they could, destroying or driving off several enemy
aircraft as the evacuation got under way, and so did their
colleagues of 263 Squadron. Between dawn and dusk on 2 June the
Gladiators flew fifty-five sorties, and the day saw some magnificent air battles.

One of the pilots involved was Pilot Officer Louis Jacobsen, a 25-
year-old New Zealander from Wellington who had joined the RAF
in 1938. During the First Norwegian Expedition he had twice

engaged enemy aircraft, being credited with one He 111 destroyed and another damaged.

Now, on 2 June, Jacobsen took off with Pilot Officer Wilkie to patrol the area between Narvik and the Swedish border. At 1445 they encountered two Junkers 88s, and Jacobsen made a beam attack on the leader while Wilkie went after the second Junkers. As Wilkie closed in, his Gladiator was hit by fire from the Ju 88's rear gunner and spun down to crash. The Junkers escaped into a bank of cloud across the Swedish border.

Meanwhile, Jacobsen had opened fire on the leading Junkers from 300 yards, but the German pilot opened his throttles and the fast twin-engined bomber quickly outpaced the Gladiator. Jacobsen chased it into Swedish airspace and fired again from 400 yards, without seeing any result. At that moment the second Junkers reappeared from cloud cover, passing directly in front of Jacobsen's fighter. He opened fire and hit the enemy aircraft, which went into an apparently uncontrolled dive. As the Junkers was flying at only 300 feet, and the terrain below was mountainous, it was unlikely that the German would have been able to pull out.

Jacobsen himself narrowly escaped colliding with the mountain peaks. Climbing at full throttle, he turned back into Norway, and soon afterwards he encountered a mixed formation of He 111s and Ju 88s flying at low level. He turned behind a Heinkel and fired a burst into its forward fuselage. The pilot was probably hit, as the bomber suddenly reared up, stalled, flicked over on its wingtip and exploded on the ground near Bjornfjell. Immediately afterwards Jacobsen was subjected to a head-on attack by three He 111s and a Ju 88. The New Zealander took evasive action and turned in behind one of the Heinkels, firing a three-second burst into it. Another Heinkel attacked him head-on and he fired a three-second burst into this bomber too before he was forced to break away. The bomber went down in a spiral dive, apparently out of control.

Jacobsen now found himself inside a circle of six He 111s and two Ju 88s which attacked him from above, below and head-on, firing at him with their nose guns. Jacobsen was now fighting for his life. One of the Gladiator's bracing wires was shot away and the engine was hit. Oil sprayed over the windscreen, and through it Jacobsen saw the vague outline of a Heinkel. He fired, and the bomber glided earthwards with both engines stopped.

His ammunition exhausted, Jacobsen managed to evade his

attackers and limp back to base. Later, the wreckage of three Heinkels was found just inside the Swedish border, and it was learned that two Ju 88s had also crashed in that area. As Jacobsen was the only pilot to have engaged Junkers 88s on 2 June, apart from the unfortunate Wilkie, the probability is that they were his victims, together with the three Heinkels. Taking the New Zealander's kill earlier in the campaign into account, this would give him six victories, and so make him the only pilot to become an ace in Norway.

Another pilot who had success on 2 June was Sergeant Herbert Kitchener. His own combat report tells the story.

I took off in Gladiator N5905 to patrol Narvik district. After being airborne I observed four He 111s in formation 2000 feet above me. After about three minutes, with F/Lt Williams, I attacked the formation. The He 111s proceeded to dive. Between us we caught up the straggling Heinkel. I attacked from the beam, F/Lt Williams from astern. Both engines and the fuselage caught alight and the aircraft dived out of control and crashed. We then caught up the next straggler and a similar attack was carried out. Both engines caught alight and it subsequently crashed. Both these aircraft can be found

The aircraft carrier HMS *Glorious* ferried RAF fighters to and from Norway. (Wright & Logan)

between five and twenty miles respectively NE of Narvik.

For the next twenty minutes, between the two of us we carried out seven more attacks of a similar nature. Both engines of the third Heinkel in formation were put out of action and it was seen to be diving out of control to the ground. We then both attacked a Ju 87; it was one of two and had a large extra tank beneath each side of the mainplanes about 4 feet from the wing tip. This aircraft put up strong resistance, but the port tank caught alight and the aircraft crashed into the top of a hill some 30 miles south of Narvik. I observed F/Lt Williams closing on a He 111 which was bobbing in and out of clouds. I was unable to catch up at the time, as while I was getting into position a Ju 87 crossed my sights and therefore I attacked. When I had finished it a white stream of smoke was coming from the engine and I lost it in cloud. Further attacks were made but no definite results can be claimed. I returned to base having run out of ammunition.

Kitchener's description of the Ju 87 shot down by himself and Williams is interesting. The only Stuka unit to operate in Norway, 1/St.G 1, was equipped with a long-range version of the dive-

The battlecruiser *Scharnhorst* firing on the British aircraft carrier *Glorious* on 8 June, 1940. (Source unknown)

The evacuation of Norway marked the first deck landings by Hawker Hurricane fighters, many of which were later adapted for naval use. Here, a Sea Hurricane lands on the escort carrier HMS *Ravager*. (John McVittie)

bomber, the Ju 87R, which carried long-range tanks under its wings. There can be no doubt about the RAF pilots' victory, but oddly enough *Luftwaffe* records admitted no Stuka losses on 2 June 1940 in Norway.

Later in the war, Kitchener flew Westland Whirlwind fighter-bombers on offensive sweeps over France and the Low Countries. In March 1941, he destroyed a Junkers Ju 88, but was hit by return fire and crashed on returning to base. He survived the war and left the RAF in 1946, having attained the rank of wing commander.

Kitchener was lucky. On 7 June 1940, when the collapse came in Norway and the final evacuation took place, the pilots of No. 263 Squadron, together with those of No 46 Squadron, were ordered to fly their remaining Gladiators and Hurricanes to the carrier HMS *Glorious*. As No. 263 Squadron had more pilots than aircraft, two stayed behind to be evacuated by destroyer. Kitchener was one of them.

All the aircraft landed safely on the carrier, which set course for Scapa Flow escorted by two destroyers, the *Ardent* and *Acasta*. In the afternoon of 8 June 1940, *Glorious* was caught in the open sea by the German battlecruisers *Scharnhorst* and *Gneisenau*, out on a sortie against Allied troop transports west of Harstad. The carrier was caught completely unawares; for reasons that were never explained, none of her reconnaissance Swordfish was airborne. Desperate attempts were made to arm and launch them as the enemy battlecruisers came in sight, but she was overwhelmed and sunk before this could be accomplished. Her escorting destroyers were also sunk, but not before the *Acasta*, already doomed, had hit the *Scharnhorst* with a torpedo.

Of all the RAF pilots on the *Glorious*, only two – both of No. 46 Squadron – survived. They were Squadron Leader Kenneth Cross and Flight Lieutenant Patrick Jameson, who found themselves clinging to a Carley raft with thirty other survivors. By the time they were picked up three days later, only seven were still alive. Both eventually reached high rank in the Royal Air Force, Cross retiring as an air chief marshal and New Zealand-born Jameson as an air commodore.

CHAPTER FIVE

Flames over France

O n 10 May 1940, while the campaign in Norway was at its height, the Germans launched their expected assault on France and the Low Countries, supported by air attacks on seventy-two Allied airfields. For some time prior to this, the *Luftwaffe* had been stepping up reconnaissance and minelaying activities in the North Sea area, but although Fighter Command had increased its patrols little contact was made with the enemy. Flying Officer Jack Rose, a Hurricane pilot with No. 32 Squadron, recalled:

During the last days of April and the early part of May our Hurricanes were commuting almost daily from Biggin Hill to Manston, which we used as a forward aerodrome for patrols, and we were at Manston when the relative peace of the Phoney War was shattered by the German invasion of the Low Countries. On 11 May word came that German paratroopers had attacked the aerodrome at The Hague and so we were sent over to try to do something about it. When we arrived we could see parachutes all over the aerodrome but there was no sign of any aircraft. There seemed to be nothing we could do so we flew around for a while and then we came back. One or two of the pilots did shoot up odd targets that they saw or imagined they saw, but I don't think we did very much.

On 10 May 1940 there were still six RAF fighter squadrons in France, four with Hurricanes and two with Gladiators. The latter,

45

Jack Rose, pictured in 1943 when he was commanding officer of No. 184 Squadron. The aircraft in the background is a Hurricane IID. (Jack Rose)

Nos 607 and 615, forming part of the BEF Air Component, had been warned to prepare for re-equipment with Hurricanes, but this plan had to be postponed when the Germans attacked. Both squadrons fought hard and with considerable success with their biplanes for three days after the invasion, when they began to receive a trickle of Hurricanes, and on 15 May they pooled their resources to provide air cover for the retreating BEF. Most of these aircraft were destroyed in a heavy attack on their airfield at Vitry-en-Artois on 18 May; the survivors, starved of fuel, were destroyed by RAF personnel, who then evacuated the airfield and made their way to Boulogne with little more than the clothes they stood up in.

Within hours of the German invasion the Air Component's two Hurricane squadrons, Nos 85 and 87, were reinforced by three more: Nos 3, 79 and 504. A fourth Hurricane squadron, No. 501, was dispatched to join Nos 1 and 73 of the Advanced Air Striking Force (AASF), which were fighting desperately to the south in the Maginot Line area. No. 501 scarcely had time to land and refuel at

The Gloster Gladiator was still an important part of the BEF Air Component's fighter strength in May 1940. (Source unknown)

its new base, Betheniville, when it was ordered to take off to intercept a force of about forty He 111s. It was not until the squadron's first action in France was an hour old that the first ground crews arrived in transport aircraft from Tangmere – one of which unfortunately crashed on landing, killing three replacement pilots and injuring six others.

On 11 May No. 501's pilots claimed the destruction of two Bf 110s, two He 111s and two Dornier 17s. The following day they shot down a further seven He 111s, three Do 17s, a Bf 110 and a Junkers 88 for the loss of two Hurricanes. It was an example of what might have happened if Hurricanes had been available in plenty: but they were not.

There were now eight Hurricane squadrons in France: Nos 1, 73 and 501 with the AASF, and Nos 3, 79, 85, 87 and 504 with the Air Component. The odds they faced were fearfully high, as is indicated by an extract from the war diary of No. 3 Squadron.

Merville, 12 May 1940. Flying Officer Bowyer, Sergeants Ford and Simms (Blue Section) and Flight Lieutenant Carter, Pilot Officer Carey and Pilot Officer Stephens (Green Section) met between 50 and 60 Ju 87s, Do 17s and He 111s between Diest and Louvain. Pilot Officer Carey destroyed one Ju 87 and one He 111; Pilot Officer Stephens destroyed two Ju 87s; Sergeant Simms destroyed two Ju 87s. Between Diest and St Trond the Squadron also destroyed two Henschel 126s.

The Pilot Officer Carey mentioned in this extract was Frank Carey, who had originally joined the RAF as an aircraft apprentice in September 1927. After serving for some years as a rigger and fitter, he was accepted for pilot training in 1935 and was eventually posted to No. 43 Squadron, flying Hawker Fury biplanes and then Hawker Hurricanes. In the winter of 1939-40, while based at Acklington in Northumberland, he shared in the destruction of three He 111s and was awarded the Distinguished Flying Medal. In April 1940 he was commissioned and posted to No. 3 Squadron, with which he fought in France. It was the start of a combat career that would see him end the war as one of the RAF's top-scoring fighter aces.

For the AASF Hurricane squadrons, Sunday 12 May was a terrible day. Committed to flying top cover for AASF Battles and Blenheims that were making hopeless and costly attacks on the enemy bridgeheads across the Meuse, they suffered appalling losses and by the end of the day they had lost around half their aircraft. The Air Component squadrons had fared little better, and

Frank Carey, seen later in the war when he was a wing commander. (IWM)

A Bristol Blenheim Mk IV of No. 139 Squadron over France, 1940.
No. 139 was one of the two Blenheim squadrons attached to the
Advanced Air Striking Force. (IWM)

to remedy what was rapidly becoming a desperate situation the
British War Cabinet authorised Air Chief Marshal Sir Hugh
Dowding, the C-in-C Fighter Command, to despatch a further
thirty-two Hurricanes and pilots to the Continent. Jack Rose was
one of the pilots who went, and his description of subsequent
events provides a classic account of the hectic and confused situation that prevailed.

On 14 May No. 32 Squadron was asked to provide four pilots
and aircraft to reinforce 3 Squadron, then stationed at
Merville near Armentières in northern France. No. 3
Squadron had suffered very heavy casualties during the
preceding few days and so in addition to the pilots and
aircraft from No. 32 Squadron they were strengthened by a
flight from No. 601. With three other volunteers from 32

Squadron, I flew the same day to Merville. We were led by a Fairey Battle as we had no maps of France; I imagine that the crew of the Battle must have been equipped with the right maps but they seemed to spend a long time flying around France before we landed, for we were very short of fuel when we pitched up at Merville.

My aircraft, like those of my three companions, was a Hurricane Mk I fitted with a Merlin II engine and a two-speed airscrew. Soon after our arrival in France, the CO of our new squadron was reported killed and so Walter Churchill, one of the flight commanders, took over. He was later killed while commanding the fighter aircraft based on Malta. Churchill proved to be a very keen tactician and a great morale booster: a first-class squadron commander.

My three companions from 32 Squadron and I soon learned that the aircraft we had joined in France had all been equipped with armour plate behind and beneath the pilot's seat; as our own aircraft were not similarly protected I think we were perhaps forgiven if our morale was marginally less receptive to the boosting process than it might have been. A further snag was that we had arrived without the appropriate crystals in our 4-channel VHF sets and spares were not available locally until damaged aircraft could be cannibalised. The result was that, at times over the next few days, we were not in contact by radio either with our new colleagues of 3 squadron when airborne, or with such ground control as there was, or both.

During this period I became more and more impressed by the robust qualities of the Hurricane. I think that some of the emergency repairs that were carried out by the maintenance crews during those few days in France would have made Sydney Camm's hair stand on end, but they worked. On 19 May, after a few hectic days, I was flying one of a formation of six Hurricanes which had been ordered to patrol between Tournai and Oudenarde, about midway between Lille and Brussels, where we had been told to expect German bombers by ground control. We soon spotted twelve or so Heinkel 111s flying in close formation roughly level with us at 12,000 feet, and after a quick check of the sky for enemy fighters we attacked the German aircraft from astern.

I was positioned to attack the Heinkel on the port flank of

the enemy formation and closed very rapidly, firing for a few seconds up to very close range, and as I was about to break away the Heinkel's port engine erupted oil which covered my windscreen, almost completely blocking off my forward vision and making the reflector sight useless. I had a quick look round above and behind and, seeing what I took to be an enemy-free sky, I throttled back, gained a little height to reduce speed and pulled back the cockpit hood. I pulled a handkerchief from my right trouser pocket but I couldn't reach far enough to wipe the front of the windscreen clear without releasing my seat harness, so I had to do that and then set about cleaning the windscreen.

As I was doing a speed of somewhere between stalling and cruising, my seat harness undone, more or less standing on the rudder stirrups and half out of the aircraft, concentrating on clearing the windscreen and with no armour plate behind, I suddenly saw tracer fly past and felt strikes on the Hurricane. I was being attacked from the rear by a 109 which had not been in sight a few seconds earlier – probably no German fighter pilots has ever had a more inviting target. At my low speed, immediate evasive action resulted in a spin, and from my point of view this was probably the best thing that could have happened. As I was spinning down I left a long trail of glycol and petrol which must have satisfied my German opponent that he need not waste any further rounds on me.

I switched off the engine as soon as I became aware of the glycol and petrol spewing out, but carried on with the spin until the immediate danger of a second attack seemed over. After I had checked the spin and adjusted the Hurricane to a glide I had to decide whether to leave the aircraft in a hurry or try a landing without engine. Then, slightly to the west and 6-7000 feet below, I spotted the airfield of Seclin, just south of Lille. The aircraft was still discharging fuel and glycol but it had not caught fire. The fire risk was now greatly reduced as the engine temperature had fallen very considerably, so I decided on a wheels-down landing at Seclin. After a long zig-zag glide approach, still with the tell-tale stream behind, I used the hand pump to lock the undercarriage down and lowered the flaps in the last few seconds before touching down.

Under all the circumstances it was a reasonably good

landing and the aircraft's run after touchdown left me near the northern boundary of the airfield, some distance from the Lysanders of No. 4 Army Co-op Squadron which was then based at Seclin. I doubt if I have ever left an aircraft as quickly or as thankfully as when my Hurricane stopped rolling. When I checked the damage it seemed almost impossible that so many hits could have been registered without one bullet passing down the centre of the fuselage and through the back of my unprotected seat. A shell from the 109 had torn a gaping hole in the radiator just below me, while another had removed much of the starboard aileron. Bullets had pierced both port and starboard main petrol tanks in several places and there were a number of holes in the fuselage and wings elsewhere.

Having taken a rough mental inventory of the damage, I slung my parachute over my shoulder and walked across the airfield towards the No. 4 Squadron Lysanders. When I arrived at the Squadron I found all ranks wearing tin helmets and packing up for an immediate evacuation as Seclin had just been attacked from the air and by now was regarded as being too close to the advancing enemy forces for comfort. Before I had fully taken in what was going on I had come across a senior maintenance NCO and enquired about the possibility of patching up my Hurricane. I soon discovered there was no prospect of this, as all concerned had other things on their minds; I had to be content with an assurance that my aircraft would be destroyed along with the unserviceable air-craft belonging to 4 Squadron and I was told that it would not fall into enemy hands. So with my parachute and helmet I was given a lift in the evacuation road convoy and dropped off at Merville, where I rejoined 3 Squadron for a few more days until we in turn made our way by various routes to England.

Three days before the above episode, on 16 May, I shot down my first aircraft, a Messerschmitt 109, and just as I had finished firing at him I saw the pilot bale out and his para-chute open. This was over Tournai, just across the Belgian border, and as far as I know he landed safely. Two days later, although I didn't know it at the time, a flight of my brother's squadron, No. 56, had recently arrived at Vitry, about 30 miles south-east of Merville. Their aerodrome was attacked and my brother's flight, led by Ian Sowden, took off to intercept bombers which were attacking the airfield. Ian Sowden and my brother (Flying Officer F.C. Rose) were shot down and killed, my brother about two miles from the aerodrome. I was later told that he had accounted for at least two of the enemy aircraft.

When 3 Squadron left France, most of the members of the Squadron went by road to the coast and eventually out via Dunkirk, but as we only had about six serviceable aircraft left on our last day the surviving pilots drew lots for the first patrol on the day of departure. I flew on the morning patrol and then drew the short straw to stay behind with a handful of ground crew who were to service the aircraft for the final flight from French soil. After a short offensive patrol, the aircraft flew back to England. With the rear party of fitters, riggers and armourers, I suppose about ten all told, I was picked up by a civilian French Douglas DC-2. The pilot was not very keen on the job. He landed at Merville, kept his engines running and gave us a bare half-minute to pile on board, so everything except what we stood up in was abandoned. Everything, that is, except the Squadron mascot, a bull terrier called Bulger, who flew back with us.

Meanwhile, the French fighter squadrons had also been battling hard, and none more so than Groupe de Chasse I/5, commanded by Capitaine Jean Accart. Born in Fécamp, Accart had begun his career as a seaman officer in the French Mercantile Marine, serving on steam packets of the Compagnie Général Transatlantique before transferring to the French Navy in 1932. In 1936 Lieutenant de Vaisseau Accart changed his allegiance yet again, this time to the French Air Force, where he soon gained his flying brevet.

For Jean Accart, the fighting began on the very first day of the German onslaught, at dawn on 10 May 1940, when he took off in his Curtiss Hawk on a patrol with a Czech pilot named Frantisek Perina. Accart's own words tell the story.

Rising out of the shadows in a rapid climb, with no instructions from fighter control, I set course eastwards, where I could see a cluster of condensation trails lit up by the rising sun. With Perina a little lower down and astern, I climbed flat out towards them but was unable to reach them, so I set up a patrol in the Second Army's sector, between Sedan and

Capitaine Jean Accart, the second top-scoring French fighter pilot of the Battle of France. (ECP Armees)

Verdun. The sun was well up when I spotted fifteen black dots, creeping westwards and to the south of our position. We headed for them, gaining altitude, for they were clearly higher than us. After a few minutes, we were close enough to positively identify them as Messerschmitt 110s.

At that moment, they began a wide turn towards us. We were still a few hundred metres below them and I didn't think that they had seen us, because our aircraft camouflage would be blending in with the terrain below. They continued their gentle turn and I decided that they had not seen us, so I gave the order to attack. We were only two against fifteen, so there was time for only one quick pass, firing on the climb. I broke away as a group of five Messerschmitts turned towards me and looked for Perina, but he was nowhere to be seen. I found out later that he had continued to fire in the climb for too long and had dropped away in a spin.

Those twin-engined Messerschmitts were pretty manoeuvrable, but I got away by gaining altitude. The enemy formation seemed to have broken up in confusion, all except for a group of five which had formed up in line astern. I attacked this group head-on and fired on the leading aircraft, which was also firing at me. I passed underneath it and fired on each of the others in turn. It was all over in just a few seconds. The last one in line pulled up just as I opened fire and I broke hard in case of a sudden attack from astern, but to my surprise the Messerschmitts regrouped and flew off to the east. I counted twelve and looked for the others; I couldn't see them against the glare of the sun, but I did see Perina climbing up to rejoin me.

I was making up my mind whether or not to chase the Germans when I heard Adjudant (Warrant Officer) Bouvard call over the radio to say that he was engaging a group of Dorniers near reims, flying at 3000 metres. Bouvard, who was accompanied by Sous-Lieutenant (Pilot Officer) Goupy, shot down one of the bombers, but then Goupy got an incendiary bullet in the thigh and just managed to make a forced landing at Wez-Thuisy before losing consciousness. Perina and I dived flat out towards the Dorniers, which were soon in sight, and attacked the bomber on the far left of the formation. He began to smoke, lost altitude and splashed himself all over a field near Suippes . . .

Events unfolded at an infernal pace throughout the day. We had hardly been refuelled when we were ordered off to escort some Potez 63s which were carrying out a reconnaissance over the Ardennes. We passed over the enemy columns which were pushing westwards and had to dodge some severe flak. . . Back at Suippes we were placed on alert. Two hours went by, and I was just about to hand over to someone else when a flare shot up from the command post, ordering us to take off. Just as I got airborne, with Perina following, the aircraft was carpeted with bomb-bursts. Looking up, I saw what seemed to be a mixture of Dornier 17s and Messerschmitt 110s, dead overhead at about 3000 metres.

A furious battle developed. In the space of a few seconds I fired on a Dornier, went to the aid of a Curtiss that was being

French pilots examine the smoking crater that is the grave of a Messerschmitt Bf 110. (ECP Armees)

attacked by two Messerschmitts, and shot down a second Dornier just outside Suippes. Then, with Perina still clinging to me, I crept up behind a Dornier hidden under his tail, and fired a long burst into him, yawing a little so as to rake him from wingtip to wingtip. I was close enough to see the bullet strikes. I ceased firing and throttled back so as not to over-shoot the target. The bomber's motors were still turning, but I saw one of the crew jump, his parachute opening as he swept past me. I pulled off to the right a little to watch the Dornier, and at the same time to keep an eye on some enemy fighters which were approaching.

I saw a second crew member jump, but his parachute opened too soon and became snagged on the fuselage. I watched him struggling to free himself, trying to drag himself along the shroud lines towards the canopy. He pulled him-self forward a little, then lost his grip and slid back towards the tail. The Dornier began to smoke, the pilot baled out and the bomber went into a vertical dive, dragging the trapped man with it. It impacted with a terrific explosion on the banks of a little river.

I returned to Suippes with Perina as dusk was falling, after destroying another Dornier near Dun-sur-Meuse. So, for me, ended the first day of the battle . . .

Jean Accart went on to destroy a total of twelve enemy aircraft, with three probably destroyed, before the battle ended in June. He was severely wounded in the closing stages and spent a long time in hospital before crossing the Pyrenees into Spain in 1942, together with a number of trainee fighter pilots. He eventually reached North Africa, where he was given command of a fighter group in the Vichy French Air Force. Following the Allied victory in North Africa in 1943, this unit was transferred to the Royal Air Force and became No. 345 Squadron, operating in Normandy and Belgium. Accart reached high rank in the French Air Force after the war, commanding France's Tactical Air Forces in the early 1960s. He retired in 1965 and died on 19 August, 1992, at the age of 80.

Frantisek Perina escaped to England after France's collapse, joining No. 312 Squadron and flying Hurricanes in the Battle of Britain. He ended the war with at least fourteen victories. Returning to Czechoslovakia, he was expelled when the communists took over in 1948 and went to Canada, then the United States where he worked for an aircraft company. He went back to Czechoslovakia in 1989 to receive many accolades, including the rank of general. He died on 6 May 2006, aged 95.

Another notable French Curtiss Hawk pilot with GC I/5 was Sergent-Chef (Flight Sergeant) François Morel, who destroyed ten enemy aircraft in a single week between 10 and 18 May 1940. During an attack on a Heinkel 111 formation of 18 May, he was hit at close range by return fire and received a bullet in the head. He remained conscious long enough to bale out, but died during the descent. It was thought at the time that he had been shot by a French infantryman in the mistaken belief that he was a German, but a subsequent examination of his wrecked aircraft revealed a bullet hole in the windscreen.

On 19 May, the day after Morel was killed, a French pilot named Sergent Edouard Le Nigen began his war in earnest. His unit was GC III/3, which was equipped with Morane 406 fighters. The

Edouard Le Nigen (second from right) with fellow pilots of GC III/3
and Morane 406 fighter. (ECP Armees)

Morane, which was roughly the equivalent of the Hawker
Hurricane in terms of its design and development history, was
cannon-armed and manoeuvrable, but it was underpowered, with
a top speed of barely 300mph, and unlike the Hurricane it was inferior to the Messerschmitt 109 on almost every count.

Le Nigen had already discovered this to his cost when, on 2
March 1940, during the 'Phoney War' period, he and two other
pilots were detailed to fly an escort mission for a Potez 63 reconnaissance aircraft over the Saar. Three more Moranes from another
unit were flying top cover.

Over the front line the Moranes were bounced by an estimated
twenty-five Bf 109s and a one-sided dogfight developed, starting at
25,000 feet and quickly descending to lower altitudes. One of Le
Nigen's colleagues, Sergent Ribo, was soon shot down in flames
and Le Nigen himself was subjected to a succession of violent
attacks that riddled his Morane with cannon shells and shot his
undercarriage hydraulics to pieces. Using all his skill, he managed
to escape and brought his crippled aircraft down for a belly-
landing on the airfield at Nancy.

Now, on 19 May, his was one of nine Moranes patrolling the

Guise-Le Cateau area at dawn. The aircraft were flying at 15,000 feet and the mission was hampered by very poor radio communications, which made it virtually impossible for the pilots to report any enemy aircraft they sighted. Suddenly, Le Nigen's Morane went into a steep dive. The other pilots followed, realising that the tall, fair-haired Breton must have spotted something. A minute later they saw his aircraft flatten out only a few feet above the forest, and only then did they sight the target: a Henschel 126 observation aircraft. Le Nigen opened fire and the German aircraft fell blazing into the trees.

During a second mission that morning, nine more Moranes – again with Le Nigen – encountered twenty-five Dornier 17 bombers, escorted by twelve Bf 109s, in the Cambrai-Le Quesnoy area. Le Nigen, ignoring two 109s that clung to his tail, shot down a third and escaped from the others by a series of tight turns, which the German fighters could not match. When he got back to base, he found that several bullets had pierced his cockpit without touching him; he had been lucky.

The next day, the pilots of GC III/3 were at readiness at Beauvais when fifteen Heinkel He 111 bombers escorted by twenty-five Bf 110s were reported to be approaching the airfield. By the time the Frenchmen reached their aircraft, the enemy formation was already in sight. Le Nigen was first off, just as the German bombers were starting to explode on the airfield. Meanwhile, the Bf 110s were strafing anti-aircraft positions around the perimeter. Le Nigen, turning hard at very low level, fired at a 100 and saw it break up, its debris falling just outside the airfield, and then – joined now by the other French fighter pilots – he pursued the remaining 110s, which were heading away towards the east. After a few minutes Le Nigen and the others returned to Beauvais, swearing fluently; their Moranes had been unable to catch up with the 110s.

The Curtiss Hawk was a much better proposition. Another unit equipped with it was GC II/4. During the first few days of the battle many of its aircraft were destroyed on the ground, so that only seven Hawks out of a normal establishment of thirty-four remained serviceable on the morning of 15 May. Nevertheless, the Group gave a good account of itself in action that day, as its war diary tells:

Wednesday, 15 May 1940. At dawn, while we were establishing ourselves in our new location, we were briefed to fly an air cover mission south-west of Charleroi. Take-off was fixed for 1100. All available aircraft were to take part; there were only seven. The pilots were selected from the 3rd and 4th Escadrilles: Lieutenant Vincotte, Sous-Lieutenant Baptizet, Sous-Lieutenant Plubeau and Adjudant Tesseraud from the 4th, Capitaine Guieu, Adjudant Paulhan and Sergent-Chef Casenobe from the 3rd.

We climbed without incident until we were over Reims, when we saw a superb V of nine twin-engined bombers heading south-west at 4000 metres. We decided to attack. They were escorted by half a dozen Messerschmitt 109s, 1000 metres higher up and a little behind. Lieutenant Vincotte attacked, perhaps a little too soon. The Messerschmitts came down on us and we were forced to break away and dive for safety. Only Lieutenant Vincotte stuck to the bombers and made several passes at the left-hand one (a Junkers 88). Meanwhile, Plubeau, Tesseraud and Baptizet were involved in a fierce dogfight with the 109s; each shot down an enemy fighter and then climbed rapidly to the aid of Vincotte. Together, they shot down one bomber; the remainder dropped their bombs haphazardly near Warmeriville and we went after them.

Plubeau's cockpit was shattered by an explosive shell and he was forced to bale out. Vincotte damaged a second Junkers, then he too was hit in his fuel tanks and also had to bale out as his cockpit was filling with fumes and his oxygen equipment was out of action. Meanwhile, Baptizet, Guieu and Casenobe had spotted a Henschel 126 at low altitude, which they attacked and shot down in the forest of Silly l'Abbaye. In the process Guieu flew through a treetop at full throttle; by some miracle he managed to reach base and land safely with great gashes torn in his wings.

Regis Guieu was the only pilot of GC II/4 to become an ace in the Battle of France, gaining five victories. He was shot down and killed in a fight with Bf 109s on 7 June, while escorting a Potez 63 reconnaissance aircraft near Soissons.

Another Curtiss Hawk ace with five victories was Lieutenant Houzé of GC II/5. He too lost his life during the Battle of France, but under very different circumstances. On 6 June, he was attacking a Bf 110 when his own aircraft was hit and set on fire.

Baling out, he landed in no-man's land and was picked up by French motor-cycle troops who were acting as rearguard. Refusing to be evacuated, Houzé seized a machine-pistol and took command of a group of French soldiers. By this time the rearguard was surrounded, and took refuge in a small wood. Houzé led his men in an attempted break-out, shooting dead several German soldiers who were lying in wait at the edge of the wood. The Frenchmen got clear, but Houzé was mortally wounded and died two hours later.

The RAF's fighter squadrons, meanwhile, continued to fight as best they could from French soil. By 17 May the Air Component's Hurricane squadrons had destroyed some sixty-five enemy aircraft for the loss of twenty-two Hurricanes and fifteen pilots, with a further fifteen Hurricanes damaged on the ground. On the 21st, realising the hopelessness of the situation, Air Vice-Marshal Charles Blount, commanding the Air Component, ordered the evacuation of the surviving Hurricanes and their pilots to bases in southern England, from where they could continue to provide cover for the BEF without the continual risk of their airfields coming under attack. Two of the squadrons, Nos 32 and 79, were immediately sent to Yorkshire to rest and re-equip, their place being taken by Nos 213 and 242. Both these units were heavily involved over Dunkirk during the last days of May, destroying twenty-six enemy aircraft for the loss of nine Hurricanes and five pilots.

The Hurricane squadrons attached to the Advanced Air Striking Force remained in France, fighting against overwhelming odds. One of the biggest air battles was fought on 27 May, as the diary of No. 501 Squadron records:

Squadron based at Anglure (50 miles east of Paris) operating from forward strip at Boos (5 miles south of Rouen). Thirteen Hurricanes were airborne at 1345 hours, led by Flying Officer E. Holden, briefed to patrol the area Abancourt-Blangy (30 miles north-east of Rouen). Intercepted twenty-four Heinkel 111Ks escorted by twenty Messerschmitt Me 110s. Eleven Heinkels definitely destroyed, three Heinkels and one Messerschmitt possibly destroyed. Flying Officers J.R. Gridland and E. Holden, Pilot Officers J.A.A. Gibson, D.A. Hewitt, R.G.H. Hulse and K.N.T. Lee, Sergeants R.C. Dafform, J.H. Lacey, A.A. Lewis and D.A.S. McKay all destroyed one

Heinkel each, while Pilot Officer Gibson and Sergeant Dafform also destroyed another between them.

The damaged aircraft was claimed by Pilot Officer E.J.H. Sylvester, who fired off all his ammunition into a Messerschmitt, which was seen falling by Sergeant P.C. Farnes, who fired further rounds into it. Sergeants Lacey and McKay also attacked two other Heinkels which started losing height, with their undercarriages down and streaming smoke. Pilot Officer Hewitt also saw another Heinkel falling after he had attacked it. It should be noted that this was the first combat for Pilot Officer Hewitt and Sergeant Lewis, who had both newly joined the squadron. Our own machines suffered hardly any damage in the above encounter, all pilots returning safely.

Some of the RAF pilots who fought in this battle already had a number of 'kills' to their credit. One of them was Sergeant J.H 'Ginger' Lacey, who had destroyed his first enemy aircraft, a Heinkel 111 and a Bf 109, on 13 May. Lacey would end the war in the Far East, with 28 victories, making him the eleventh-ranking British Commonwealth fighter ace.

By 27 May, 'Cobber' Kain of No. 73 Squadron had amassed a total of seventeen enemy aircraft destroyed. His superiors decided that it was enough; he was awarded a Bar to his DFC, and then 73 Squadron was ordered back to England. On 6 June, Kain took off from the squadron's airfield at Echmines and, as a farewell gesture, launched into an impromptu aerobatic routine. Eye-witnesses saw his Hurricane enter a series of rapid flick-rolls to the left, then it suddenly lost flying speed and went into a spin. There was insufficient height for the pilot to recover, and the Hurricane hit the ground and burst into flames. Kain, the first Allied air ace of the war, was thrown from the cockpit, and died instantly from head injuries.

Kain's closest rival in France during the 'Phoney War' was Flying Officer Leslie R. Clisby, an Australian who had started his Service career as a cadet in the RAAF and who had come to England on a short-service commission in 1937. Clisby was credited with six victories while flying with No. 1 Squadron up to the end of April 1940; three of them all Bf 109s, were destroyed on two consecutive days in that month. He destroyed eight more during the first four days of May, bringing his score to fourteen. He shot down three more Bf 109s in a furious battle on 11 May, then the rudder of his Hurricane was partially shot away by another enemy fighter.

Barely able to control the aircraft, he headed earthwards to make a forced landing. Suddenly, he saw a Heinkel 111 below and ahead of him. Manoeuvring his Hurricane cautiously, he fired a burst into the German bomber, which crash-landed. Clisby landed nearby, drew his revolver as he jumped from the cockpit, and chased the German crew over the fields, firing as he gained on them. The Germans stopped, raised their hands, and the Australian took them prisoner, handing them over to the French authorities in a nearby village before returning to his squadron.

Three days later, Leslie Clisby's Hurricane was seen going down in flames near Reims. He was never seen again.

On 15 June, with the bulk of the British Expeditionary Force evacuated from the Dunkirk area, the remnants of the Hurricane squadrons were ordered to cover the final evacuation of British forces from the ports still held by the Allies, and for this purpose two more units – Nos 17 and 242 Squadrons – were temporarily transferred to France. Nos 1, 73 and 242 Squadrons were given the task of defending Nantes, Brest and St Nazaire, while Nos 17 and 501 – operating from Dinard and later from the Channel Islands – were assigned to St Malo and Cherbourg. Finally, on the 18th, the squadrons were ordered back to England, although all but a handful of their Hurricanes had to be left behind because of unserviceability and lack of fuel.

The last two fighter squadrons to leave, on the 18th, were Nos 1 and 73, which had been the first to arrive in France in 1939. One of the last RAF victories of the campaign was scored on the 17th by pilots of No. 1 Squadron, who shot down the Junkers 88 that had attacked and sunk the former Cunard

A superb fighter pilot, Pierre Le Gloan also fought against the British during the Syrian campaign of 1941.

liner *Lancastria*, which sank in the Channel with the loss of at least 5000 troops and civilians who were being evacuated from St Nazaire. It was Britain's worst maritime disaster.

The last French air ace of the campaign was Sergent-Chef Pierre le Gloan of GC III/6, which was equipped with the excellent Dewoitine D.520 fighter. Le Gloan already had three German bombers to his credit, together with a Dornier 17 reconnaissance aircraft shared with his wingman. All his latest victims were Italian aircraft, and he destroyed five of them in one air battle on 15 June, five days after the Italian dictator Benito Mussolini – sensing a quick victory and anticipating a share in the spoils – declared war on France and Britain.

In his first skirmish with Italian aircraft, on 13 June, Le Gloan destroyed two Fiat BR.20 bombers. Now, two days later, the pilots of GC III/6 were just landing at Luc-en-Provence after a patrol over Marseille when a formation of Fiat BR.20s, escorted by Fiat CR.42 biplane fighters, appeared overhead. Commandant Paul Stehlin, III/6's commander, at once ordered those pilots who had not yet landed to engage the enemy. The first pilot to do so was Le Gloan, who attacked a flight of CR.42s which was trying to gain altitude. Within seconds, two of the Italian fighters were spinning down in flames. Le Gloan's comrades stood on the airfield below and watched, spellbound, as he destroyed a third and fourth CR.42 in quick succession. He then went after a BR.20, which he also shot down. The crew of the latter aircraft, together with one of the CR.42 pilots, baled out and was dined by the officers of GC III/6 before going off into their brief captivity. For his exploit, Le Gloan received immediate promotion to Sous-Lieutenant.

After the fall of France, Pierre le Gloan escaped to Algeria with GC III/6. The unit, still with D.520s, was later transferred to Rayak, in the Lebanon, as part of the armed forces of the Vichy French regime there. In the summer of 1941, when a mixed force of British Empire and Free French troops invaded Syria and the Lebanon to secure these territories against Axis intervention, with its potential dire threat to the Suez Canal, Le Gloan found himself in action again, this time against former allies. On 8 June 1941, the day the invasion began, Le Gloan shot down an RAF Hurricane over Damascus, and on the following day he destroyed two more. On the 15th he claimed a Gloster Gladiator, but in the air battle his D.520 was damaged and he crash-landed at Rayak.

On 23 June, Le Gloan was one of nine pilots of GC III/6 who took off to intercept RAF Hurricanes of No. 80 Squadron which were strafing Rayak. He shot down two of them, but was himself hit and slightly wounded. He returned to action on 5 July and shot down another Hurricane. It was his eighteenth victory and his seventh in the Syrian campaign, during which he had shown himself to be the best fighter pilot on either side. Shortly afterwards, with Vichy resistance in Syria collapsing, Le Gloan was evacuated to Algeria with the surviving pilots of GC III/6.

After the Allied invasion of North Africa in November 1942 GC III/6 was absorbed into the Free French forces, and in May 1943 the unit received Bell P-39 Airacobra fighters. On 11 September, 1943, Pierre Le Gloan was on a coastal patrol when smoke began to come from the P-39's engine. He turned towards the shore but the engine stopped. He tried to make a belly landing on the beach, but his under-fuselage fuel tank was still attached and it exploded as the aircraft touched down, killing him instantly.

CHAPTER SIX

Aces of the
Battle of Britain

In June 1940, while the Battle of France still raged, the *Luftwaffe* began to turn its attention to 'fringe' targets, such as ports, on the English coast. The defeat of France was followed by a growing number of incursions into British air space by enemy aircraft at night. Many of these raids were intercepted by both day fighters and Blenheim night fighters, the latter having already registered some successes as intruders during the Battle of France. At 0050 19 June, for example, a Heinkel He 111H-4 of 2/KG54 was shot down into the sea off the Norfolk coast by Flight Lieutenant R.M.B Duke-Woolley in a Blenheim of No. 23 Squadron, the German crew being captured; on the same night two Heinkels of 4/KG4 were also destroyed, both at 0115. The first was shot down off Felixstowe by Flight Lieutenant A.G. Malan in a Spitfire of No. 74 Squadron, and the second was shot down jointly by a Spitfire of No. 19 Squadron and a Blenheim of No. 23 Squadron at Fleam Dyke, Cambridgeshire. Unfortunately, the Spitfire pilot, Flying Officer Petra, was forced to bale out during the combat after his aircraft was hit, while the Blenheim pilot, Squadron Leader O'Brien, baled out after losing control. Both his crew members were killed. The third victory of the night was achieved at 0215 by Flying Officer G.E. Ball of No. 19 Squadron, who shot down a Heinkel 111H of 6/KG4 into the sea off Margate. Three more Heinkels were destroyed in the early hours of 26 June. The first, a Heinkel He 111P-2 of 3/KG4,

Bomben auf England:
the view from a
Heinkel He 111's
cockpit. (ECP Armées)

was shot down into the sea off Hull by Pilot Officers R.A. Smith
and R. Marples at 0017, while two He 111H-3s of 3/KG26 were
shot down by pilots of Nos 602 and 603 Squadrons off the Scottish
coast. Interceptions of this kind were aided by the clear, translucent
nature of the summer nights, with their attendant good visibility.
In the following months the *Luftwaffe*'s main effort switched to
attacks on coastal shipping. There were still opportunities for the
day fighter pilots to make night interceptions, however; at 0055 on
26 July, for example, a Heinkel He 111H-4 of 1/KG4 on a minelaying sortie over the Bristol Channel was shot down by Pilot
Officer Cock of No. 87 Squadron, flying a Hurricane.

These 'fringe' attacks were a prelude to larger-scale *Luftwaffe*
operations, starting early in July, against shipping in the English
Channel, the aim being to probe Fighter Command's defences and
reaction times, in addition to inflicting physical damage on its
fighter squadrons. The convoy attacks continued during July and
the first week of August. Although there were several major air
battles during this phase, usually in the Dover area, the enemy
formations were usually intercepted by only half a dozen British

Although it enjoyed later success as a night fighter, the Boulton Paul
Defiant suffered appalling losses in the daylight battle. (Source unknown)

fighters, and were often able to carry out their attack and head for
home before any British fighters arrived. But Air Chief Marshal Sir
Hugh Dowding, C-in-C Fighter Command, was husbanding his
valuable fighter resources; he had earlier turned down repeated
requests to send more RAF fighter squadrons to France, knowing
that the decisive battle would be fought over the British Isles. His
fighter assets at the beginning of July 1940 numbered about 600
aircraft – twenty-nine squadrons of Hurricanes, nineteen of
Spitfires, seven of Blenheim fighters (most of which were assigned
to night defence) and two of Boulton Paul Defiants. One of the
latter squadrons, No. 141, lost six aircraft in an encounter with Bf
109s on 19 July, and after that the Defiant played no further part in
the daylight phase of the battle.

Dowding's approach was essentially a scientific one; he believed
that Britain's air defences should have the benefit of the very latest
technological developments. This was reflected in Fighter
Command's operations rooms, linked with one another by an
elaborate system of telephone and teleprinter lines to provide
an integrated system of control. This enabled fighter aircraft to be
passed rapidly from sector to sector and from group to group,
wherever they were most needed. It was No. 11 Group, in the
crucial south-east area of England, that would bear the brunt of the

fighting throughout the battle; twenty-nine of Dowding's squadrons were based there, with another eleven in No. 12 Group, north of the Thames, and seventeen in No. 13 Group, covering northern England and Scotland.

Nowhere was modern technology more apparent in Britain's defences than in the use of radar, or radio direction finding (RDF) as it was then known. Developed by Robert Watson-Watt from earlier experiments in thunderstorm detection by the use of radio waves, the use of radar as an integral part of the British air defence system was largely the fruit of Dowding's initiative; he had worked with Watson-Watt in the 1930s and had not been slow to recognize the potential of the new invention.

The Germans knew all about the British warning radar system, and the destruction of the radar stations on the south coast of England was recognized as a vital preliminary to the main air offensive against England. Planning for the offensive was completed by 2 August 1940. Air Fleets (*Luftflotten*) 2 and 3 were to attack simultaneously, their main tasks being to bring the RAF's fighters to combat, to destroy their airfields and the coastal radar stations, and to disrupt the RAF's ground organisation in southern

Controllers and plotters at work in one of Fighter Command's operations rooms. (IWM)

England. The attacks on the south coast radar stations began on 12 August; one station, at Ventnor on the Isle of Wight, was damaged beyond repair, but although others suffered damage they were operational again within hours.

On 13 August, the day designated as *Adlertag* – Eagle Day – the Germans struck hard against the RAF's key airfields in south-east England. Three airfields were badly hit, but none was a fighter base, and the *Luftwaffe* lost thirty-four aircraft against Fighter Command's thirteen. Bad weather frustrated operations on the 14th, but the next day – which would turn out to be the most hectic of the entire battle – the *Luftwaffe* launched a two-pronged offensive against northern and southern England.

Several noteworthy fighter pilots were airborne to face the attack on the north, among them Archie McKellar, now a flight lieutenant and a flight commander with No. 605 Squadron, flying Hurricanes from Drem. On this Thursday, 15 August, sixty-three Heinkel He 111s of KG26 took off from bases in Norway to attack the northern airfields. The bombers were escorted by twenty-six Bf 110s of ZG76. The fighters would be operating at the limit of their range, but the Germans did not expect serious trouble; according to *Luftwaffe* intelligence, most of the RAF's northern fighter squadrons had been transferred south, to help counter the heavy attacks in No 11 Group's area. Once again, however, German in-

Scramble! RAF fighter pilots race for their Hurricanes. (IWM)

Brought down on British soil, this Heinkel 111 is equipped with a fender for penetrating balloon barrages. (IWM)

telligence was at fault. Unknown to the incoming Heinkels and Messerschmitts, five squadrons of Spitfires and Hurricanes lay in their path. One of them was No. 605 Squadron.

At 1300 hours, the Messerschmitts, sweeping ahead of the bombers, were heavily engaged over the Farne Islands by the Spitfires of No. 72 Squadron ahd the Hurricanes of No. 79, both from RAF Acklington in Northumberland. When the pilots of No 605 Squadron sighted the Heinkels approaching the river Tyne from the north-east, they consequently found that the bomber formation was unescorted.

McKellar's 'B' Flight was the first to make contact with the Heinkels, which were flying in groups of twenty to twenty-five, straggling back across the sky for several miles. McKellar ordered his pilots into line astern and told them to follow him into the sun. Then he led a diving attack on the rear aircraft of the leading group. Lining up on a Heinkel, he opened fire at 250 yards. After one three-second burst the bomber fell away in a spiral dive and McKellar was forced to break away sharply as he came under fire from a pair of Heinkels behind him. 'We were by then over Newcastle,' he wrote later in his combat report, 'and I ordered my flight to make individual attacks as I considered harrying tactics were the best way of defeating the object of bombing Tyneside.'

Some of the bombers, in fact, jettisoned their loads over the Tyne shipyards and veered away out to sea. The remainder flew on towards Sunderland, still harried by No. 605 Squadron. Archie McKellar attacked another Heinkel, which took violent evasive action and got away, then he selected the leading bomber in the formation and swept down in a beam attack, giving the aircraft a long eight-second burst. It started to go down, with both engines pouring smoke. McKellar turned steeply and fired at a Heinkel which flashed across his nose; that, too, began to burn. Looking round, he picked up a straggler and closed in astern, firing off the remainder of his ammunition. He saw the bomber's dorsal gunner suddenly throw up his hands and disappear beneath his cupola; an instant later the Heinkel's starboard engine began to trail grey smoke. Low on fuel, and with his ammunition exhausted, McKellar left the bomber to its uncertain fate and headed for the nearest airfield.

By the end of October 1940, Archie McKellar – known to his friends as 'Wee Mac' – had been officially credited with the destruction of twenty enemy aircraft, and had been awarded the DSO and DFC and Bar. On 1 November, he took off on a sortie and never returned. His Hurricane was seen to fall from a high level before crashing into the grounds of a country mansion in Kent. A Bf 109 was shot down during his squadron's morning patrol, and since no other pilot claimed it, it could have been McKellar's last victim.

During the engagement over the Tyne, the pilots of No. 605 Squadron destroyed four enemy aircraft and damaged six more. The remainder, under attack now by the Spitfires of No. 41 Squadron from Catterick and the Hurricanes of No. 607 Squadron from RAF Usworth, near Sunderland, unloaded their bombs more or less at random and made their escape as quickly as possible. Behind them, scattered along the coast, they left the wrecks of eight Heinkels and six Bf 110s.

One of the Catterick-based fighter pilots was Flying Officer Eric Lock of No. 41 Squadron. His combat report described his experience of 15 August:

I was flying in formation with 41 Squadron when we were ordered to patrol north of base at 20,000 feet. After flying for a while we saw a formation of Junkers 88 (they were actually He 111s – author) and Messerschmitt 110. The squadron then

These two photographs show typical Battle of Britain dispersal scenes, not to mention an interesting collection of vehicles! (Jack Rose)

went into line astern and we made an attack. During our second attack, I fired two short bursts into the starboard engine of a Messerschmitt 110. I followed it down to 10,000 feet, firing at the fuselage. The machine-gunner stopped firing. Continuing my dive I fired at the port engine, which caught fire. I left it at 5000 feet still in a vertical dive, with both engines on fire.

Lock did not see his victim crash, but a fellow pilot saw it plunge into Seaham Harbour.

Lock got into the thick of the fighting in the first week of September, when No. 41 Squadron moved to RAF Hornchurch in Essex. On 5 September, he destroyed two Heinkel 111s and a Messerschmitt 109, and the next day he shot down a Ju 88 into the Channel. Three days later he destroyed two Bf 109s over Kent, and on 11 September he shot down a Ju 88 and a Bf 110. This brought his total kills so far to nine, all of them confirmed; he had destroyed eight of the enemy aircraft in one week, a feat that brought him the award of a DFC. He went on to destroy seven more aircraft before the end of October, and shared in the destruction of another, bringing his tally to sixteen.

On 17 November, by which time he had scored six more kills, Lock was badly wounded in a battle over the Thames Estuary. He brought his Spitfire down to a crash-landing at Martlesham Heath and was hospitalised until May 1941, being awarded the Distinguished Service Order in the interval. In June 1941, having undergone fifteen operations for the removal of shell splinters from his right arm and both legs, he was pronounced fit again and posted as a flight commander to No. 611 Squadron, flying Spitfires from Hornchurch. Fighter Command was just beginning its offensive 'sweeps' over occupied France, and during the next few weeks Lock added four more enemy aircraft to his score. He now had twenty-six victories. On 3 August 1941, he failed to return from an operation over northern France and was posted missing, presumed killed. No one ever found out what had happened to him.

On 2 September 1940, a Hurricane pilot was on patrol over Dover when he sighted two Messerschmitt 109s and attacked one of them head-on. At a range of 100 yards the 109 broke away and the Hurricane pilot turned after it, firing several bursts into it. The 109 began to stream smoke and went down to crash two miles from Dover.

It was the pilot's first victory over England, but he already had eleven German aircraft to his credit in other skies. His name was Josef Frantisek, and he had been a Czech regular airman when the Germans occupied his country in the spring of 1939. He escaped to Poland, where he flew and fought with the Polish Air Force in September 1939, gaining his first victories against the *Luftwaffe*. After Poland's collapse he escaped to Romania, where he was interned, but he managed to make his escape and made his way through the Balkans to Syria, where he took ship for France.

During the battles of May and June 1940, flying Morane 406 fighters with the French Air Force, he added to his score and was awarded the Croix de Guerre. When France fell, Frantisek escaped again, this time to England, and after converting to Hurricanes he was posted to No. 303 (Polish) Squadron at RAF Northolt. This unit, known as the Kosciuszko Squadron, was one of the first two Polish fighter units to reach operational status in Britain, and went into action at a crucial stage of the battle.

Frantisek was the only Czech pilot on the squadron, but he did not seem to mind. He was very much a lone wolf by nature, and many of his successes were gained while flying lone patrols. He gained his second victory, a Bf 109, on 3 September, and two days later, in a hectic engagement with fifty Bf 109s and Ju 88s over the Thames Estuary, he added two more enemy aircraft to his tally. Disposing of a Bf 109 which attacked him and overshot, he joined

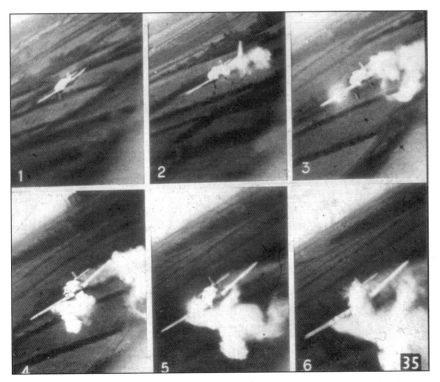

Gun camera sequence showing the destruction of a Messerschmitt
Bf 109. (IWM)

his flight commander, Flight Lieutenant Forbes, in an assault on the bomber formation, and sent a Ju 88 down into the sea. The next day, he destroyed a Bf 109 over Sevenoaks.

His score continued to mount steadily during the remainder of September. On the last day of the month he shot down a Bf 109, his seventeenth victory over England. A few days later, on 8 October, he was landing after an early morning patrol when his Hurricane's wingtip struck a slight rise in the ground and the aircraft somersaulted on its back. The fighter exploded in flames and its pilot, trapped in the cockpit, had no chance of escape. No other Czech fighter pilot was to surpass his score of twenty-eight victories, and he was to remain the top scorer of the Battle of Britain.

Three days after Frantisek gained his first victory with the RAF, a Polish pilot, attached to No. 501 Squadron, fought a hectic early morning air battle. He attacked a Heinkel 111 and set its starboard engine on fire, then shot down one of the escorting Bf 109s, whose pilot baled out. A few minutes later, climbing to 24,000 feet, the Pole attacked and shot down another 109, but was then attacked in turn by another enemy fighter, which set his Hurricane on fire. The Polish pilot baled out, having suffered burns that were to keep him in hospital for six weeks. For the time being, Stanislaw Skalski's combat career with the RAF was at an end.

Behind Josef Frantisek and Eric Lock, three pilots competed for third place in the table of Battle of Britain aces, each shooting down fifteen enemy aircraft during the battle. They were Sergeant J.H. 'Ginger' Lacey of No. 501 Squadron, Flying Officer Brian Carberry of No. 603, and Pilot Officer Bob Doe of No. 234. Lacey was already a very experienced fighter pilot when the battle began, having destroyed five enemy aircraft in the Battle of France, and he briefly made the headlines of 13 September 1940, when he shot down a Heinkel 111 that had just bombed Buckingham Palace, but apart from that his achievements were mostly overlooked. For the popular Press, there was little mileage in the activities of a mere sergeant pilot. For the same reason, the activities of Josef Frantisek remained relatively unknown until long afterwards.

By the end of October 1940 Lacey had increased his score to twenty-three and been awarded a Bar to the DFM he had earned in France. Early in 1941 he was commissioned and the squadron converted to Spitfires, with which it began to fly fighter sweeps across the Channel. At the end of July 1941 Lacey's score stood at twenty-seven and he had been awarded the DFC. After a spell as

Sergeant (later Squadron Leader) J.H. Lacey, one of the finest fighter pilots of World War Two. (RAF)

an instructor he was posted as a flight commander to No. 602 Squadron at Kenley, and in November 1942 he was appointed chief instructor at the Special Attack Instructors' School at Milfield, Northumberland.

In 1943 he was posted to India, first as an instructor and then as officer commanding No. 17 Squadron, flying Spitfire VIIIs in Burma. It was in one of these aircraft that he destroyed his twenty-eighth and last enemy aircraft, a Nakajima Ki.43 Oscar, on 19 February 1945. Granted a permanent commission after the war, Lacey remained in the RAF until 1967 as a fighter controller, reaching the rank of squadron leader. He then ran an air charter business. James Harry Lacey died of cancer on 30 May, 1989.

More important, perhaps, than Lacey's prowess in air combat was his skill as an air combat instructor. Few of the fighter pilots who were put through the mill by 'Ginger' Lacey were ever taken by surprise by the enemy, and several went on to achieve respectable scores in their own right. They thought the world of him.

A score of twenty-eight victories placed 'Ginger' Lacey in joint eighth place in the pecking order of RAF fighter aces. The pilot who shared the position with him was Frank Carey, a contemporary of Lacey's who had also fought in the Battles of France and Britain but who, unlike Lacey, rose from sergeant pilot to squadron leader in the space of six months. Carey first saw action with No. 43 Squadron at RAF Acklington, Northumberland, early in 1940, when he shared in the destruction of a Heinkel 111; a few days later he shot another Heinkel down in flames over the North Sea. At the end of February he was awarded the DFM, commissioned, and posted to No. 3 Squadron, which rotated flights of Hurricanes to France when the *Blitzkrieg* began.

During the Battle of France Carey destroyed four enemy aircraft, together with two probables, before being wounded on 14 May. On his return to England he was posted back to No. 43 Squadron as a flight commander, and destroyed a Bf 109 over the Channel on 19 June. During July Carey added two more aircraft – a Bf 109 and a Bf 110 – to his score. Then, on 12 and 13 August, the first two days of heavy *Luftwaffe* attacks on the RAF airfields in the south of England, Carey claimed two Junkers 88s, and on the 16th he was involved in a fierce air battle over the south coast. His combat report describes the action:

> I was leading 'A' Flight behind the leader of the squadron, having taken off at 1245 hours to patrol Selsey Bill at 11,000 feet when I gave Tally Ho on sighting waves of Ju 87s. The leader ordered the squadron to attack one formation of Ju 87s from the front and immediately on closing the leader of the enemy aircraft was hit by Squadron Leader and crew baled out.
>
> I pulled my flight over to the left to attack the right hand formation as we met them. Almost as soon as I opened fire, the enemy aircraft's crew baled out and the machine crashed into the sea, just off Selsey Bill. I turned to continue my attack from the rear as enemy aircraft were completely broken up by frontal attack and several other waves behind me turned back to sea immediately although we had not attacked them. I picked out one Ju 87 and fired two two-second bursts at him and the enemy aircraft burst into flames on the port wing-root. I did not wait to see it crash as I turned to attack another. After one burst at the third enemy aircraft, two large pieces of metal broke off the port wing and the enemy aircraft seemed to stop abruptly and go into a dive, but I did not see the machine crash as two other Ju 87s were turning on to my tail. I eventually picked on a fourth, but after firing two bursts and causing the engine to issue black smoke, the enemy aircraft turned out to sea and I ran out of ammunition. I noticed firing behind me and turned to see a pair of Me 109s behind me, one firing and the other guarding his tail. After a few evasive actions the enemy aircraft broke off and I returned to land and refuel and rearm at 1340 hours.

Two days later, while leading No. 43 Squadron on patrol, Carey encountered another large formation of Ju 87s near Chichester. He shot down one Stuka, but his own aircraft was repeatredly hit by machine gun fire and he was wounded in the right knee. He brought his Hurricane down for a successful forced landing, and spent the next couple of weeks recuperating.

Frank Carey ended the Battle of Britain with a total score of enemy aircraft destroyed. In 1941 he was appointed to command the newly-formed No. 135 Squadron, and on 6 December that year this unit sailed for Rangoon – just in time to meet the Japanese offensive in Burma.

At the end of August 1940 No. 43 Squadron received a new commanding officer: Squadron Leader Caesar Hull, veteran of the Norwegian campaign. In the afternoon of 7 September, Hull led the squadron into action against German bombers that were attacking the London docks. He was last seen diving down to the attack, and it is thought that he was shot sown by Bf 109s of JG 54. The wreckage of his Hurricane was found at Purley, Surrey. He was twenty-seven years old.

One of the top-scoring pilots during the Battle of Britain was a Pole, Squadron Leader Witold Urbanowicz, who destroyed fourteen enemy aircraft. Like so many of his fellow countrymen, Urbanowicz reached Britain by way of the Balkans and France, and after operational training he was posted to No. 303 Kosciuszko Squadron. He gained his first victory on 15 August, when, on patrol over the Channel off Portsmouth, he caught a Bf 109, pursued it out to sea and shot it down. Soon afterwards he was given command of No. 303 Squadron's 'A' Flight, and then, when the squadron commander was injured, he was promoted to lead the unit. Under his command, the pilots of No. 303 Squadron soon distinguished themselves. On 31 August, six Hurricanes of 'A' Flight engaged some Bf 109s escorting bombers, and destroyed four of them for no loss to themselves, and on 7 September, intercepting a formation of Dornier 17s attacking the London docks, the Poles were credited with sixteen per cent of the enemy destroyed by Fighter Command that day. Three of the Polish squadron's own aircraft were lost in the battle, and two pilots wounded.

On 11 September, No. 303 Squadron claimed fourteen victories for the loss of two of its own pilots. On 26 September, during a visit by King George VI, the squadron was scrambled to intercept enemy bombers attacking Portsmouth and the pilots claimed the destruction of eleven enemy aircraft – a great success, particularly as the King was following proceedings in the operations room.

During the critical month of September No. 303 Squadron was credited with just over eleven per cent of all enemy aircraft destroyed by the RAF – the highest score for any unit in Fighter Command, and more than double that achieved by the nearest rival.

Witold Urbanowicz's last combat in the Battle of Britain took place on 30 September, and it was his best day yet. Leading his squadron into action over Kent, he destroyed a Dornier 17 and then came up behind two Bf 109s, which failed to see him until it was too late. Closing in, he gave each of them a short burst and sent them down into the Channel.

For his exploits in the battle, Urabanowicz was awarded the DFC, the Virtuti Militari, Poland's highest decoration, and the Cross of Valour, the Polish equivalent of the DFC. In 1941, he was appointed CO of the Polish Fighter Wing in the RAF, but flew only a few more missions until he was sent to Washington as Assistant Air Attaché. In 1943, he transferred to the USAAF and flew on operations with the Fourteenth Air Force in the China-Burma-India theatre. He left the USAAF in 1946 and took US citizenship, working successively for Eastern Airlines, American

New Zealander Colin Gray, seen here with his Spitfire, was one of Fighter Command's unsung heroes. (RNZAF)

Airlines and Republic Aviation. He died in New York on 17 August, 1996.

Another pilot who scored fourteen kills during the Battle of Britain was Flying Officer Colin Gray, a New Zealander who flew Spitfires in No. 54 Squadron alongside another New Zealander, Flying Officer Alan Deere. Whereas Deere, who was later to lead the famous Biggin Hill Wing on fighter sweeps and escort missions over France in1943, was much publicised, Gray's achievements went largely unrecorded until long after the war.

Colin Gray's first taste of action came over Dunkirk in May 1940, when he shared in the destruction of a Bf 109. His next victory came on 24 July, during the preliminary phase of the Battle of Britain, when he shot down a Bf 109 over Margate. When the main battle began on 12 August, Gray destroyed two Bf 109s, repeating this success three days later. On 18 August he attacked a Bf 110 and sent it down on fire, and later that day he crippled a Bf 109 which crashed in the middle of Clacton. On 24 August he chased a Bf 110 almost all the way across the Channel and shot it down off the French coast, and two days later he added a Bf 109 to his score. In the four days from 31 August to 3 September he destroyed six more enemy aircraft and had a number of lucky escapes, one when a cannon shell exploded behind his cockpit without injuring him. On his last day of action No. 54 Squadron was sent north to RAF Catterick for a rest, which probably saved his life.

Colin Falkland Gray, who later reached the rank of group captain, subsequently fought over France, in Malta and North Africa. His official final score of enemy aircraft destroyed was 27.5. He died in Waikanae, New Zealand, on 1 August 1995, aged eighty.

While Britain's Air Ministry remained reluctant to publicise the exploits of the leading fighter pilots in the Battle of Britain, the Germans had no such inhibitions. Two names, those of Werner Mölders and Adolf Galland – whose respective number of victories reached 54 and 52 by the end of the battle – were featured constantly in the German propaganda organs. But it was a young fighter pilot who had been one of Mölders' pupils in the 1930s who surpassed both of them.

A forester's son, Helmut Wick had been a poor scholar as a child, constantly playing truant to escape into the woods. His sole ambition, then, had been to follow in his father's footsteps, but in 1936 he joined the new *Luftwaffe* and, under the instruction of

Mölders and other skilled pilots, he soon showed exceptional flying talent. He scored his first kill in November 1939, during the 'Phoney War' period, and when the Battle of France began his score mounted with phenomenal speed. He was aggressive and impetuous, and intensely patriotic. His unit was JG 2 'Richthofen', named after the celebrated flying ace of the previous war, and it was the ambition of every German fighter pilot to better Richthofen's score of eighty enemy aircraft destroyed.

At the end of October 1940, Helmut Wick's score stood at forty-nine, and he was itching to catch up with his old instructor, Mölders. Wick, at the age of twenty-five, was now commanding JG 2. On 6 November he led his Bf 109s on a fighter sweep over the Southampton area of southern England, and a day or two later wrote an account of what happened.

We met a formation of Hurricanes flying lower than ourselves. Just as I was about to start the attack, I saw something above me and immediately called 'Look out, Spitfires ahead.' The Spitfires were still far enough away to permit an attack on the lower-flying Hurricanes.

At that moment the Hurricanes made a turn, which proved to be their downfall. We shot down four of this group, one of which fell to me. The remaining Hurricanes turned away but began to climb again, and during the climb I caught one of them flying on the right-hand side of the formation. The Hurricanes then dived steeply. I cannot fully explain my next experience – perhaps I was not quite fit or my nerves were frayed – but after my second Englishman went down, I only wanted to fly home. I still had fuel for a few more minutes of action . . . I saw three Spitfires coming in from the sea in front of me. I saw them first and caught up with them quickly and the first one went down immediately. Now, I said to myself, we must get them all. If we let them get away they will probably kill some of my comrades tomorrow, now away with them!

I gritted my teeth and started the next attack. The second Spitfire fell after only a few bursts, leaving only one . . . I fired at him with my machine guns and soon white smoke poured from him. The pilot appeared to be hit because the aircraft went down out of control, but suddenly it recovered and I was forced to attack it again. The Spitfire slowly turned over and crashed to the ground. Now it really was time to fly home. When I arrived back over my airfield, I did not perform the usual stunts to indicate my victories as my fuel was almost exhausted. When I jumped out of the aircraft I hugged the first person who came across to me, who by chance turned out to be an old friend from my training days. I now have scored fifty-three victories and need only one more to draw level with my old instructor Werner Mölders.

The next day, Wick led fifty Bf 109s on an offensive sweep over the Isle of Wight. They encountered the eleven Hurricanes of No. 145 Squadron, which had just returned south to RAF Tangmere after a spell at Dyce, near Abderdeen. The 109s split up and boxed in the Hurricanes, whose pilots tried to escape by climbing. It was the signal for the 109s to dart in, attacking in pairs and picking off one Hurricane after another. Five Hurricanes were shot down, two of their pilots being killed, and Helmut Wick gained his fifty-fourth victory. On 28 November, he failed to return from a fight between JG 2's Messerschmitts and RAF Spitfires over the Channel; it was

Reichsmarschall Hermann Göring, the *Luftwaffe* C-in-C, in conversation with one of his 'Young Turks'. (via J.R. Cavanagh)

later established that he had escaped from his crippled aircraft, but had drowned.

Wick was succeeded as commander of JG 2 by Wilhelm Balthasar, another very experienced fighter pilot and splendid leader, although his manner was less flamboyant than Wick's. Balthasar had fought in the Spanish Civil War, claiming six victories – four of which, Russian SB-2 bombers, he destroyed in six minutes in February 1938 – and in the Battle of France he had shot down twenty-one aircraft in as many days. During the Battle of Britain he commanded III/JG 3, and recorded a combat that took place on 23 September 1940:

> Over London my Schwarm (flight) encountered a formation of about sixty Spitfires. I made a head-on attack on one of them. The enemy's tracer flew past my canopy, but the Englishman went spinning down in flames. Perhaps he had lost his nerve. Now a wild dogfight began. It was best to break away. Now I had four Spitfires on my tail. I was at 8000 metres, and I pushed the stick forward and dived away at full speed, pulling out at ground level with my wings fluttering. No British fighter could have followed my wild dive. I looked behind me. Damn! There were two Spits on my tail again. There was no time to draw breath. My only chance of escape lay in my flying ability at low level, hedge-hopping to the Channel over houses and around trees. It was no use, one of them was always there and I couldn't shake him off. He hung a hundred metres behind me. Then we were over Dover. I thought; he can't keep this up, as I fled out over the wavetops, but the Spitfire stayed right behind.
>
> I jinked to the right and left as the pilot opened fire and the bullets splashed into the water in front of me. I blinked the sweat out of my eyes. The French coast was now in sight. My fuel was getting low. I kept squinting behind so as not to miss the moment when he broke away. Wait, my friend, I though, you must return soon, and then I will be the hunter.
>
> Cap Gris Nez loomed up in front, and I skimmed over it one metre above. Suddenly the Tommy climbed steeply and slowed down. At once I turned my Me 109 and zoomed up in a tight bank, engine howling, straight at him. I fired one burst from close range – I nearly rammed him – and the Spitfire went straight into the sea. He flew fantastically.

Wilhelm Balthasar achieved forty-seven victories. He was killed on 3 July, 1941, when a wing of his Bf 109 folded up during a combat with RAF fighters near St Omer.

Another Spanish Civil War veteran who fought in the Battle of Britain was Walter Oesau, who in July 1940 was *Staffelkapitän* (squadron leader) of 7/JG 51. One of his early successes was a Hurricane of No. 111 Squadron, which he shot down on 10 July while escorting a force of Dorniers attacking British convoys. His jubilation was marred by the fact that the Hurricane collided with a Dornier on the way down, both aircraft crashing in the Channel. By 20 August, Oesau had scored twenty victories and had been promoted to *Hauptmann*. He took command of III/JG 51 towards the end of 1940, and succeeded Wilhem Balthasar as commander of JG 2. Oesau, who already had eight victories in Spain, went on to achieve a total score of 125 enemy aircraft destroyed, forty-four of them on the Eastern Front. He was shot down and killed by USAAF P-38 Lightnings on 11 May 1944, while he was engaged in attacking American bombers over Belgium.

Herbert Ihlefeld also fought in Spain, destroying nine Republican aircraft. In August 1940, at the age of 27, he was commanding I/*Lehrgeschwader* 2, which was based on the Channel coast and operating Bf 109s; its function was to test new equipment and tactics under combat conditions. On 13 September, having gained twenty-one victories, he was awarded the Knight's Cross. Later, during the Russian campaign, he became the fifth German fighter pilot to claim more than 100 kills; he was to end the war with a total of 130 to his credit, including nine in Spain. By this time he was flying Heinkel He 162 jet fighters with LG 1 at Leck, although the war ended before he could take the type into combat. Herbert Ihlefeld died in 1952.

On 14 September 1940, the day after Ihlefeld received his medal, *Hauptmann* Joachim Müncheberg was also awarded the Knight's Cross. In 1939, as a lieutenant in III JG 26, Müncheberg had opened his scoring by destroying a Bristol Blenheim reconnaissance aircraft over northern Germany. August 1940 found him commanding 7/JG 26, and a month later he had twenty victories. He was later transferred to the Mediterranean, where he claimed nineteen RAF fighters destroyed during the attacks on Malta. In March 1943, by which time his total number of kills stood at 103, he was killed when his Bf 109 collided with a Spitfire over Tunisia.

These were the men whom Hermann Göring, C-in-C *Luftwaffe*,

called his 'Young Turks'; men who had been brought in to replace the veteran *Geschwader* commanders early in the Battle of Britain. Some, like Adolf Galland, survived the war; most did not, although a few came very close to seeing the conflict through. One such was Günther 'Franzl' Lützow, who fought with JG 3 during the Battle of Britain. By January 1945 he had amassed 103 kills, 85 of them on the Russian Front. At that time, he was one of several senior *Luftwaffe* officers who were pressing both Hitler and Göring to use the Messerschmitt 262 in an interceptor role, rather than as a fast bomber; Göring flew into a rage, accused Lützow of mutiny and banished him to Italy, forbidding him to set foot on German soil again.

But Lützow did return, in the last weeks of the war; and it was in an Me 262, flying with Adolf Galland's elite *Jagdverband* 44, that he met his end while intercepting USAAF B-26 Marauders. His body was never recovered, and the wreckage of his aircraft was never found.

Following its heavy losses in September 1940 the *Luftwaffe* turned to night attacks on Britain's cities, and it was in countering these that the RAF produced the first of a new breed of fighter 'ace' in the men who stalked and destroyed the enemy bombers in the night sky. The development of airborne radar in Britain had proceeded well in the summer of 1940, by which time the RAF had five squadrons assigned to night fighting; these were equipped with Bristol Blenheims and two of them, Nos 29 and 604, were just starting to carry out trials with rudimentary Mk III AI radar. The real pioneering work, however, was undertaken by the Fighter Interception Unit at RAF Tangmere, and on the night of 22/23 July 1940 the long-awaited breakthrough came when a radar-equipped Blenheim of this unit intercepted and destroyed a Dornier Do 17 bomber. Flying Officer G. Ashfield, Pilot Officer G.E. Morris and Sergeant R.H. Leyland were patrolling at 10,000ft when the Chain Home (CH) radar station at Poling established contact with a group of enemy raiders crossing the coast at about 6,000ft. Information on the enemy's progress was passed to Tangmere Sector Operations Room where the FIU's CO, Wing Commander Peter Chamberlain, was acting as controller. Following Chamberlain's instructions, Ashfield closed on one of the enemy aircraft, the last phase of the interception being controlled by Morris's AI, and at a range of 400 yards the pilot identified it as a Do 17 and opened fire. The bomber, of II/KG3, went down into the sea off the Sussex coast. All four crew members, although wounded, were picked up. This was the first recorded success of a radar-assisted fighter, and although to some extent it was a lucky interception it showed that the concept was feasible, and the conversion of Blenheims to the night-fighter role continued.

However, a few squadrons of Blenheims, converted to carry airborne radar, did not provide a solution to the night defence problem; they were too slow, the equipment was very unreliable, and its operators lacked experience. A solution was on the horizon in the shape of the fast, heavily armed Bristol Beaufighter, which was just entering service; but this aircraft was beset by more than the usual crop of teething troubles. In November and December 1940, Beaufighters and radar-equipped Blenheims flew over 600 sorties, made seventy-one radar contacts, and succeeded in destroying only four enemy aircraft. In an attempt to fill the gap Fighter Command was compelled to adopt what might best be described as desperation measures to counter the enemy night raiders, especially when the *Luftwaffe* began to step up its night offensive against Britain after the failure of its massed daylight attacks in August and September. In the latter month, Air Chief Marshal Sir Hugh Dowding, the AOC-in-C Fighter Command, was ordered by the Air Council to allocate three squadrons of Hawker Hurricanes to night defence, this decision having been taken following the creation of a high-level Night Air Defence Committee earlier in the month. Added to these were three squadrons of Boulton-Paul Defiants, which, armed solely with a four-gun power-operated turret, had suffered appalling losses in the day-fighter role during the Battle of Britain. During the closing weeks of 1940, these six squadrons of single-engined fighters flew 491 sorties on forty-six nights and destroyed eleven enemy bombers. Operating on a hit-or-miss basis, pilots would seek out enemy bombers trapped in the glare of searchlights and would then go into the attack, risking being shot down by friendly anti-aircraft fire.

One such pilot was Flight Lieutenant Richard Stevens, a Hurricane pilot with No. 151 Squadron at RAF Manston. A former civil pilot who had flown the cross-Channel mail route at night and in all weathers, Stevens was 30 years old and a very experienced man by the time he joined No. 151 Squadron at the tail-end of the Battle of Britain, in October 1940. At this time the Germans had switched most of their effort to night attacks, and night after night

Stevens watched in frustration as the German bombers droned overhead towards the red glare of burning London. He constantly sought permission to try his hand at intercepting the raiders, and at last, one night in December, it was granted.

His early night patrols were disappointing. For several nights running, although the Manston controller assured him that the sky was stiff with enemy bombers, Stevens saw nothing. Then, on the night of 15 January 1941, the shellbursts of the London anti-aircraft defences led him to a Dornier 17 of 4/KG3, which he chased up to 30,000 feet and then almost down to ground level as the German pilot tried to shake him off. But Stevens hung on, and after two or three short bursts the bomber went down and exploded on the ground. It was No. 151 Squadron's first night victory, and there were more to come. On a second patrol that night, Stevens caught a Heinkel 111 of 2/KG53 at 17,000 feet, heading for London, and shot it down into the Thames estuary. Three of the four crew members baled out and were captured. The night's work earned Stevens a Distinguished Flying Cross.

Somehow, it seemed as though Stevens' brace of kills had been a good omen. After that, the RAF's night-fighter squadrons appeared to enjoy more success. Men like Flight Lieutenant John Cunningham of No. 604 Squadron, now flying Bristol Beaufighters, began to carve out reputations for themselves as bomber destroyers. Cunningham, known by the nickname of 'Cat's Eyes' bestowed on him by the popular press, and which he thoroughly detested, was to destroy no fewer than eight enemy bombers at night in April 1941, having been led expertly to his targets by his AI operator, Sergeant Jimmy Rawnsley. He was to end the war with a score of twenty enemy aircraft destroyed, two probably destroyed and seven damaged, most of them at night. (The 'Cat's Eyes' nickname, of course, was designed to divert attention from the AI radar, which was still highly secret and about which the public as yet knew nothing.)

It was eyesight alone, however, with a little help from search-lights and shellbursts, that brought Richard Stevens to his victims. Shortly after the award of his DFC, he developed ear trouble and was grounded for a while, but he celebrated his return to action on 8 April 1941 by shooting down two Heinkel 111s in one night. Two nights later he got another Heinkel and a Junkers 88, and a few days later he received a Bar to his DFC. He destroyed yet another Heinkel on the 19th, and on 7 May he accounted for two more.

Three nights after that, his claim was one Heinkel destroyed and one probably destroyed. He shot down a further Heinkel on 13 June, damaged one on the 22nd, and on 3 July sent a Junkers 88 down in flames. There seemed to be no end to his success; at this time he was the RAF's top-scoring night-fighter pilot, enjoying a considerable lead over pilots who flew the radar-equipped Beaufighters.

Stevens experienced a lot of frustration during the summer months of 1941. In June the Germans invaded the Soviet Union, and by the end of July they had withdrawn many of their bomber units from the Western Front. Raids at night over Britain became fewer, and although Stevens continued to fly his lone patrols, for weeks he never saw an enemy bomber. Then, one evening in October, he spotted a Junkers 88 slipping inland over the coast of East Anglia and attacked it. The Junkers jettisoned its bombs and turned away, diving low over the water, but Stevens caught it with a burst of fire and sent it into the sea. It was his fourteenth victory. Soon afterwards, Stevens was posted to another Hurricane unit, No. 253 Squadron, as a flight commander, and he immediately set about devising a plan to take the war to the enemy by flying night intruder operations over the German airfields in Holland and Belgium. Later in the war, offensive operations of this kind would become routine, but in December 1941 Stevens was virtually pioneering a new technique. He flew his first night intruder operation on the night of 12/13 December, the day when it was announced that he had been awarded the Distinguished Service Order. He loitered in the vicinity of the bomber airfield at Gilze-Rijen, in Holland, but saw no aircraft and returned home in disappointment.

Three nights later he took off again, heading for the same destination, and never returned. The signal that his squadron commander sent to Group HQ was simple and concise. 'One Hurricane IIC (long range), 253 Squadron, took off Manston 1940 hours, 15.12.41, to go to Gilze. It has failed to return and is beyond maximum endurance.' Richard Stevens, who had fought a lonely, single-handed battle in the night sky for over a year, had met an equally lonely fate.

The majority of the home-based Hurricane II squadrons took part in night intruder operations at one time or another during 1942, and some became specialists in the role. No. 1 Squadron, for example, which was based at RAF Tangmere, destroyed twenty-

Flight Lieutenant Karel Kuttelwascher destroyed at least eighteen enemy aircraft, mostly at night. (Roger Darlington)

two enemy aircraft over occupied Europe between 1 April and 1 July that year before moving to Northumberland to convert to Typhoon fighter-bombers, and no fewer than fifteen of these victories were gained by one pilot, Flight Lieutenant Karel Kuttelwascher. A highly competent and experienced pilot, Kuttelwascher – known by the simpler abbreviation of 'Kut' to his squadron colleagues – had flown with the Czech Air Force for four years before his country was overrun by the Germans, after which he had made his way to Britain via France. He scored his first three kills – all Messerschmitt 109s – while flying convoy protection and bomber escort missions over the Channel in the spring and early summer of 1941, but it was when

A Hurricane Mk IIc. This example bears the code letters of No 87 Squadron. (Flight International)

No. 1 Squadron went over to night intruder operations in April 1942 that Kut really got into his stride. In April 1942 he destroyed three Junkers 88s, three Dornier 217s and a Heinkel 111, and on the night of 4/5 May he shot down three Heinkel 111s over St André. He destroyed a Dornier 217 off Dunkirk on 2/3 June, and on the following night he visited St André again to destroy a Heinkel 111 and a Dornier 217, as well as damaging another Dornier. St André was once again the target on 21/22 June, when Kut shot down a Junkers 88 and damaged another. A Dornier 217 went down before his guns near Trevières on 29/29 June, and his last two victims, also Dornier 217s, were brought down near Dinard on the night of 1/2 July, when he also damaged a third Dornier.

That brought Kut's score to eighteen destroyed, with one probable (a Messerschmitt 109, his first combat in the RAF, on 2 February 1941) and five damaged. In addition, he may have claimed up to six victories while flying Morane 406 fighters in the Battle of France. After the war, he became a captain with British European Airways, flying Vikings and Elizabethans. He died of a heart attack on 17 August 1959, at the untimely age of 42.

CHAPTER SEVEN

Mediterranean Combat

For Flight Lieutenant Marmaduke St John Pattle, Sunday, 4 August 1940 was a day of mixed fortunes. It began early that morning, when he and three other pilots had taken off in their Gloster Gladiator biplane fighters from No. 80 Squadron's base at Sidi Barrani, Egypt, to escort a Lysander observation aircraft. The Lysander completed its mission successfully and lumbered away

A Fiat CR.42 lies crumpled in the desert after being shot down by British fighters. (IWM)

The Gloster Gladiator bore the brunt of the early desert air fighting.
(IWM)

safely over friendly territory, while the Gladiators climbed over the front line to look for some action.

The enemy found them first. The first indication Pattle had of danger was when machine-gun bullets ripped through his aircraft's wings and an Italian Fiat CR.42 fighter shot past, diving out of the sun. Pattle and the other Gladiator pilots broke hard into a climbing turn to find themselves confronted by a whole swarm of enemy machines – at least seventeen CR.42s and ten Breda 65 light bombers. One of the latter drifted into Pattle's sights and he opened fire. Thick smoke poured from its engine and the Breda nosed over into a dive. At the last moment it flattened out and hit the desert heavily in a cloud of sand.

An instant later, Pattle loosed off a short burst at a Fiat that came into his sights. It was excellent deflection shooting; the enemy fighter began to trail smoke immediately and went down in a vertical dive. Then Pattle's own aircraft shuddered as bullets struck it. The control column went sloppy and lifeless in his hands and the aircraft spun down, out of control. There was no alternative but to bale out. Pattle made a safe landing as the air battle raged over-head. Discarding his parachute, he took his bearings from the sun and began to walk in the direction of the British lines.

No one had seen him bale out, and when he failed to return to Sidi Barrani he was listed as missing, believed killed. But Pattle was still very much alive, and although he twice narrowly escaped capture by Italian patrols during his walk across the sands he was picked up by a British patrol some twenty-four hours after he was shot down, arriving back at Sidi Barrani the next day.

Pattle – known simply as 'Pat' to his friends – was born in Butterworth, Cape Province, South Africa in 1913. He came from a strong military background, and as soon as he had completed his education he joined the South African Air Force as a cadet. To his great disappointment he was not accepted for aircrew training, so he returned to civilian life and worked for some time with a mining company.

In 1936, with the urge to fly strong in him, he made his way to England and applied to join the Royal Air Force. He was quickly accepted, and soon showed that he had the makings of a born pilot. His aerobatics and marksmanship were excellent, and in 1937 he graduated from flying training school in the top three of his course. As a newly-commissioned pilot officer he was posted to No. 80 Squadron, which deployed to Ismailia, Egypt, in 1938. By the outbreak of war Pattle had become a flight commander, but he had to wait nearly a year to experience his first taste of combat, as Italy – the principal threat to the Middle East – did not enter the conflict until June 1940.

On 29 June 1940 Pattle was temporarily attached to No. 33 Squadron, also equipped with Gladiators, to replace a wounded flight commander. His first serious action came on 24 July, when six Gladiators led by the South African encountered eighteen Italian fighters and bombers over Sollum. Pattle destroyed one and the other Gladiator pilots accounted for three more without loss to themselves. The next day Pattle and three other Gladiators inter- cepted seven enemy aircraft over Bardia and destroyed five of them, Pattle himself shooting down three.

On 1 August No. 33 Squadron moved back to Helwan and its place at Sidi Barrani was taken by No. 80, Pattle rejoining his old unit. The squadron spent its first week at the front escorting the reconnaissance Lysanders of No. 208 Squadron, and sustained its first combat losses; on 4 August, the day Pattle was shot down, one Gladiator pilot was killed and another had to take to his parachute.

Four days later, however, the squadron had its revenge. On 8 August, thirteen Gladiator pilots – including Pattle – were carrying out an offensive patrol when twenty-seven Fiat CR.42 biplanes were sighted near El Gobi. The Gladiators had all the advantages, attacking out of the sun, and in the dogfight that followed nine Italian aircraft were destroyed for certain, two of them by Pattle. Six more Fiats were claimed as probably destroyed. One Gladiator pilot was killed and a second baled out safely.

In November 1940 No. 80 Squadron, together with No. 112 and two squadrons of Blenheims, deployed to Greece in support of the Greek Army, fighting hard against Italian invasion forces. During operations in November Pattle destroyed two Fiat CR.42s, sharing two more with other pilots and damaging two Savoia SM.79 bombers. On 2 December he shot down two Ro 37 observation biplanes, and on the 4th he destroyed three CR.42s, also claiming a fourth probably destroyed and a fifth damaged.On the 20th he claimed two more bombers – an SM.79 and an SM.81 – and the next day he added another CR.42 to his list. Pattle's growing reputation as a superlative air fighter, a brilliant tactician who launched his attacks with split-second timing and who rarely missed, had an electrifying effect on the morale of the other pilots. By the end of December the squadron had destroyed forty enemy aircraft for the loss in action of only six Gladiators, and the rumour that No. 80 would shortly re-arm with Hurricanes brought a promise of even greater achievements to come.

Nevertheless, it was with its ageing Gladiators that No. 80 Squadron entered the New Year of 1941. During January air activity on both sides was severely curtailed by bad weather, but on the 28th three Gladiator pilots, one of them Pattle, shared in the destruction of a CANT Z.1007 bomber. Shortly afterwards, Pattle received the news that he had been awarded the DFC.

There was a big squadron effort on 7 February, when the Gladiators encountered nearly forty CR.42s over the front line near Yannina. The British pilots shot down four of the enemy and claimed three more probably destroyed. Pattle did not score on this occasion, but two days later he claimed a CR.42. This was followed, on 10 February, by an air battle in which he damaged a CANT Z.1007 and also a Fiat BR.20 bomber.

It was Pattle's last action in the cockpit of a Gladiator. On 7 February the first Hurricanes had arrived in Greece, and these were allocated to Pattle's 'B' Flight of No. 80 Squadron. The South African's first combat in a Hurricane took place on 20 February, when Pattle's flight was attacked by a squadron of Fiat G.50

The Bristol Blenheim, seen here taking off from a Greek airstrip,
provided one component of the RAF's commitment in Greece. (IWM)

fighters while providing escort for thirty Blenheims. The British
pilots showed how well they could handle their new aircraft by
shooting down four of the enemy in as many minutes, Pattle
himself making short work of the leader.

By this time the Italian drive into Greece had become hopelessly
bogged down in the face of the Greek Army's determined stand,
and in the last week of February the Greeks launched a major
offensive that was designed to push the Italians out of Albania,
which they had used as a springboard for the assault on Greece.
The RAF fighter squadrons supporting the Greek Army – Nos 33,
80 and 112 – flew almost non-stop during this phase, and it was
while providing top cover for the Greek drive on Tepelini on 27
February that the British pilots scored their greatest success of the
campaign. In just ninety minutes of air combat, Nos 33 and 80
Squadrons destroyed twenty-seven enemy aircraft over the front
line, every one of them a confirmed victory.

Pattle, who had shot down a CR.42 the day before, was in the
thick of the fighting right from the start. After shooting down two
more CR.42s he was forced to land in order to refuel and rearm,
but when he took off again he saw that the battle was still raging.
Climbing hard, he sighted three CR.42s over Valona and
manoeuvred for an attack out of the sun. The Italians had not seen
him, and Pattle dived on their tails, opening fire at close range and
observing his bullets striking all three. The leading CR.42 went into

a steep dive and Pattle followed it, giving it a second burst. It finally burned and plunged into the sea. Climbing and turning to face the other two enemy fighters, he was just in time to see them both spinning down trailing smoke, with their pilots' parachutes drifting overhead. The entire action had taken less than three minutes.

The next day Pattle shot down a pair of Fiat BR.20s, and on 4 March he was involved in another big fight while leading his Hurricane flight on an offensive patrol over Himara. The pilots sighted and attacked a mixed formation of Fiat CR.42s and G.50s; on his first firing pass Pattle hit one of the latter in the fuel tank and the enemy fighter exploded. Breaking hard to port Pattle found himself nicely placed behind a pair of CR.42s, one of which went into a steep climbing turn. A short burst from the Hurricane's guns and the Fiat went down, smoking; the pilot baled out. The other CR.42 dived to ground level and tried to get away by hedge-hopping. For two minutes the Italian and his pursuer leap-frogged over trees and hills, until a burst from Pattle's guns found its target and the enemy biplane dived into the ground with a big explosion. The Hurricane was caught in the blast wave and slightly damaged by flying debris, but Pattle reached base safely.

Soon afterwards, Pattle was awarded a Bar to his DFC. He celebrated this on 24 March by shooting down a G.50, probably destroying another, and setting three more on fire during an attack on an enemy airfield. A few days later, he was posted to command No. 33 Squadron. Pattle had been with his new unit less than a week when, literally overnight, the battle situation took a dramatic turn for the worse. On 6 April, 1941, German forces simultaneously invaded Yugoslavia and Greece, and from dawn onwards the RAF fighters began to encounter Messerschmitt 109s and 110s in increasing numbers. Against the 1200 combat aircraft of *Luftflotte* 4, operating in the Balkans, the Allies could muster only about 200 machines, and of these only about fifty were modern Hurricanes.

Despite their numerical inferiority the RAF pilots fought valiantly, and Pattle's score continued to grow. On the first day of the German invasion he destroyed two Messerschmitt 109s and other pilots of 33 Squadron accounted for three more for no loss to themselves. The next day Pattle shot down a CR.42, and on the 8th he knocked out a pair of 109s during an attack on an enemy airfield. On the 9th he shot down his first German bomber, a Junkers 88; on the 10th a Messerschmitt 109 and 110; on the 11th

Hawker Hurricanes fitted with long-range tanks, seen here over the desert, arrived too late to save the situation in Greece. (RAF Museum)

a Heinkel 111 and a Junkers 88; and on the 12th a Dornier 17 and an SM.79.

The enemy advance continued relentlessly, and by the middle of April the Greeks and the Commonwealth forces supporting them were engaged in a fighting withdrawal, all the while under heavy attack by the *Luftwaffe*. The RAF fighter squadrons did what they could, but the number of combat aircraft at their disposal dwindled steadily as the *Luftwaffe* launched heavy raids on their airfields.

Finally, under overwhelming enemy pressure, it was decided to withdraw all the Hurricane squadrons to the Athens area in readiness to provide air cover for the evacuation of Allied forces. By this time there were only fifteen Hurricanes left in the whole of Greece, and these were assembled at Eleusis under Pattle's command.

Pattle himself was now suffering from extreme exhaustion, aggravated by a bout of influenza. Despite this he continued to fly and fight, and on 19 April he claimed two 109s and a Junkers 88 and shared a Henschel 126 with two other pilots. The next day, still feeling ill, he took off at the head of the surviving Hurricanes to intercept a formation of Ju 88 dive-bombers which was heading for Athens, escorted by a swarm of Bf 109s and 110s – over a hundred aircraft in all. Pattle led his Hurricanes right into the midst of the enemy, setting a 110 on fire with his first burst. A second 110 also went down in flames a few moments later, and as he climbed away Pattle found himself pursued by a pair of 109s.

Throwing his Hurricane into a very tight turn he got one of the enemy fighters in his sights and loosed off a short burst; the 109 fell apart as its fuel tanks exploded. Looking round, Pattle saw a lone Hurricane being harassed by two more 109s and turned to help. As he did so, he apparently made a serious omission – one that had almost cost him his life months earlier, when he had been shot down over the desert. He neglected to secure his tail. With eyes only for the aircraft ahead of him, he probably never even saw the Messerschmitt 110 that closed in behind him; at any rate, he took no evasive action. His Hurricane, riddled with cannon shells, fell into the waters of Eleusis Bay. The pilot did not bale out.

To this day, there remains some doubt as to Pattle's exact score of enemy aircraft destroyed. Some sources put it at twenty-eight, others at thirty-four. But men who flew alongside him swear that it was over forty, perhaps as high as fifty. No one will ever know for certain.

April 1941, the month in which Pattle was killed, saw the arrival in North Africa of an elite German fighter unit, I/ JG 27, commanded by Major Eduard 'Edu' Neumann. On the flight from Tripoli to Gazala, the unit's main base, one Messerschmitt 109 developed engine trouble and its pilot had to make a forced landing 500 miles short of his destination. His name was Hans-Joachim Marseille, a young and debonair Berliner with eight victories to his credit, gained over the English Channel.

Marseille arrived at Gazala after hitching a lift in an Italian truck and an Italian general's staff car, and a few days later he shot down the first British aircraft, a Hurricane, to be claimed by I/ JG 27 since its arrival.

Marseille was determined to prove that he had the makings of a first-rate fighter pilot, for he had an unfortunate reputation. His personal file was littered with remarks such as "showed bravado and played pranks while under training" and "committed offences in contravention of flying regulations." There was even an entry, underlined in red by one furious flight commander, that labelled him a "flying obscenity."

Marseille's eagerness was almost his undoing. Time after time, regardless of personal danger, he dived into the middle of a British formation and often returned to base with his aircraft full of bullet holes. On one occasion, during a dogfight, he leaned forward in the cockpit – and a burst of gunfire ripped the back of his helmet. Had it not been for his sudden movement, the bullets would have shattered his head. In another dogfight over Tobruk his 109 was badly hit and he had to make a forced landing in no-man's land, but he managed to reach the German lines safely. A few days later his aircraft was hit in the engine and he crash-landed at Gazala, walking unscathed from the wreck.

Edu Neumann thought it was time to have a word with Marseille. 'You are only alive,' he told him, 'because you have more luck than sense. But don't imagine that it will continue indefinitely. One can overstrain one's luck like one can an aeroplane. You have the makings of a top-notch pilot, but to become one you need time, maturity and experience – certainly more time than you have left if you go on as you have been doing.'

The message sank home, and from now on Marseille devoted much of his time to improving his tactics. He practised shooting from every angle, making dummy attacks on the other aircraft of his squadron, and as the weeks passed his skill increased. During Rommel's summer offensive of 1941 his score grew to eighteen aircraft destroyed and his name was frequently mentioned in dispatches. The high point of this period came on 24 September, when Marseille destroyed a Martin Maryland bomber, and in the afternoon he destroyed four Hurricanes in a fierce half-hour battle between Halfaya Pass and Sidi Barrani.

In October the rains came, flooding Allied and German airstrips alike and severely curtailing air activity on both sides. At the same time the British launched an autumn offensive, pushing Rommel back to the point from which he had started several months earlier. During this defensive period Marseille's score rose to forty-eight, bringing the award of the Knight's Cross. He was also accorded certain privileges, being permitted to fly his 'personal' Messerschmitt, with a large and distinctive yellow 14 painted on its fuselage just aft of the cockpit.

All three groups of JG 27 were now in North Africa, and in April 1942 Marseille was given command of III Gruppe. On 3 June, during the battle for the Gazala Line, Marseille led III/JG 27 on a mission to Bit Hakeim, escorting Stukas which were dive-bombing the Free French positions there. The Stukas were attacked by the P-40 Tomahawks of No. 5 Squadron, South African Air Force, which had inflicted heavy losses on the dive-bombers during earlier raids.

A Curtiss P-40 Kittyhawk taxiing in a cloud of desert sand. (IWM)

Together with his wingman, *Feldwebel* Reiner Pöttger, Marseille dived his Bf 109 into the middle of the South Africans, who, doubt-less believing that they were being attacked by a far superior force, immediately formed a defensive circle. Marseille got inside it, turning steeply, and gave a P-40 a short burst. The fighter went down vertically and exploded in the desert. Marseille's tactics were unorthodox; turning continually inside the circle of enemy fighters, keeping his airspeed low, he fired in short, accurate bursts. In less than twelve minutes, he had accounted for five more Tomahawks, all of which were seen to crash by Pöttgen.

During the next few days Marseille destroyed fourteen more aircraft. His score was now ninety-one and, as he approached the magic figure of 100, the other pilots of JG 27 were laying bets on when he would claim his 100th victory. On 16 June he shot down four aircraft, and the following day he claimed a further six, making his score 101. After that, he was sent home on leave. He was away for two months, and when he returned he found that considerable changes had taken place.

A fierce argument had broken out between General Rommel, commanding the German forces in Africa, and *Feldmarschall* Albert Kesselring, the commander of the German forces in the Mediterranean. In June, when Tobruk fell to the Germans, Rommel had declared his intention to push straight on to the Nile delta and

Cairo, giving the British no time to regroup. Kesselring's argument was that such a move would create an enormous logistics problem for the *Luftwaffe*, whose crews were exhausted and aircraft badly in need of overhaul. Moreover, the strength of the British Desert Air Force was continuing to grow and the Luftwaffe was in no position to mount attacks on its airfields; this meant that if Rommel persisted in an all-out drive on Cairo, there was no guarantee that the *Luftwaffe* would be able to provide the necessary air support. Rommel, however, emerged victorious from the conflict of wills and the advance continued. The *Luftwaffe* threw its dwindling resources into the battle, attacking enemy supply depots and troop concentrations. At the end of June, JG 27 took its Bf 109s to Sidi Barrani, and for days on end the pilots flew sortie after sortie. Rommel's drive finally ground to a halt before El Alamein, and it was at this point that Marseille returned to the battle.

For a week he saw little action. Then, on 1 September 1942, Rommel made a last attempt to break through the British Eighth Army's defences, and fierce air battles developed over the front when the *Luftwaffe* put every available fighter into the air in a maximum effort. For Marseille, the day began at 0628 when he shot down a Kittyhawk. A second P-40 followed quickly, and ten minutes later he claimed a pair of Spitfires. In an incredible ten-minute period between 10.55 and 11.05, while escorting Stukas on

A Junkers Ju 87 Stuka shot down in the desert. (Source unknown)

a raid against Alem el Halfa, he claimed no fewer than eight Kittyhawks. In a third sortie between 1747 and 1753 he destroyed five more aircraft south of Imayid, raising his score for the day to the unbelievable total of seventeen.

Later, this claim was to be the subject of controversy. It was bitterly contested by the RAF, who stated that Marseille's claim exceeded the total British losses for that day. Yet every one of Marseille's claims on 1 September was confirmed by his wingmen, who noted precise times and locations. Moreover, the losses of the RAF, Australian and South African fighter squadrons for 1 September, taken together, did in fact exceed the claims of all German fighter pilots by about ten per cent.

Two days later, Marseille was awarded the Diamonds to the Knight's Cross. He was now the *Luftwaffe*'s most highly-decorated pilot, possessing the Knight's Cross with Oak Leaves and Swords, and the Italian Gold Medal for Bravery, the latter being only of only three awarded in World War Two.

During September 1942, Marseille's score rose to 158 enemy aircraft destroyed. His 158th victim, a Spitfire, almost succeeded in shooting him down, but Marseille gained the advantage and despatched his opponent after a dogfight that lasted fifteen minutes.

It was his last victory. On 30 September 1942, together with eight other Bf 109s, he took off to provide top cover for a formation of Stukas. The dive-bombers attacked their targets without incident; no enemy aircraft were sighted and the Bf 109s turned for base, their task completed. At 1135, as the fighter formation cruised at 4500 feet, Marseille's voice suddenly came over the radio, telling the others that there was smoke in the cockpit and that he could no longer see clearly. The other pilots saw him open the small ventilation hatch in the side of the canopy, and a stream of dense smoke poured out. Marseille kept repeating that he was unable to see, and the others passed directions to him over the radio. Ground control, which had heard his radio call, advised him to bale out, but the Messerschmitts were still three minutes' flying time away from the German lines and Marseille refused.

The smoke grew worse, pouring back from the cockpit and engulfing the rear fuselage and tail. At last, the formation entered friendly territory. The other pilots saw Marseille jettison his cockpit canopy, and a second later he fell from the aircraft as he turned the aircraft over on his back. His body struck the tailplane

A Hurricane fighter-bomber of the Desert Air Force strafing enemy transport in the Western Desert. ((IWM)

a glancing blow, then dropped away towards the desert. There was no parachute.

They buried Hauptmann Hans-Joachim Marseille in the War Heroes' Cemetery at Derna. On his gravestone was inscribed a single word: 'Undefeated'. In the desert where he fell, Italian engineers erected a simple pyramid, a monument renewed in 1989 by Edu Neumann and others survivors of JG 27.

A few weeks after Marseille was killed, the tanks of General Montgomery's Eighth Army, fresh from its victory at El Alamein, rolled past the spot.

The Allied victory in North Africa, leading to the subsequent landings in Sicily and Italy, would not have been possible without one factor: the tenacious resistance, under months of almost cease-less air attack, by the garrison and people of the island of Malta, deservedly awarded the George Cross in 1942. Defended originally by three Gloster Sea Gladiators (named Faith, Hope and Charity by the popular press, and more correctly as the Malta Fighter Flight) in the weeks following Italy's declaration of war, the full weight of the early onslaught against the island was borne by the Hawker Hurricane for over a year before the arrival of the first Spitfires in March 1942, at which time only thirty serviceable Hurricanes were left.

Code-named Operation Spotter, the first reinforcement, on 7 March, involved the flying-off of fifteen Spitfires from the aircraft carriers *Eagle* and *Argus* at extreme range; all arrived safely, as did nine aircraft on 21 March and seven more on 29 March. These precious assets were divided among the three Hurricane squadrons defending the island, Nos 126, 185 and 249.

By the middle of April 1942 the position was once again desperate, and on the 20th of that month Operation Calendar was mounted, in which the American aircraft carrier USS *Wasp* flew off forty-seven Spitfires, of which forty-six reached the island. By the end of the next day, after further heavy air attacks, only eighteen remained airworthy. Operation Calendar involved, for the first time, the deployment of a complete Spitfire squadron to Malta; this was No. 603, transferred to the island from Peterhead in Scotland.

On 9 May the USS *Wasp* returned, together with HMS *Eagle*, and between them the carriers flew off sixty-four Spitfires. Of these, sixty reached Malta, and the next day they played an important part in a major battle that developed over the island when the Luftwaffe made a determined effort o sink the fast minelayer HMS *Welshman*. The defending Spitfires and Hurricanes flew 124 sorties, destroying fifteen enemy aircraft. Three Spitfires were lost, two pilots were picked up by the air-sea rescue service, and the *Welshman*, with her vital cargo of supplies and ammunition, escaped.

On 18 May 1942 seventeen more Spitfires arrived safely on Malta, again flown from the carriers *Eagle* and *Argus*. On 3 June the same carriers launched thirty-one more, of which twenty-seven arrived, and on 9 June they flew off another thirty-two, all of which reached the island.

Led by a Lockheed Hudson, Hurricanes head for the besieged island of Malta. (RAF Museum)

Malta's ordeal: a rescue team at work in the rubble after an air attack. (IWM)

Among the replacement pilots who reached Malta that day was a Canadian, Flight Sergeant George Frederick Beurling, posted to No. 249 Squadron. Born in Verdun, a suburb of Montreal, in 1922, George Beurling's future was shaped from the moment his father presented him with a model aeroplane on his sixth birthday. By the time he was ten he was reading every book he could lay his hands on about the fighter aces of World War One and spending most of his time watching aircraft at the local airport. His parents were disturbed by their son's growing obsession; his father wanted George to become a commercial artist, like himself, or as a second choice to study medicine.

George would have none of it. As soon as he was old enough he learned to fly and went to night school to gain the necessary qualifications to become a professional pilot, having already applied to join the Royal Canadian Air Force and been rejected. Working his passage to England, he was accepted for flying training in the RAF on 7 September 1940, and a year later he reported for duty with No. 403 (Canadian) Squadron as a sergeant pilot. Soon afterwards he was posted to No. 41 Squadron, destroying two Focke-Wulf 190s in fighter sweeps over France, but he never fitted in with squadron discipline and he applied for a posting to Malta.

Beurling's arrival on the island was dramatic. Seconds after he taxied his Spitfire clear of the runway at Luqa a big enemy raid developed and he was bundled unceremoniously into a slit trench while waves of Junkers 88s and Italian bombers pounded the airfield. Buerling watched the action unfolding all around him, and craved to be part of it. His craving was satisfied sooner than he expected. At 1530 he was strapped into the cockpit of a Spitfire on immediate readiness, with eleven other Spitfires of No. 249 Squadron ready to taxi from their dispersals. The pilots, even though they wore only shorts and shirts, were dizzy with the heat as the sun beat down mercilessly; although it would be up to thirty degrees below freezing at 20,000 feet, to don heavier flying clothing would be to risk sunstroke on the island's baked surface.

It came as a relief when the squadron was ordered to scramble to intercept an incoming raid over Gozo, Malta's neighbouring island. The Spitfires climbed in sections of four, the pilots searching the sky to the north. Suddenly they saw the enemy: twenty Ju 88s, escorted by fifty Bf 109s and Macchi C.202s. Beurling's section went for the fighter escort while the remaining Spitfires tackled the bombers. There was no time for manoeuvre; the opposing sides met head-on at 18,000 feet over the sea and within seconds a fierce battle spread out across the sky. Beurling loosed off an ineffective burst at a Messerschmitt that flashed across his nose; a moment later he got another enemy fighter in his sights, but it skidded out of the line of fire and dived away.

The next moment, Beurling himself came under fire and brought his Spitfire round in a maximum-rate turn. His adversary shot past him; it was a Macchi C.202, and now it hung squarely in the Canadian's sights as he turned in behind it. The Macchi shuddered as the Spitfire's cannon shells struck home and then went down in a fast spin, shrouded in white glycol vapour. There was no time to see whether the Italian had crashed. The sky was full of aircraft and Beurling went after a section of Ju 88s which was diving in the direction of Valetta harbour. Closing to within fifty yards of the nearest bomber he opened fire. It burst into flames and the crew baled out.

As he was preparing to select another target, Beurling heard a frantic call over the radio from a fellow pilot who, short of fuel, was being prevented from landing on Safi airstrip by Messerschmitts. Beurling at once dived over the island towards Safi, squeezing off a short burst at a Bf 109 on the way. It was a lucky shot; the German fighter spun down and crashed. Arriving over Safi, Beurling quickly assessed the situation. A lone Spitfire, desperately trying to land, was being menaced by a Bf 109, closing in on its tail. Beurling came down and opened fire, roaring over the top of the landing Spitfire and attacking the Messerschmitt head-on. The enemy fighter flashed past him and vanished. A moment later, more Spitfires arrived and circled watchfully overhead as Beurling himself went in to land.

An hour later he was airborne once more, together with every available fighter on the island, intercepting thirty Junkers Ju 87s that were attacking HMS *Welshman*, once again unloading a vital cargo of fuel and ammunition. The Spitfires and Hurricanes ran the gauntlet of their own AA fire to get at the Stukas as they dived over Valletta, and a free-for-all developed over the harbour as over a hundred enemy fighters joined the fray. Beurling shot down a 109 and severely damaged a Junkers; pieces from the enemy bomber whirled back and damaged his propeller, but he made a successful belly landing near the clifftops.

During the remainder of June there was a comparative lull in the air fighting over Malta. The Germans and Italians had suffered considerable losses in their air offensive of April and May, which had all but beaten the island to its knees, and were now gathering their strength for a renewed offensive. In July, however, the fighting flared up again, and on the 11th Beurling destroyed three Macchi C.202s in the course of the afternoon, an exploit that earned him the award of the Distinguished Flying Medal. From then on, his score began to mount with remarkable speed. On the 18th he shot down a Reggiane 2001 fighter-bomber, on the 27th he destroyed two Macchis and two Messerschmitts, damaging two more; and on the 29th he shot down another Bf 109. He opened his August score on the 8th with yet another 109, and on the 13th he shared a Ju 88 with two other pilots.

The air battles of July 1942, in which the RAF claimed 149 victories (much exaggerated) for the loss of thirty-six, was the end of the Hurricane's combat career over Malta; from now on the defence of the island rested solely upon the Spitfire. August and the early part of September passed fairly quietly, but towards the end of the month, with Malta's torpedo-bombers and submarines taking a growing toll of Rommel's vital supply lines to North Africa, the *Luftwaffe* made a last attempt to knock out the island's offensive and defensive capability.

On 25 September there was a fierce air battle over the island, and Beurling, now commissioned as a pilot officer, shot down two more Bf 109s. On 9 October he shot down three more, together with a Junkers 88, a score that was repeated three days later. On the 13th he got another Bf 109, bringing his score to twenty-four. His last day of combat came on 15 October. He engaged a Junkers 88 and shot it down, but not before the enemy gunner had hit his Spitfire and wounded him in the heel. Despite this, he managed to shoot down two Messerschmitts before taking to his parachute. He landed in the sea and was picked up by an air-sea rescue launch.

Beurling (who, incidentally, was known as 'Buzz' by his colleagues, and never by the rather derogatory nickname of 'Screwball', bestowed on him by the popular press) was flown back to the United Kingdom at the end of October, narrowly escaping death when the Liberator bomber in which he was a passenger ran off the end of the runway at Gibraltar and crashed into the sea. Soon after his return, he attended an investiture at Buckingham Palace and received from King George VI no fewer than four decorations at the same time: the DSO, DFC, DFM and Bar to the DFM, all earned in Malta.

Beurling ended the war as a squadron leader. Unable to settle in

The announcement in the Times of Malta that the island and its people had been awarded the George Cross. (IWM)

civilian life and yearning for more action, he volunteered to fly and fight for the new State of Israel. On 20 May 1948, while ferrying a Noorduyn Norseman to Israel, the aircraft crashed on take-off from Rome's Urbe Airport. He was twenty-six years old.

Beurling was buried in Rome, but two years later, at the request of the Israeli government, his remains were re-interred at Mount Carmel, in Israel.

A week before Beurling flew back to England, on 23 October, 1942, General Bernard Montgomery's Eighth Army launched the offensive that would ultimately drive the Axis forces out of Africa. The fate of Rommel's *Panzerarmee Afrika* was sealed in November, when Anglo-American force landed in Morocco and western Algeria. By early 1943 the German-Italian forces were retreating into Tunisia, where the terrain favoured defensive operations. But the Germans were dependent on their trans-Mediterranean supply lines, which were being hammered mercilessly by the RAF's Malta-based anti-shipping squadrons while British and American fighters roved the skies over Tunisia and Tripoli, hounding the remnants of the *Luftwaffe* to destruction.

In March 1943, a group of fifteen fighter pilots arrived in North Africa. They were soon to distinguish themselves as the Polish Fighting Team, and they were led by Squadron Leader Stanislaw Skalski, who since June 1942 had commanded No. 317 'City of Wilno' Squadron at Northolt. His new team, which soon became known as 'Skalski's Circus', was attached to No. 145 Squadron, flying Spitfire Mk IXs at Bou Grara in Tunisia. In eight weeks of operations, the exploits of the Polish pilots became legendary. During that two-month period, they shot down more enemy aircraft than any other Polish fighter unit in 1943, and the pilots achieved such reputations that they were subsequently offered post as commanding officers of other RAF fighter squadrons. Skalski, who shot down two Bf 109s and a Ju 88 over Tunisia, became the first Pole to command an RAF fighter squadron, the famous No. 601, then in Malta.

In 1944 Skalski was given command of No. 133 Wing, covering the D-Day landings. On 24 June, flying a Mustang during the fighting in Normandy, he scored his twenty-second and last victory, a Bf 109. In October 1944 he was sent on a staff course to the USA, and on his return he was posted to the staff of No. 11 Group and later to the Second Tactical Air Force in occupied Germany. By the end of the war he had attained the rank of group captain, and as well as the highest Polish decorations he had been awarded the DSO, the DFC and three Bars, and the American DFC.

In June 1947, having turned down offers of exciting positions in the RAF and USAAF, he returned to Poland and joined its new Soviet-controlled air force with the rank of major. Then, in June 1948, together with other Polish RAF veterans, he was arrested, accused of espionage, tortured and imprisoned. He was condemned to death, but the sentence was reduced to twenty-five years. He languished in prison until 1956, when he was amnestied and rehabilitated. He rejoined the Polish Air Force a year later, retiring in 1968 with the rank of brigadier-general. In his later years he lived quietly and humbly in a small flat in Warsaw,where he died on 12 November 2004, at the age of eighty-nine.

On 7 April, 1943, following desperate fighting in North Africa, the American II Army Corps linked up with the British Eighth Army and the drive northwards into Tunisia began. At the same time, the Allied air forces began an all-out campaign to destroy the remnants of the *Luftwaffe* in North Africa; they also launched a series of heavy attacks on enemy airfields in Sicily, where the enemy was assembling fleets of transport aircraft – Junkers Ju 52s and massive, six-engined Messerschmitt Me 323 'Giants' – in a desperate attempt to get supplies and reinforcements through to the *Afrika Korps*.

On Palm Sunday, 18 April, long lines of battle-ready German and Italian troops, fresh from training camps, filed aboard ninety Junkers 52s that stood waiting on their Sicilian airfields. There were 1800 soldiers in all, twenty to each aircraft. By 16.30 the armada was airborne and heading south-westwards, flying low over the sea to avoid detection by the radar stations on Malta. With the transports came the fighter escort, thirty Messerschmitt 109s and 110s, as well as a few Macchi 202s.

Three hundred miles away, on the other side of the Mediterranean, forty-eight P-40 Warhawks of the USAAF's 57th and 324th Fighter Groups lifted away from their desert airfield of El Djem. Climbing steadily, they flew northwards along the Tunisian coast. The pilots' orders were to patrol the Cape Bon area and the Gulf of Tunis. Over Sousse, halfway to the Gulf, twelve sleek aircraft came up from the east and slipped into position above the American formation, at 15,000 feet. They were the Spitfires of No. 92 Squadron, RAF.

The big fighter formation reached Cape Bon and began its

patrol. For ninety minutes the pilots flew back and forth over the sea, the squadrons wheeling lazily at heights of between 7000 and 15,000 feet. By 1800, the sun was a great orange ball in the west and it was becoming hard to see.

Captain Roy Whittaker was a pilot with the 57th Fighter Group. He had already flown one lengthy patrol that day without seeing anything.

> Suddenly, something caught my eye: the flash of sunlight on a wing, low over the sea. A moment later, I made out a large formation of enemy fighters, weaving from side to side. Behind them, looking like a massive flight of geese in three v-shaped formations, Junkers 52s stretched as far as the eye could see. They were flying in perfect formation as though at an air show, heading on towards the Tunisian coast. It was a fighter pilot's dream.

While twelve P-40s and the Spitfires of 92 Squadron went for the enemy fighter escort, the remaining thirty-six P-40s dived on the transports. Roy Whittaker swept down on the leading formation and fired at a pair of Ju 52s, seeing pieces fly off one of them, then climbed and circled for another attack. This time he was more successful; two Junkers went down in flames and a few moments later they were joined by a third. Pulling up sharply, Whittaker

A giant Messerschmitt Me 323 transport under attack over the Mediterranean. (RAF Museum)

One of the leading British fighter aces, who scored the majority of his
kills in the Middle East and Italy, was Squadron Leader Neville Duke,
with twenty-eight victories. He is seen here in the cockpit of the
prototype Hunter jet-fighter when he was Chief Test Pilot with Hawker
Aircraft. (British Aerospace)

found the belly of a Messerschmitt 109. He fired, and the enemy
fighter spun into the sea. The American glanced at his watch: he
had destroyed four enemy aircraft in just three minutes.

Everywhere it was the same story. Young pilots for whom this
was the first taste of combat suddenly found themselves turned
into aces in a matter of minutes. Lieutenants Arthur B. Cleaveland
and Richard E. Duffy destroyed five Junkers apiece, while another
57th Group pilot, Lieutenant MacArthur Powers, shot down four
Ju 52s and a Messerschmitt 109.

As they attacked again and again, the fighter pilots began to run
into a storm of small-arms fire from the transports. Hatches and
doors were jettisoned and the German troops crouched in the slipstream, blazing away at the attackers with rifles and light machine
guns.

Deprived of their fighter cover, by this time scattered all over the
sky, the slow transports had no chance. Some were lucky, but only

because shortage of fuel compelled the Allied pilots to abandon the chase. Behind them, the fighters left a scene of carnage; patches of oil and wreckage drifted on the water, with a handful of survivors struggling among them; tall columns of smoke rose from the crashed aircraft that littered the coast.

In just ten minutes, for the loss of six of their own number, the Allied fighters had destroyed seventy-seven enemy aircraft – more than the RAF had destroyed in the heaviest day's fighting in the Battle of Britain. Fifty-nine of those aircraft were Junkers 52s, and with them a thousand men of the Afrika Korps went to their deaths. So ended the great air battle that was to go down in history as the Palm Sunday Massacre.

Four days later the Germans tried again, this time with huge Messerschmitt 323s. Sixteen aircraft, all from *Transport-Geschwader* 5 and fully laden with fuel, were heading for Tunis with a small fighter escort when they were caught off Cap Bon by two squadrons of RAF Spitfires and four squadrons of South African Air Force P-40s. In five minutes, the fighters shot down fourteen of the mighty transports and seven of the escorting fighters, leaving the coastal waters aflame with burning petrol. Two hundred and forty tons of fuel never reached the Axis forces that day, and of the 140 aircrew of TG 5 who took part in the operation, only nineteen survived.

CHAPTER EIGHT

Holding On: Burma and the Pacific, 1942

I first flew a Hurricane in July 1941 at RAF Ternhill, where I was awarded my wings and commissioned, and after further Hurricane flying at the OTU at Sutton Bridge I was posted to 136 Squadron with a grand total of 190 flying hours, of which some seventy-five were on Hurricanes. When I joined 136, preparations were in hand to go overseas, and we thought we were off to the Caucasus. Because of the possibility that we would be flying off a carrier, the last few flights were in Hurricanes fitted with long-range tanks and we practised very short take-offs. Our CO, who had formed 136 Squadron in August that year, was T.A.F. Elsdon, who had been at Cranwell just before the war began and who subsequently flew with 72 Squadron in the Battle of Britain, gaining a DFC for some seven or eight destroyed by September 1940. My flight commander in 'B' Flight was Barry Sutton, a journalist, who flew in France and the Battle of Britain with 56 Squadron; he had been burnt and off flying for some time.

So spoke Wing Commander Gordon Conway DFC, who was to fly Hurricanes with No. 136 Squadron for two years – not in the Caucasus, as anticipated, but in the far different climate of India and Burma.

November was a month of great change within the squadron. We received several new officers to fill specialist ground posts and some dozen of the sergeant pilots were hastily commissioned to bring us up to overseas manning tables. 'A' Flight commander was Murray-Taylor; he and five other pilots became our advance party and, together with most of the ground officers and airmen, who formed the main party, were seen off by the twenty or so remaining pilots.

The rest of us were soon at Padgate transit camp awaiting a ship. We were to be a four-squadron Wing; the pattern of each was similar, with experienced squadron and flight commanders heading teams of young pilots, most of whom had very little operational flying experience, and some of whom, like me, were completely raw. No. 17 Squadron was commanded by 'Bunny' Stone, who had shot down three or four enemy aircraft while serving with No. 3 Squadron in France; 232 Squadron was under Squadron Leader Llewellyn; and 135 Squadron, recently formed like us, was commanded by the redoubtable Frank Carey, who had scored eighteen victories while flying with No. 43 Squadron in 1940 and who already wore three decorations.

We sailed from the Clyde in the P&O cruise liner Strathallan as part of a large convoy of escorted troopships bound for the Middle East, but within a week the Japanese launched their attack in the Far East, which caused us to be diverted to Singapore. In a signal to General Wavell, Winston Churchill announced that four fighter squadrons of the RAF, now en route to the Caucasus and Caspian Theatre, were to be placed under his Far East Command together with the 18th Division, which was then rounding the Cape. This Cape convoy contained the advane aircrew parties of the four squadrons, together with most of the ground parties.

On 3 January 1942, the diverted convoy arrived in Singapore with fifty-one crated Hurricane Mk Is and the advance parties of Nos 17, 135, 136 and 232 Squadrons. The Hurricanes earmarked for the defence of Singapore operated as No. 232 Squadron under Llewellyn. The pilots fought on against mounting odds and achieved some notable successes, as on 20 January, when they shot down eight of a formation of twenty-seven unescorted Japanese bombers over Singapore. The next day, however, the enemy

A Hawker Hurricane strafing Japanese troops in Burma. (IWM)

bombers were escorted by Zero fighters, and this time five Hurricanes were shot down. These actions cost the lives of Flight Lieutenant Murray-Taylor, Pilots Officers Hackforth and Fleming, and Sergeant Leetham; Pilot Officers Williams and Mendizabel were also shot down and wounded. In a matter of days, the pilots who had formed 'A' Flight of 136 Squadron when it left England had been wiped out.

By 28 January, only twenty Hurricanes remained airworthy, and of these only ten were serviceable at any one time. Added to these were six Brewster Buffaloes, the remnants of four squadrons – one RAF, one RNZAF and two RAAF – which had been responsible for the air defence of Malaya. By 9 February the Buffaloes had been virtually destroyed, but the Hurricanes continued to register successes; on that day, for example, six Japanese bombers were shot down over Singapore and fourteen damaged, for the loss of one RAF fighter. But it was the end; on 10 February the last Hurricanes were withdrawn to Sumatra, and five days later Singapore surrendered.

The decision had already been taken to concentrate any fighter reinforcements on Sumatra, and on 26 January forty-eight

Hurricane Mk IIAs arrived on the aircraft carrier HMS *Indomitable*. They were flown by a mixture of pilots drawn from Nos 242, 258 and 605 Squadrons, all of whom had been originally destined for Singapore. The aircraft were dispersed between P.I, the airstrip at Palembang, and P.II, a new and secret strip further south. Unfortunately, five of the Hurricanes crashed on landing at Palembang, and, because their guns were choked with anti-corrosion grease and had to be stripped and cleaned, it was some time before the remainder could go into action.

Conditions on Sumatra were appalling, with airfields severely congested and their surfaces in a fearful state as a result of the heavy rains. The task of the air units in Sumatra became doubly difficult after 14 February, when the Japanese launched a heavy attack on Palembang airstrip and then captured it using airborne forces. From then on, the Allied units had to operate from P.II, and it was from here that reconnaissance aircraft detected a Japanese naval force en route to occupy the island. On the morning of 14 February the convoy was attacked by every available bomber that could be mustered by the RAF and RAAF. They enjoyed a conspicuous success by sinking six enemy transports for the loss of seven aircraft, and the next day, escorted this time by Hurricanes, they attacked the enemy landing force again, inflicting enormous destruction on the landing ships in the Banka Strait and the mouth of the Palembang river. The enemy landing plan was completely dislocated, and thousands of troops killed. In addition, the Hurricanes destroyed a number of Zero fighters on the ground at Banka Island. Unfortunately, no Allied troops or naval forces were available to exploit this success, and the position in Sumatra quickly became untenable. With stocks of food and ammunition running dangerously low, the order was given for a move to Java.

The evacuation was completed on 18 February. By that time, twenty-five Hurricanes remained, of which eighteen were serviceable; these were divided between Nos 232 and 605 Squadrons and immediately thrown into the defence of Batavia. Twenty-four more Hurricanes – Mk Is which had been diverted in crates from Singapore to Batavia – were also operated by the Royal Netherlands Indies Army Air Corps and were divided into two squadrons, one for the defence of Batavia and the other for ground attack. At that time twenty-four more Hurricanes were still in crates at Batavia; these had been destined for the RAF, but as there were simply not enough pilots to fly them it was decided to turn them over to the Dutch too, along with about forty airmen and an engineer officer. The latter was Squadron Leader John David, who had earlier been responsible for the Buffaloes of No. 243 Squadron at Kallang, Singapore. He provided this unique account of the Dutch Hurricane operations.

No spares, ammunition or supplies of any kind were included and no training was offered. At the handing-over ceremony the Dutch colonel receiving the aircraft, not understanding the safety ring on the firing button, enlivened the proceedings by firing a long burst just over the heads of the RAF VIPs on parade! This set the scene for a remarkable do-it-yourself private air force, which survived for several weeks and really gave the Japs quite a bad time, although at great cost.

We moved to an improvised grass airfield north of Bandoeng in central Java and lived in grass huts in the local village. The squadron CO was Lieutenant-Colonel Animaat, a saturnine individual of daemonic courage (his family had been wiped out in the Celebes Islands). He came from Dutch Guiana, in South America, and was of very mixed blood. He was also a gentleman of the old school and spoke perfect English. His No. 2 in charge was Captain Bruning, who had fought in the Battle of Britain and who now acted as training and conversion man. He, too, spoke perfect English and never hid from me his assessment of how hopeless the situation was; at the same time, he did a remarkable job of building the pilots' morale even higher. As their experience had been confined to the Curtiss Mohawk (Hawk 75A) and the even earlier Curtiss-Wright CW-21, the Hurricane was an eye-opener for them and they revelled in its speed, rate of climb and, above all, armament and toughness.

We worked about twenty hours a day, cutting out dispersal pens in the rubber plantations around the airstrip, getting the locals to dig trenches, checking out the assembly work, stripping the aircraft down, teaching the Dutch pilots to handle liquid-cooled engines and constant-speed props and, above all – vital to morale, it seemed – painting the orange triangle insignia of the Royal Netherlands Indies Army Air Corps on the aircraft.

Knowing the familiar glycol problem, to which was now added a critical shortage of .303 ammunition (the Dutch only had .300 calibre) as well as batteries and equipment for the Hurricanes' TR9D radios, I made many visits to Bandoeng and Batavia to squeeze the official channels – with almost complete failure. I was then reduced to begging from my engineer colleagues dotted about Java and finally to finding out where the most recent crash had occurred. It was then a matter of trying to beat the RAF recovery team to the site. Thanks to our Dutch native airman driver, we usually got there first.

The Hurricanes' first operation was a total success, because eight of them – all we could get into the air – caught a formation of Japanese Navy single-engined carrier aircraft (probably Kates) returning unescorted after a maximum-range trip and shot the lot down. That was their only easy one; after that it was nearly always fighter to fighter. We were lucky to get five minutes warning of a raid coming in, so we were usually at a disadvantage.

The Dutch were, however, brilliant pilots, having had years of training in the peacetime Netherlands East Indies, and the strength of the Hurricane allowed them to take ridiculous liberties with it. Inevitably, we irritated the Japanese too much

An armourer at work on a Hawker Hurricane. (C.W. Gudge)

and they located our airfield, which was cutting up badly, and mounted a major low-level bombing and strafing attack just after our morning patrol had come in. Six aircraft were re-fuelling, and all were destroyed when the petrol bowsers exploded. About fifteen of my men were killed or seriously wounded, as were several Dutch pilots. My life was saved by Bruning, who pushed me into a slit trench and fell on top of me just as another strafing wave came in.

Our dispersed aircraft were not hit, however, and we managed to get six out of eight serviceable. The Dutch played cards to decide who was first in the queue to fly. A few days after the major raid, with even petrol almost unobtainable, Animaat was ordered to move to Surabaya in east Java, which had been flattened and was expected to be invaded. It was obviously to be a last stand and he absolutely refused to take me with him, saying that they would probably manage only one take-off and that his own ground crew of about ten men could look after that. We were returned to Bandoeng, already in chaos; some of us were ordered to evacuate and some to stay. I was lucky . . .

Meanwhile, Nos 232 and 605 Squadrons had been in almost constant action from 17 to 27 February in the defence of Batavia, and on the 28th the few remaining Hurricanes were concentrated in No. 232. The squadron was now under the command of Squadron Leader Brooker, his predecessor, Llewellyn, having been killed when his aircraft struck the mast of a sampan on take-off. On 1 March the RAF pilots, together with a few Dutch Mohawks and Buffaloes, carried out a gallant attack on Japanese forces landing at Eretanwetan and inflicted considerable casualties. The surviving Hurricanes were then flown to Bandoeng, from where they covered the remaining ground forces as best they could until 7 March, when only two serviceable aircraft were left. On 8 March all organised resistance in the Dutch East Indies ceased. Some of the RAF air and ground crews who had taken part in the spirited defence of the islands managed to escape; most were captured to face the horror and misery of Japanese prison camps, a three-and-a-half-year nightmare from which more than half did not awake.

There remained Burma, whose seizure by the Japanese would mean an abrupt cessation of foreign aid to China and would also give Japan a base from which to launch an invasion of India. The

A tactical reconnaissance Hurricane suffers a mishap while operating from an airstrip in India. (C.W.Gudge)

original Allied plan had been to provide an air defence of some 280 aircraft, and for this purpose No. 221 Group was established under the command of Group Captain E.R. Manning. Under his direction, seven new airstrips were built between Mingaladon in the south and Lasio in the north; these were supported by a series of satellite landing grounds. There was another airfield at Akyab, on the west coast. By December 1941, therefore, the facilities for the air defence of Burma were well established; unfortunately, the aircraft that were to form No. 221 Group's offensive and defensive power were not.

On 7 December 1941, the air defence of Burma comprised sixteen Buffaloes of No. 67 Squadron, RAF, and twenty-one P-40s of the 3rd Pursuit Squadron, American Volunteer Group (AVG), the remainder of which was based on Kunming in China. When the Japanese attack came the British and American pilots fought with great gallantry and achieved considerable success; in one memorable battle on Christmas Day the AVG destroyed twenty-four Japanese aircraft and the Buffaloes of No 67 Squadron accounted for twelve more. But the losses sustained by the small Anglo-American force were high, and by early January it was apparent that it would soon be powerless to stem the Japanese onslaught.

Meanwhile, the main parties of Nos 17, 135 and 136 Squadrons – originally intended for the defence of Singapore – had arrived in Cairo, the pilots having literally hitched rides in various aircraft from Takoradi, and by mid-January twenty Hurricanes had been made available to be flown to the defence of Burma by a small party from each squadron. Led by the three squadron commanders, Carey, Stone and Elsdon, the Hurricanes took off from an airfield just outside Cairo and then flew via Palestine, Iraq, down the Persian Gulf of Bahrain and then on to Karachi, and from there across India to Calcutta and finally down the length of Burma to Mingaladon, near Rangoon. So pressing was the need for fighters that Carey, Stone and Elsdon, the most experienced pilots, were all in action before the ground crews had time to remove the long-range tanks from their Hurricanes. All were badly hit and only their considerable fighting experience saved them.

Frank Carey's experiences typify the bitter, losing battle for

Frank Carey pictured after the war in the cockpit of a Hawker Tempest II fighter-bomber, when he was OC Flying at Gütersloh, Germany. (Doreen Clegg)

command of the air in Burma during those early weeks of 1942. He destroyed his first aircraft, a Nakajima Ki.27, on 29 January, shortly after his arrival; a few days later he was promoted to wing commander and placed in command of the combined fighter force at Mingaladon, bringing in Barry Sutton to taker command of No. 135 Squadron. Japanese air activity was increasing all the time, and on 23 February Carey intercepted and destroyed an enemy reconnaissance aircraft over Rangoon. Three days later, in the course of three separate sorties, he shot down three Nakajima Ki.43 Oscar fighters, bringing his score in the Far East to five and his total score to twenty-three. Soon after this exploit he received a second Bar to his DFC.

The main task of the Mingaladon Wing was to cover the progressive withdrawal of the Allied forces, who were being pushed back towards the Indian frontier by the relentless Japanese advance. For operational purposes the Hurricanes, operating in close conjunction with the AVG and No. 67 Squadron, which was still using what was left of its Buffaloes, were dispersed over a number of makeshift airstrips in the Rangoon area. This reduced the risk of losses during enemy air attacks, but made it difficult to mount a sizeable force of fighters for either attack or defence at short notice.

This was the problem that faced Carey when, at the beginning of March, he received information that a large number of Japanese fighters and bombers were moving into the captured airfield at Moulmein, just across the Gulf of Martaban and close to the border with Thailand. Carey immediately mustered his eight remaining serviceable Hurricanes and ordered them to take off for an attack on the enemy field. However, just as the Hurricanes were leaving their respective airstrips, Japanese aircraft appeared overhead and it was not possible for the RAF fighters to make rendezvous with one another.

Carey accordingly set course for Moulmein accompanied by only two other Hurricanes, one of which got lost en route. Carey and the other pilot, Pilot Officer Underwood, pressed on and arrived at Moulmein to find that the intelligence report had been correct. The airfield was crammed with enemy fighters, many standing in neat rows while ground crews refuelled and rearmed them.

Carey went after two Oscars which were approaching to land, well committed with their wheels and flaps down, and shot one of them down over the end of the runway. The second tried to take evasive action by means of a steep turn, stalled and crashed. Carey looked around for Underwood, but there was no sign of him. By this time the Japanese were thoroughly aroused, and Carey found himself being attacked by several enemy fighters, one of which he shot down as it turned in front of him. For five minutes the Japanese had him boxed in, and he needed all his considerable skill to stay alive. Then the enemy fighters started getting in each other's way in their eagerness to bring him down, and eventually he spotted an opening and headed for it at full throttle. The Japanese chased him across the jungle for some distance, then gave up. Carey landed at Mingaladon with his aircraft riddled like a colander. Later, he learned that Underwood had been hit by anti-aircraft fire and taken prisoner after baling out.

At the end of the Burma Campaign Frank Carey went back to the United Kingdom to attend the central Gunnery School, but returned to India to Air HQ Bengal and then to command the Air Fighting Training Unit at Calcutta. He ended the war as a group captain in command of an operational training unit, and in 1949, having been granted a permanent commission and dropped rank temporarily to wing commander, he became Wing Commander (Flying) at RAF Gütersloh in Germany, flying Hawker Tempest IIs and then Vampires. His last appointment as a group captain was as Air Adviser to the British High Commission in Australia. He retired from the RAF in 1960 and subsequently worked for the Rolls-Royce Aero-engine Division in Australia, returning to the UK in 1974.

Group Captain Frank Carey, CBE, DFC and two Bars, AFC, DFM, died in West Sussex on 6 December, 2004, aged ninety-two. Many of his wartime colleagues remained adamant that he was the RAF's top-scoring pilot of World War Two, with perhaps as many as fifty victories – a claim that could never be verified because so many records were lost during the retreat from Burma.

With the arrival of the Hurricanes, the Japanese switched almost entirely to night bombing, which caused the RAF some problems, as there were no dedicated night fighter squadrons in Burma. An early warning system of sorts was devised, relying on a network of ground observers to give warning of the Japanese bombers' approach by telephone. Ten minutes' warning was usually just enough to enable the defending fighters to gain a height advantage over the bombers as they approached their target. After that, the

The men of the American Volunteer Group, the 'Flying Tigers', played a valiant part in the defence of Burma. (USAF)

fighter pilots relied on their eyesight, moonlight and searchlights (of which there were very few) to locate the enemy.

War correspondent O.D. Gallagher, an accurate eye-witness to events in Burma (as far as censorship would allow) described a night battle early in 1942.

At last two night-fighter pilots arrived from Britain. We were in front of the club [the Mingaladon Golf Club – author] on the big lawn, with some twenty Blenheim pilots, observers and gunners. We heard the distant sirens of Rangoon . . . We heard the night fighter take off [the pilot was Squadron Leader Stone, DFC] and begin its sinister, unseen prowling of the sky. The moonlight was brilliant, although there were some high, patchy, still clouds. Indeed, they seemed to add to the brilliance of the moonlight by reflecting it. 'The Japanese night formation arrived with a trembling drone that filled the air. They were at a great height but we spotted them. They circled the airfield once or twice with their customary arrogance, their usual contempt for the feeble defences. Tonight it was a pleasure to see them keep tight formation, supremely ignorant of the single, higher-pitched sound that manoeuvred around them. They could not, of course hear the Hurricane with its old night-fighter pilot in the cockpit. They certainly could not see it, any more than we could. It was perfectly blacked out – not a twinkle of light from its shielded exhausts . . .

A line of red tracer bullets pierced the sky and shot up verti-cally. Another – the tracers chased each other upwards until they burned out. Seconds later we heard the rat-tat-tat of Stone's guns . . . Tracers shot from another point, obviously fired by the gunner of a Japanese bomber. But at that same moment a new line of red tracers poured downward from an invisible source above them. It was Stone, who had drawn their attention to a spot below the formation, then climbed all out above them and caught them unawares . . .

One of the bombers burst into fire and crashed to the ground. An immense flash as it hit, and later a heavy crump . . . In the light of the following day they found the bodies and remains of five Japanese around the wreck. That was the first night-fighter success from Mingaladon airfield . . . (O.D. Gallagher, *Retreat in the Far East*, Harrap, London, 1942).

On 8 March 1942 the Japanese entered Rangoon, and it was no longer possible for the Allies to carry out an organised defence of Burma. The army now began the long retreat northwards along the Irrawaddy and Sittang rivers, protected by the handful of fighters that remained. The remnants of No. 221 Group were moved north to the civil airport at Magwe and the island of Akyab, where they were formed into Burwing under Group Captain S. Broughall and Akwing under Group Captain N.C. Singer. Burwing comprised No. 17 Squadron, which had absorbed the remnants of Nos 135 and 136 Squadrons, together with the Blenheims of No. 45 Squadron; Akwing consisted of No. 67 Squadron, now operating a small number of Hurricane Mk IIAs and its last surviving pair of Buffaloes, and No. 139 Squadron, equipped with Lockheed Hudsons.

On 20 March, ten Hurricanes and nine Blenheims from Magwe attacked Mingaladon, where they destroyed sixteen Japanese aircraft and eleven in the air. The enemy reprisal was swift; in a period of twenty-four hours more than 230 aircraft struck at Magwe, destroying all but six Blenheims and eleven Hurricanes.

The survivors flew out to Akyab, while the AVG's three remaining P-40s were evacuated to Lashio. On 27 March, the enemy launched a three-day air assault on Akyab, destroying seven Hurricanes and some transport aircraft.

It was the end. The surviving Allied aircraft were evacuated to India, and Burma's towns, together with the long columns of troops and refugees struggling towards India, were at the mercy of the Japanese Air Force. Yet the Allied fighters in Burma had given a magnificent account of themselves, claiming the destruction of 233 enemy aircraft in the air and fifty-eight on the ground, with a further seventy-six probably destroyed and 116 damaged, for the loss in air combat of thirty-eight of their own number, of which twenty-two were Hurricanes. At least some of the success was probably due to the relatively low calibre of the Japanese Army pilots. Elsewhere, when the Allies encountered the highly-trained squadrons of the Imperial Japanese Navy, it was a very different story.

Meanwhile, on 3 February 1942, the remaining aircrews of the original four-squadron wing that had been assigned to the defence of Singapore had arrived in Karachi, together with a cargo of crated Hurricanes. With the victorious Japanese fleet now poised to enter the Bay of Bengal, it was decided that the first eight Hurricanes to be assembled were to be flown to Colombo to defend Ceylon. The pilots assigned were Flight Lieutenant Peter Fletcher, a Rhodesian; Flying Officer Joe Edwards, a Canadian; Pilot Officer Ian Adamson, a Scot from the Argentine who wore the shoulder flashes BLAV (British Latin American Volunteers); Pilot Officer Gordon Conway; Warrant Officer Thomas Taggart Young, an American in RAF uniform; Flight Sergeants Barney Banikhin and Bill Higgins; and Sergeant 'Ginger' Hicks. It would have been hard to find a more cosmopolitan team.

Of the eight, all the officers were to survive the war and all the NCOs would be killed within a year.

The Hurricanes made the long flight south over India guided by a Blenheim and landed at Ratlamana, the home of the Ceylon Flying Club. There was also a detachment of Blenheims of No. 11 Squadron; they were worn out and several crashed as they took off, fully bombed-up, to search for the Japanese fleet. On one occasion, one of them collided on take-off with Ian Adamson, the volunteer from Argentina; both aircraft were destroyed but Adamson survived although with severe burns.

On another occasion, a Dutch Lockheed Lodestar landed on the airstrip and out stepped half a dozen British officers, among them 'Dizzy' Mendizabel, No. 232 Squadron's French-Canadian pilot who had fought over Singapore and Java and had survived being shot down. They had found the old Lodestar and repaired it, tying on its broken tailwheel with rope and filling its fuselage with four-gallon petrol cans from which they passed a hose to the main wing tanks via a hole knocked in the skin. They had managed to get airborne and had then set course for India using a hand pump to refuel and a school atlas for navigation. 'Not surprisingly,' Gordon Conway remembered, 'they missed India, but not by much! It was a storybook escape spoiled a little when the pilot damaged his ankle badly on climbing out!'

The Hurricanes were scrambled several times to intercept suspected enemy aircraft, but these usually turned out to be false alarms caused by the island's sole and rudimentary radar set. At the beginning of 1942, following the arrival of reinforcements, the air defences of Ceylon comprised about fifty Hurricanes, together with a small number of Royal Navy Fairey Fulmar fighters. On 4 April, a reconnaissance Catalina of No. 205 Squadron, RAF, reported that the enemy fleet was approaching Ceylon, and at dawn the following day – Easter Sunday – a strong force of about 150 Japanese carrier aircraft attacked Colombo harbour in the hope of surprising the Royal Navy's Eastern Fleet at anchor. In fact the fleet was at sea, having sailed in an abortive bid to launch a night strike against the Japanese task force.

Thirty-six Hurricanes of Nos 30 and 258 Squadrons, together with six Fulmars, took off to intercept the enemy. The radar had given plenty of warning of the incoming raid and the engagement took place initially far out to sea, the air battle gradually creeping back towards the island. Both the RAF and Fleet Air Arm pilots elected to intercept the enemy at the extreme limit of their range in an attempt to knock down as many of the Japanese as possible over the sea, in the full knowledge that after the battle they would hardly have any hope of regaining the island because of lack of fuel. Fifteen Hurricanes and four Fulmars, hopelessly outclassed by the Zero fighter escort, were shot down. At the time, it was estimated that the Japanese had lost eighteen aircraft in combat and five more to anti-aircraft fire, but these claims have never been substantiated. A more accurate assessment is that the enemy lost seven aircraft, most of them falling victim to Colombo's AA barrage.

The next morning, a dozen Hurricanes of No. 261 Squadron and six Fulmars operated by No 273 took off at 0700 to intercept a raid on China Bay airfield and the neighbouring dockyards. On this occasion fifteen enemy aircraft were claimed destroyed for the loss of eight Hurricanes and three Fulmars.

The surviving Hurricanes and Fulmars suffered heavily in subsequent Japanese air attacks, particularly in the defence of Trincomalee. On 9 April, the remnants took off in a desperate bid to provide air cover for the carrier HMS *Hermes*, which was being attacked by enemy torpedo-bombers and had no fighters of her own on board. By the time the fighters arrived the *Hermes* was on fire and sinking, as were the Australian destroyer *Vampire*, the corvette HMS *Hollyhock* and two Fleet Auxiliaries. Earlier, Admiral Nagumo's carrier aircraft had also sunk the cruisers *Dorsetshire* and *Cornwall*.

Fortunately for Ceylon's depleted defences, and for the Eastern Fleet, Japanese carriers never again made an appearance in the Indian Ocean. After the attacks on Ceylon, Nagumo withdrew his task force to the Pacific in readiness for the next big Japanese adventure: the planned occupation of Midway Island. It was an action that would cost him the carriers *Akagi*, *Kaga*, *Hiryo* and *Soryu*. Ultimately, it would cost Japan the war.

The focus now shifted to Calcutta, the assembly area for the units and individuals straggling back into India following the collapse in Burma. The Hurricane squadrons that had fought so valiantly there now had time to rest and re-equip and, for the first time since leaving the United Kingdom, become established as cohesive units. With the squadrons fully established, flying concentrated on essential training – battle formations, interceptions and combat – and each squadron automatically kept a sharp lookout no matter what the nature of the exercise and attacked any other fighter formation seen in the sky. For the pilots who had yet to see action, it provided invaluable experience that would stand them in good stead during the months to come. Gordon Conway remembered the period well, and some of the accidents that occurred during it.

For the next three months we were based at Alipore. Frank Carey was our wing leader and Jimmy Elsdon our CO, but we had two new flight commanders with Battle of Britain experience who had flown in the last few days at Akyab: Piers

Worrall now commanded 'A' Flight of 136 Squadron and 'B' Flight was commanded by Guy Marsland. Equipped with replacement Hurricanes, mostly old ones, we trained as a fighting unit, waiting for the Japanese and the daily routine was much the same as it is for all fighters: a proportion of us were at a high state of readiness while other squadrons would be at various lower states, and the dawn shift always started long before dawn. A period of readiness was from first light to last light for the day boys, but since we dispersed our aircraft every evening by flying them out to one of the many satellite strips around Calcutta in order to minimise losses from a surprise attack at dawn or dusk, the first pre-dawn task was to drive by car – or, worse still, 15-cwt open truck – over rough and very rudimentary tracks to the satellite strip to be in the cockpit for readiness at first light. This was followed by a short flight to main base before settling down to a long waiting game in the growing heat.

We lost two pilots at this time. To test Japanese reaction a sweep was flown over Chittagong, on the far side of the Bay of Begal. On the way back Barney Banikhin made a successful forced landing, but Hamish Weatherall developed a bad glycol leak and was killed when he spun in, apparently overcome by fumes. A fortnight later I handed over my aircraft to Piers Worrall, who took over readiness in it. I had flown it twice the previous day, but when he took off later in a scramble he lost his engine in a dead cut and was burned to death when he crashed into a pillbox at the end of the runway.

In mid-1942, No. 136 Squadron moved to Red Road, a strip in the centre of Calcutta, from where it could operate as a single unit. Because of the severe camber on Red Road, the Hurricanes normally took off singly on the crown of the road to assist in keeping straight. Failure to do so could have disastrous consequences, as Gordon Conway discovered one day when, while taking off as number two of a pair, he failed to keep on top of the camber and progressively drifted to port as engine torque and adverse camber combined. Just as he got airborne the port wing took the top off a sentry box that had foolishly been sited right on the edge of the road (it never was again). Thanks to the Hurricane's ruggedness and some skilful flying, Conway got down with several feet of wing missing.

Early in September 1942, Nos 135 and 136 Squadrons deployed to Vizagapatam, a newly constructed all-weather strip about 500 mioes south of Calcutta, in response to a Japanese air threast to Allied coastal shipping in the Bay of Bengal. Japanese reconnaissance aircraft had been sighted over the Andamans, and patrols were flown to intercept them. On one such sortie Squadron Leader Elsdon and Gordon Conway spotted a Japanese seaplane dropping bombs near a ship and gave chase, but the enemy escaped in cloud. However, the Japanese were now aware that British fighters were in the area and their aircraft made no further appearances.

After three weeks the two squadrons moved to Dum Dum, the strip at Red Road having been occupied by No 17 Squadron. No 136 suffered two more losses in 1942 when Barney Banikhin flew into the ground during a practice attack and was killed instantly, and a month later the squadron's American pilot, Thomas Taggart Young, hit a tree in the same exercise area and died from his injuries three days later.

By the end of 1942, it was apparent that the Japanese were gathering their forces for the big push that would take them into India. It was equally apparent that the British commanders in the theatre, and one in particular, whose I Burma Corps had just conducted the longest fighting retreat in the history of the British Army, were determined to stop them. The name of the I Corps commander, soon to command the Fourteenth Army, was General William Slim.

While British Commonwealth and Chinese forces were engaged in the fighting retreat through Burma during those long months of 1942, the Americans had been fighting a very different kind of war in the Pacific, a war in which naval air power was to be the decisive factor.

In the Philippines, the Army Air Corps' P-40 squadrons suffered appalling losses from the first day of the Pacific War. The islands were defended by five USAAC P-40 squadrons totalling abnout ninety aircraft; one-third of this force was wiped out on the ground in the first day of the Japanese attack. Fifteen more P-40s were lost in air combat on 10 December, victims of the highly skilled Zero pilots of the Imperial Japanese Navy.

One of the P-40 units in the thick of the fighting was the 17th Pursuit Squadron, whose P-40s were based at Del Carmen alongside those of the 34th Pursuit Squadron. The 17th Squadron's commander was Lieutenant Boyd D. 'Buzz' Wagner, who on 11 December was leading a flight of P-40s on patrol north of Aparri when they were attacked by five Zeros. In two days of air fighting Wagner had learned how to cope with the agile Japanese fighters. Now, as two Zeros dived on him, he waited until they were in firing range and then suddenly throttled back. Taken by surprise, the Zero pilots shot past his aircraft. Wagner opened the throttle again, quickly caught up with them in the dive and shot both of them down. A week later, on 18 December, Wagner destroyed three more enemy aircraft to become the first US Army Air Corps ace of World War Two. A few days later he was almost blinded when a cannon shell exploded in his cockpit, filling his eyes with Perspex splinters, but he brought his aircraft home and recovered to fly P-40s and P-39s in New Guinea, raising his score to eight. He was killed in a flying accident later in the war.

In February 1942, with the battle for the Philippines lost and their aircraft destroyed, the surviving P-40 pilots evacuated to Australia, where they joined the 49th Fighter Group at Darwin in time to provide the principal fighter defence of the vital northern Australian port. The 49th was equipped with a more modern version of the Warhawk, the P-40E, and as the Japanese stepped up their air attacks on Darwin in the spring and summer of 1942 a number of American pilots became aces.

The nimble Mitsubishi Zero fighter was more than a match for any
Allied type at the outset of the Pacific war. (via J.R. Cavanagh)

Lieutenant John D. Landers delivered a new P-40 to Darwin on 3 April and was in action the next day, shooting down an enemy bomber. Almost immediately afterwards, he was pounced on by several Zeros, who shot his P-40 full of holes. He dived away and shook them off, then climbed over Melville Island in the hope of picking off any Japanese stragglers returning from the battle over Darwin. A while later, three Zeros passed directly under him and he dived on them, shooting one down. They were the first of six victories Landers was to score during his tour with the 49th. Later, flying with the Eighth Air Force in Europe, he added eight and a half more kills to his total.

Lieutenant James B. Morehead had already destroyed two Ki 21 Sally bombers over Java before joining the 49th FG in March 1942. On 29 April 1942, ANZAC Day, the Japanese launched a major attack on Darwin and all three squadrons of the 49th Group were scrambled to intercept the incoming bombers and their fighter escort. Morehead, leading the 8th Squadron, shot down three Mitsubishi G4M Betty bombers, closing right in to make certain of his kills and braving very heavy return fire. His P-40 was hit by thirty-nine machine-gun bullets and two cannon shells, which

The Curtiss P-40 Warhawk was the principal fighter type used in the air defence of northern Australia. (USAF)

An American pilot of the 49th Fighter Group with his shark-nosed P-40 in northern Australia, 1942. (USAF)

damaged it so badly that Morehead had to make a belly landing back at base. During his tour with the 49th, Morehead shot down two Zeros over Darwin, bringing his total to seven. He later added a Messerschmitt 109 to his tally while serving with the 1st Fighter Group in Italy. He retired from the USAF after the war with the rank of colonel.

In the months that followed the Japanese attack on Pearl Harbor in December 1941, the fighter aircraft that really held the line for the United States was the Grumman F4F Wildcat. Powered by a Pratt & Whitney Twin Wasp radial engine and armed with four .50 calibre machine guns, the tubby little Wildcat was the standard single-seat fighter in service with the US Navy and US Marine Corps at that time. Although completely outclassed by the Mitsubishi A6M Zero, it fought valiantly against hopeless odds in those early months of the Pacific War, and many American aces scored their first victories while flying it.

The Wildcats first met the Japanese in action during the heroic defence of Wake Island in December 1941, shooting down nine Japanese aircraft before they were overwhelmed. The first kill by a carrier-based Wildcat in the Pacific was scored by Lieutenant (Jg) W.E. Rawie, who was strafing Japanese positions during an attack on the Japanese-held Marshall and Gilbert Islands by the aircraft carriers USS *Yorktown* and USS *Enterprise* on 1 February 1942 when he was attacked by two Mitsubishi A5M Claude fighters. He turned into them and shot one of them down as they went past.

A second US carrier strike was laid on later in the month, this time by the USS *Lexington* against Rabaul, the idea being to try to relive growing Japanese pressure on Port Moresby in New Guinea. Part of *Lexington*'s carrier air group was VF-3, a Wildcat squadron commanded by Lieutenant-Commander John S. Thach. An excellent shot and the US Navy's leading exponent of air tactics, Thach had developed a defensive manoeuvre which became known as the Thach Weave. This involved elements of two aircraft, with about 300 yards' spacing between each aircraft so that each pilot could watch his partner's tail. If a pilot was attacked from astern, he would break towards his partner, who would also break outwards towards the second pair. This pair would then break inwards in order to meet the threat head-on; the attacking aircraft would effectively be drawn into a trap. It proved an excellent tactical manoeuvre, and with modification it is still used today.

Thach had insisted on his pilots constantly striving to improve their marksmanship, so that in February 1942 VF-3's gunnery record was probably the best in the US Navy. Their skill was to stand them in good stead, and compensated in part for the Wildcat's shortcomings. It was also appropriate that Thach himself had the privilege of scoring VF-3's first kill, a Kawanishi H6K Mavis reconnaissance flying boat which he shot down in flames 400 miles north-east of Rabaul. The Japanese crew made no attempt to abandon their aircraft and the gunners kept on firing until the Mavis exploded on the sea.

It was soon clear that the Japanese had remained at their posts long enough to alert their HQ on Rabaul to the presence of an American aircraft carrier. Late that afternoon, nine Mitsubishi G4M Betty bombers were seen approaching the USS *Lexington*. They were engaged by the carrier's combat air patrol (CAP) and the Wildcats shot down four of them, but the rest continued on course and bombed in formation from 11,000 feet. The bombing was accurate, but the carrier took evasive action and escaped damage. Then, as the Wildcats were preparing to land-on in order to refuel and rearm, a second formation of nine Bettys was detected by the carrier's radar.

Only two Wildcats were in a position to intercept this second attack, and their pilots showed no hesitation. In the leading fighter, Lieutenant H. 'Butch' O'Hare ripped into the Japanese formation and sent down two Bettys in flames on his first pass. The Betty had an excellent range, but this had been achieved by saving weight at the expense of armour protection for the crew and fuel tanks; as a result, when the Betty was subjected to a determined attack it usually exploded into flames. O'Hare braved heavy defensive fire to destroy another bomber, quickly followed by two more. In just five minutes, he had become the US Navy's first air ace.

By this time, John Thach and other Wildcat pilots had arrived to join the fight, and they followed the surviving bombers for as long as their fuel permitted. Of the eighteen Japanese bombers that tried to attack the *Lexington* that day, thirteen went blazing into the sea. For his personal exploit, Butch O'Hare was awarded the Medal of Honor. He went on to score a total of twelve kills before being killed in action during a strike on the Gilbert Islands on 26 November 1943.

Later in the war, John Thach was assigned to the Fast Carrier Task Force as Air Operations Officer, where he developed tactics that played a major part in destroying Japan's offensive air capability. He continued his distinguished career after the war, eventually reaching the rank of rear-admiral. He died on 15 April, 1981.

On 7 August 1942, a division of United States Marines stormed ashore on Guadalcanal, in the Solomon Islands. For the Americans, it was the first step on a long journey back across the Pacific, a journey that would end almost exactly three years later with the nuclear destruction of Hiroshima and Nagasaki. One of the main American objectives in the invasion of Guadalcanal was to capture an airstrip which had been built there by the Japanese. The Marines went in and took it, and the land battle subsequently centred on the struggle to retain it. In one of the most tenacious and heroic actions of the Pacific war the Marines clung grimly to the perimeter they had set up around the strip, which they called Henderson Field in honour of Major Lofton R. Henderson, a squadron commander and Marine Corps pilot lost in the Battle of

US Marines tackle a burning F4F Wildcat at Henderson Field,
Guadalcanal, after a Japanese air attack. (US Navy)

Midway, and by 20 August it had been made sufficiently secure
for the first US fighters to fly in.

They were the Wildcats of Marine Fighter Squadron VMF-223,
led by Major John L. Smith, and they were followed by Major
Robert E. Galer's VMF-224 a few days later. The day after their
arrival on Guadalcanal, the pilots of VMF-223 intercepted six Zeros
at 14,000 feet over the island, and Major Smith shot down one of
them to score the squadron's first victory. The following afternoon
the Japanese came again, this time with fifteen bombers escorted
by twelve Zeros. All VMF-223's serviceable Wildcats took off to
intercept the enemy, and in the course of a savage air battle they
destroyed sixteen Japanese aircraft for the loss of three Wildcats.
John Smith and one of his flight commanders, Captain Marion E.
Carl, each shot down three.

Day after day, while the ground forces strove desperately to
hold the thin perimeter around Henderson Field, the Marine pilots
went into action against the Japanese squadrons that were making
determined efforts to wipe out the primitive airstrip. At the same
time, Japanese warships shelled the base every night, and individual enemy aircraft carried out nuisance raids to ensure that the
American personnel got little rest. As the weeks went by, malaria,

dysentery and fatigue began to have a telling effect, yet the Americans, flying to the limits of their physical endurance, somehow managed to retain air superiority. By the time VMF-223 was relieved in October 1942, the pilots had destroyed 110 enemy aircraft. John Smith's score was nineteen, while his close rival Marion Carl had shot down sixteen. Major Robert E. Galer, of VMF-224, had chalked up thirteen victories; both he and Smith were awarded the Medal of Honor. All three survived the war.

The replacement squadrons of Guadalcanal were VMF-121 and VMF-212. One of the former's pilots was Captain Joe Foss, a farm boy from South Dakota whose marksmanship, thanks to his father's tuition with rifle and shotgun, was superb. Foss rose to fame with incredible speed over Guadalcanal; by the middle of October he was averaging one victory a day, and by the end of the month three a day. On 23 and 25 October he destroyed a total of nine enemy aircraft, all of them Zeros. By the time VMF-121 left Guadalcanal in January 1943 its pilots had destroyed 123 Japanese aircraft for the loss of fourteen Wildcats. Joe Foss's personal score was twenty-six, which made him the first American to equal the personal score of Eddie Rickenbacker, the leading American ace of World War One. His outstanding combat record earned Joe Foss the Medal of Honor. He never flew in combat again (American policy being that outstanding combat pilots who had been awarded the Medal of Honor should not be required to risk their lives in action again) and, after the war, he became Governor of South Dakota. Brigadier-General Joseph J. Foss died in hospital on 1 January, 2003 at the age of 87, having suffered an apparent aneurism.

The exploits of Joe Foss tended to overshadow all others in the embattled sky over Guadalcanal; but in the hectic days of October and

USMC ace Joe Foss survived the war to become Governor of South Dakota. (US Navy)

November 1942, when the Japanese were making their most determined attempts to recapture the island, the effective resistance of
the American pilots was due in no small measure to the dedicated
leadership of one man. He was Lieutenant-Colonel Harold W.
Bauer, known throughout US Marine Aviation as 'Indian Joe'.

Bauer was the commanding officer of VMF-212, which was
based on Hefate in the New Hebrides when the battle for
Guadalcanal began. His initial task was to provide a pool of trained
replacement Wildcat pilots for the two Marine squadrons already
in action on the island, and before long he was making frequent
visits to Guadalcanal himself, flying combat air patrols with the
others. On 28 September, he destroyed an Aichi D3A Val dive-
bomber, his first victory, and on 3 October he claimed four Zeros,
part of a Japanese fighter force which was escorting a large group
of G4M Betty bombers. He shot down four more enemy aircraft –
all Vals – on 16 October, the day that he led his own VMF-212 into
action on the island.

It was Bauer who instructed his Wildcat pilots to dogfight with
the Zeros. This had been attempted earlier, with disastrous results
because the Zero was more manoeuvrable than the Wildcat, but
Bauer had shrewdly assessed that the Japanese must now be
fielding less experienced pilots. He was right, and in a big air battle
on 23 October, twenty-four Wildcats and four Army P-39s took on
a big formation of Bettys and Zeros and shot down twenty fighters
and two bombers. All the enemy aircraft fell in the vicinity of the
airfield in clear view of the exhausted defenders, providing a
massive boost to their morale.

On that day, Bauer was appointed Commander of Fighters on
Guadalcanal. On 14 November, after shooting down another Zero
– his eleventh victim – while providing top cover for US bombers
which were attacking Japanese shipping off the island, he was
himself hit and sent down into the sea. The other pilots saw him in
his lifejacket, waving, and sent out a Grumman Duck amphibian to
pick him up, but despite an extensive air and sea search Indian Joe
Bauer was never found. He was posthumously awarded the Medal
of Honor.

On 26 October, 1942, US and Japanese naval forces – the latter
covering and supporting a major land attack designed to seize
Henderson Field – met head-on in a major engagement that was to
become known as the Battle of Santa Cruz. It developed into a slog-
ging match between carrier aircraft of the opposing sides, and in

US Navy pilot Stanley Vejtasa destroyed seven Japanese aircraft in one air battle. (US Navy)

the fierce air battles one US Navy Wildcat pilot particularly distinguished himself. His name was Lieutenant Stanley W. Vejtasa, who destroyed no fewer than seven enemy torpedo bombers in a single engagement. Vejtasa was then flying with VF-10 aboard the USS *Enterprise* and he already had three victories to his credit, gained during the Battle of the Coral Sea in May 1942. These kills were also claimed in a single fight, but the extraordinary thing was that Vejtasa notched them up while flying a Douglas SBD Dauntless dive-bomber from the USS *Yorktown*.

On 8 May, Vejtasa's SBD was one of a formation searching for Japanese aircraft carriers when the American bombers were attacked by about twenty Zeros. Two SBDs were soon shot down and the remainder formed a defensive circle, turning hard and firing at the Zeros whenever the chance presented itself. The fight went on for forty minutes, and in that time Vejtasa shot down three of the Zeros. The fact that he applied for a transfer to fighters soon afterwards came as no surprise to anyone. Stanley 'Swede' Vejtasa was the only US Navy pilot to be awarded Navy Crosses for both dive bombing and aerial combat. He remained in the Navy after the war, rising to the rank of captain and commanding the carrier USS *Constellation* in 1963-64.

Another US Navy Wildcat pilot who distinguished himself by becoming an ace in one day was Lieutenant (jg) E.S. 'Scott' McCuskey of VF-42, which operated from the USS *Yorktown* during the Battle of Midway in June 1942. Sighting a formation of enemy torpedo-bombers heading for his carrier, he attacked the first wave head-on and sent three of them down in flames. He then turned in behind another three and damaged them before running out of ammunition. Later in the day, he destroyed two more torpedo-bombers. McCuskey was to survive the war with a score of thirteen kills. He died in 1997.

The Battle of Midway cost the Imperial Japanese Navy four fast attack carriers – the ships that had launched the devastating attack on Pearl Harbor seven months earlier – as well as 258 aircraft and many of its most experienced naval pilots. It was a decisive defeat from which the Japanese never recovered, and it was Midway, more than any other action, that destroyed Japan's hopes of further expansion in the Pacific.

At this time, many of the leading pilots of the Imperial Japanese Navy were based at Lae, on the east coast of New Guinea, with the Tainan Air Group, whose Zeros were tasked with providing air support for Japanese bomber operations against Port Moresby. The Japanese, pushing through the Owen Stanley Mountains, were making ceaseless attempts to capture this vital objective, which was to serve as the springboard for an invasion of northern Australia, and were meeting fierce resistance from Australian and American troops. Lae was only 180 miles from Port Moresby, and day after day in that summer of 1942 the sky over the mountainous jungle terrain separating the two bases became the scene of bitter air battles as the Allies threw in all their resources to halt the Japanese advance. For the first time, the Zero squadrons began to sustain real losses in combat with fighters – mostly Bell P-39 Airacobras and Curtiss P-40 Tomahawks – flown superbly by USAAF and Royal Australian Air Force pilots.

One of the latter was Squadron Leader Keith 'Bluey' Truscott, who had destroyed at least fourteen German aircraft while flying Spitfires with No. 452 Squadron in England and had received the DFC and Bar. In 1942 he was posted back to Australia with No. 76 Squadron RAAF, armed with P-40 Kittyhawks, which he flew in combat during the Battle of Milne Bay, Papua. In July 1942 Truscott was saddened to learn of the death of his close friend and former rival, Wing Commander J.B. 'Paddy' Finucane, whose Spitfire had gone down in the English Channel after being hit by ground fire. Three days before Christmas, Finucane's father broadcast over the radio to Australia. His message ended: 'Especially do we remember and send our sincere wishes for a happy landing to Squadron Leader Bluey Truscott who, before he left his country, led the immortal band of fighter pilots who formed the first Australian Spitfire squadron.' And then, in Gaelic, 'God's blessing be with you.'

In March 1943, after adding three Japanese bombers to his score, Bluey Truscott was flying his Kittyhawk on a practice interception detail against an RAAF Catalina flying boat. After one run, the fighter swept beneath the larger aircraft; the location was just off the coast of New Guinea, near Port Moresby. The flying boat crew waited for the fighter to reappear and make another dummy run. When it failed to do so, they circled in time to see the tell-tale oil slick on the glassy water that marked Truscott's grave. Like Paddy Finucane, the sea had claimed him.

The Japanese commander of the Lae Wing, as the detachment of the Tainan Air Group was known, was Sub-Lieutenant Hiroyoshi Nishizawa. As far as it is possible to establish, Nishizawa became the leading Japanese ace of the Pacific war. He was born in 1920 in a mountain village in Nagano Prefecture, and following gaduation from higher elementary school, he worked for a time in a textile factory before volunteering for flying duties in the Imperial Japanese Navy. He completed his flying training in March 1939, graduating seventeenth out of a class of seventy-one, and was assigned to the Chitose Air Group in 1941. In February 1942 he was transferred to the 4th Air Group and moved to Rabaul, scoring his first victory on the 3rd. In April he was transferred to the Tainan Group. On 7 August, the day that saw the American assault on Guadalcanal, he shot down six F4F Wildcats in a single air battle, and only just recovered to his base with a damaged aircraft. By November 1942, when the Tainan Air Group was redesignated Air Group 251, his score had risen to thirty aircraft destroyed.

Hiroyoshi Nishizawa in the cockpit of his Mitsubishi A6M3 Zero fighter.
(Via J.R. Cavanagh)

After a spell in Japan Nishizawa rejoined Air Group 251 and moved with it to Rabaul in May 1943. It is recorded that he destroyed six aircraft in mid-June, but his subsequent achievements are not clear because the air groups discontinued the practice of recording the scores of individual pilots around this time. In September 1943 he was transferred to Air Group 253 for a brief period before returning to Japan, where in November he was promoted to Warrant Officer and assigned to Air Group 203, which was engaged in air defence duties in the northern Kuriles. In October 1944 the unit moved to the Philippines, and on the 25th Nishizawa led a flight of three Zeros that flew in direct support of the first planned kamikaze attack of the war. He shot down two Hellcats during this operation, but had to make an emergency landing on the island of Cebu, short of fuel. The next day, he was returning to base in a transport, having been compelled to leave his own aircraft behind, when it was attacked and shot down by two Hellcats over Calapan, Mindoro Island. Nishizawa was killed, along with everyone else on board. He was posthumously promoted to lieutenant-commander, a not uncommon practice in the Japanese Navy. Some sources put his final score as high as 150, which is unlikely; for a long time, the 'official' tally was fixed at 102, although this has since been revised to eighty-seven in the light of more recent documentary evidence.

Although Nishizawa was officially Japan's top-scoring pilot, probably the best-known Japanese air ace was Sub-Lieut Saburo Sakai, mainly because he wrote a book (Samurai) about his exploits, which was translated into several languages. Born into a farming family in Saga Prefecture on 16 August 1916, Sakai enlisted as a seaman in the Imperial Japanese Navy in 1933. Selected for aircrew training, he graduated top of his class at flight school, and in September 1938 he was posted to the 12th Air Group for operations in central China, claiming his first combat victory on 5 October near Hankow while flying a Mitsubishi A5M. In June 1941 he was promoted to Petty Officer 1st Class, and in October he was transferred to the Tainan Air Group. As a flight commander, he took part in the air battles during the Philippines and Dutch East Indies campaigns, afterwards operating from Rabaul and Laea. Early in the battle for Guadalcanal Sakai was hit by return fire from the gunner of a TBD Avenger and received severe head wounds, but despite his injuries he managed to return to Rabaul and was shipped back to Japan. According to official records, his score at this point was twenty-eight. In Japan, he found that he had lost the sight of one eye completely, and only retained the use of the other after a surgeon carried out a painful operation without the use of anaesthetics. Despite his injuries, he was passed fit for duty as a flying instructor, training new pilots in fighter tactics. In 1944 he was promoted to the commissioned rank of ensign, an almost unheard-of honour for someone who had begun his career as an enlisted man. He returned to operations later in the war and took part in the desperate air battles off Iwo Jima, but failing eyesight compelled him to give up combat flying once more and he ended the war as a fighter instructor, with a score of around sixty-four aircraft destroyed. (Sakai himself never laid claim to that figure, which was calculated by others). After the war Sakai opened a printing business. He died on 22 September, 2000.

It was Sakai who was the Lae Wing's true tactician, and who instilled the value of tactical air fighting into the younger pilots. His teaching paid dividends. On 23 April 1942, for example, Sakai's squadron engaged six Martin B-26 Marauder bombers, fifteen P-40s and a number of P-39s in the Port Moresby area and claimed the definite destruction of two bombers and six P-40s. The next day, the Zeros shot down six out of seven P-40s and also

A youthful Saburo Sakai pictured in the cockpit of his Mitsubishi A5M fighter. (Via J.R. Cavanagh)

CHAPTER NINE

Holding On: Russia, 1941–42

I n the bitter air fighting that raged over the Eastern Front between 1941 and 1945, many Soviet fighter pilots achieved high scores; but these pilots achieved most of their successes during and after the great air battles fought in the summer of 1943, when the Soviet fighter regiments had aircraft which were as good as, and in some cases better than, their German adversaries.

For the pilots who fought to stem the German onslaught in the weeks that followed the attack of 22 June 1941, it was a different story. Their aircraft were outclassed, their tactics hopeless, their experience lacking, and as a result they suffered appalling losses. Most of the Red Air Force's fighter units were still equipped with I-15 and I-16 aircraft, which had been considered first class when they fought on the Republican side during the Spanish Civil War, but which now proved no match for the *Luftwaffe*'s Messerschmitts. Their brave endeavours to protect the bomber formations that were thrown into battle against the advancing German divisions cost them dearly, and the sheer hopelessness of their position sometimes led to desperate tactics. On the morning of 22 June, for example, Lieutenant Dmitri V. Kokorev of the 124th Air Regiment, having exhausted his ammunition in a dogfight, deliberately manoeuvred his I-16 to ram a Bf 110, destroying both aircraft. Lieutenants P.S. Ryabtsev and A.S. Danilov of the 123rd Air Regiment also made ramming attacks that day, as did First

Lieutenant Ivanov of the 46th Air Regiment. Ivanov alone survived.

Soviet fighter regiments equipped with more modern types fared somewhat better, although they too suffered from sadly inferior tactics. It was not until 1939-40 that the prototypes of three Soviet fighters that could really be classed as modern made their appearance. The first was the LaGG-1 (I-22), which took its name from the initials of the three engineers who conceived it: Lavochkin, Gorbunov and Gudkov. It was a remarkable little aircraft, built entirely of wood and bearing a strong resemblance to France's Dewoitine D.520. The LaGG-1 flew for the first time in March 1940 and was superseded by an improved variant, the LaGG-3, after 100 examples had been built. These still equipped two air regiments at the time of the German invasion of June 1941, but it was the LaGG-3 that held the line during the first critical months of the German onslaught. Production ended in 1942 after 6427 had been built.

The second type, the MiG-1 (I-200) was developed to meet a Soviet Air Force requirement, issued in 1938, for a high-altitude fighter, and although it was unstable and difficult to fly it was rushed into production because of its high performance. The prototype flew in April 1940, having been built in a record time of only four months. The aircraft was of composite construction, the forward fuselage up to the rear of the cockpit consisting of a steel frame with fabric covering, while the rear sectioon was all wood. The wing centre section was of duralumin, the outer panels

LaGG-3 fighters on the flight line. (Via J.R. Cavanagh)

wooden. The MiG-1 was redesignated MiG-3 after the 100th machine had been produced, the main improvements being a fully enclosed cockpit and the addition of an auxiliary fuel tank. Because of the increased combat radius that resulted, MiG-3s were used extensively for fighter reconnaissance. Total MiG-3 production was 3322 aircraft.

The third type was the Yak-1 Krasavyets (Beauty), which made its first public appearance during an air display on 7 November 1940. It was Aleksandr S. Yakovlev's first fighter design, and it earned him the Order of Lenin, the gift of a Zis car and a prize of 100,000 roubles. The Yak-1 was of mixed construction, fabric and plywood covered; it was simple to build and service, and a delight to fly. Production of the Yak-1 was accelerated following the German invasion of Russia in June 1941, and in the second half of the year 1019 aircraft were turned out.

Two of the units equipped with the MiG-1 at the time of the German invasion were the 401st and 402nd Fighter Regiments, commanded respectively by Lieutenant-Colonel Stepan Suprun and Lieutenant-Colonel Pyotr Stefanovsky. The unusual thing about these two regiments was that their flying personnel were almost all test pilots, both civil and military, and their collective experience soon paid dividends.

The 401st Fighter Regiment went into action for the first time on 1 July 1941, and on that first day destroyed four Bf 109s for the loss of one of their own number. During the next two days the regiment shot down eight enemy aircraft for no loss, but the record was marred on the 4th when three MiGs were shot down by flak while strafing an enemy armoured column. One of the pilots who failed to return was Stepan Suprun, whose aircraft was hit and burst into flames as it climbed away from an attack. Suprun, who had been born in the United States, had been made a Hero of the Soviet Union (HSU) during the Soviet-Japanese war on the Manchurian border in the summer of 1938. On 22 July 1941 he was posthumously awarded a second HSU gold star.

Suprun's place as commander of the 401st Fighter Regiment was taken by Vladimir V. Kokkinaki, a famous pilot who had made several record-breaking intercontinental flights before the war and who was later to test Russia's early jet fighters. By the beginning of October the 401st, which was based at Borisov, near Minsk, had fifty-four victories to its credit, and a close rivalry existed between this unit and the 402nd, based at Idritsa. The 402nd first saw action

The Soviet Union was the only belligerent to permit women to fly in combat. Foremost among them was Lydia Litvak, seen here (centre) with her Yak-1 fighter. Litvak scored eleven victories. Known as the 'White Rose of Stalingrad', she was killed in action on 1 August 1943, aged twenty-two. (Via J.R. Cavanagh)

on 3 July 1941 and destroyed six enemy aircraft, followed by six more the next day The 402nd's primary task was close support and low-level reconnaissance, and its pilots had orders to avoid combat if possible – but the regiment's adjutant, Major K.A. Gruzdev, devised tactics to bring the enemy to battle. These involved a steep spiral climb to between 15,000 and 18,000 feet, where the MiG-3 enjoyed a performance advantage over the Bf 109. The German pilots almost always followed the spiral, doubtless believing that they were chasing a novice instead of an aerobatic champion, which Gruzdev had been before the war. They discovered their mistake too late when Gruzdev stall-turned out of the climb and shot them down. By the end of 1941, this talented pilot had nineteen victories to his credit.

On the southern front, where the German armies were thrusting towards the Crimea, one MiG-3 unit which distinguished itself from the beginning was the 55th Fighter Regiment, commanded by

Lieutenant-Colonel Vladimir P. Ivanov. Many pilots who were to become Russia's leading air aces saw their first combats with the 55th; foremost among them was Aleksandr I. Pokryshkin, who was to survive the war as the second-ranking Soviet ace with fifty-nine victories. It was Pokryshkin who, more than any other pilot, developed the air fighting tactics that were to become standard throughout Soviet Fighter Aviation from 1943.

In the Moscow sector, the most successful MiG-3 unit during the first months of the war was the 34th Fighter Regiment, commanded by Major L.G. Rybkin and based at Vnukovo. The top-scorer in 1941 was Lieutenant Stepan I. Platov, with twenty victories, followed by Lieutenants N.E. Tarankantchikov with ten and Semyon D. Baykov with nine. Other units assigned to the air defence of Moscow were equipped with Yak-1s. One of them was the 177th Fighter Air Regiment, and on the night of 7 August a pilot with this unit, Second Lieutenant V.V. Talalikhin, made a night interception of a Junkers 88 which was bombing the capital. Having exhausted all his ammunition, Talalikhin rammed the enemy aircraft and then took to his parachute. He destroyed four more aircraft before being killed in an air battle on 27 October 1941.

Another Yak-1 unit was the 69th Fighter Air Regiment, which was based at Odessa on the Black Sea and was commanded by Lieutenant-Colonel L.L. Shestakov. The 69th's war began in August 1941, when the Germans launched a major offensive on the Southern Front. The regiment was under-strength in terms of both manpower and aircraft, and during the air battles over Odessa the Russian pilots each flew four or five sorties a day. On 9 August, led by Shestakov, they engaged a formation of twelve Bf 109s and destroyed nine of them without loss. During the next two and a half years, before the Germans were driven from the Crimea, twelve of the 69th's pilots were made Heroes of the Soviet Union; Shestakov himself flew 200 combat sorties and took part in thirty-two air battles, shooting down fifteen enemy aircraft. He was shot down and killed in the course of a dogfight near Proskurov on 13 March, 1944.

On the Northern Front, many Russian fighter units were equipped with ex-RAF Hawker Hurricanes and American Curtiss P-40 Tomahawks, both of which were shipped to the USSR in substantial numbers soon after the German attack developed. Some Hurricanes were issued to the 3rd Fighter Regiment of the Soviet Baltic Fleet, and the Russian pilots, used to the much lighter

One of the Hawker Hurricane fighters supplied by Britain to the Soviet Union in 1942. (British Aerospace)

and more nimble Yak-1s and LaGG-3s, viewed the British fighter with mixed feelings.

'I thought that the name "Hurricane" hardly matched the technical qualities of the machine,' wrote Lieutenant Viktor Kaberov. 'The armament on it was now good – two 20mm cannons and two heavy calibre machine guns. One burst and pieces would fly off any aircraft. The armour plating (taken from our LaGG) was fine. Such protection was like a stone wall. The horizon indicator was also a wonderful instrument. It was easy to fly in the clouds with it. The radio worked perfectly, like a domestic telephone: neither noise nor crackle. But the speed, the speed . . . No, this aircraft was far from being a Hurricane. It was slow to gain height and was not good in a dive. As for vertical manoeuvrability – not good at all!'

To improve the Hurricane's firepower, its 0.303 calibre machine guns were replaced by 0.50-calibre weapons removed from P-40s or P-39s that had been scrapped for one reason or another. The 20mm cannon were of Soviet manufacture.

Hurricanes were also used by the 72nd (Naval) Fighter Air Regiment, which also flew Curtiss P-40s. The unit was commanded by Lieutenant-Commander Boris F. Safonov and was based on the Murmansk Front. The war in this sector intensified in the spring of 1942, as the *Luftwaffe* made determined efforts to destroy the Allied convoys that that were bringing supplies to Russia via the Arctic route, and fierce air battles took place between Russian fighters and the Germans over the Kola Inlet. In the course of these battles, Boris Safonov's score rose to twenty-two enemy aircraft destroyed and by May 1942 he had twice been awarded the HSU, the first pilot to achieve this double distinction during the war.

The unserviceability rate among the 72nd's P-40s was high, and when the fighters were ordered to provide air cover for the incoming convoy PQ 16 on 30 May 1942, only four aircraft could be made airworthy. The convoy, which was 60 miles offshore, was being attacked by forty German bombers escorted by Bf 109s of the *Luftwaffe's* JG 5 Polar Wing, and the four Russian fighters, led by Safonov, raced up to intercept. The other three P-40s were flown by Lieutenants Kukharenko, Pokrovsky and Orlov; the first was compelled to return to base soon after take-off with engine trouble, reducing the fighter force to three machines. In spite of the formidable odds, the Russians did not hesitate to attack; Pokrovsky and Orlov shot down a Ju 88 apiece and Safonov got two. He had just damaged a third when he radioed that his engine had been hit

British and Russian fighter pilots in conference at Murmansk in 1942. In the centre, with pencil, is Wing Commander H.N. G. Ramsbottom-Isherwood, commanding the RAF contingent; Boris Safonov is on the right. (Flight International)

and that he would have to ditch. The crew of a Russian destroyer, escorting the convoy, saw him glide down and hit the sea about two miles away. The warships raced to the spot but Safonov had gone, dragged down into the icy depths inside his aircraft. His final score was twenty-five enemy aircraft destroyed.

The air battles that accompanied the German offensive towards the Caucasus oilfields in the summer of 1942 produced a crop of Soviet fighter aces. One of them was Senior Lieutenant Mikhail D.Baranov, a flight commander with the 183rd Fighter Air Regiment. On 6 August, leading a patrol of four Yak-1s, he encountered a formation of enemy bombers escorted by twenty-five fighters. Baranov attacked, shooting down a Bf 109 on his first pass, and then engaged the bombers, damaging one so badly that it crash-landed behind the Russian lines. Looking round, he saw that the Messerschmitts were attacking some Russian Il-2 Shturmovik ground-attack aircraft. Diving down, he destroyed a Bf 109 and then, with all his ammunition gone, he sliced off another 109's tail with his wing before baling out. Baranov went on to score a total of twenty-four victories before his death in action in 1943.

During the German push towards Stalingrad, in August 1942, some Soviet fighter regiments began to re-equip with the latest Russian fighter type, the Lavochkin La-5, which was developed from the LaGG-3. Towards the end of 1941, Semyon A. Lavochkin had fitted a standard LaGG-3 airframe with a 1600 hp Shvetsov M-82A radial engine, and during flight testing the type was found to be 30 mph faster that the Messerschmitt Bf 109F. The improved fighter, designated La-5, was extremely promising and was ordered into quantity production. The aircraft soon lived up to its promise: on 20 August, the 287th Fighter Air Division (Colonel S.P.Danilin) arrived with its La-5s to reinforce the 8th Air Army on the Stalingrad Front, and in just under a month its pilots destroyed ninety-seven enemy aircraft in the course of 299 engagements.

Although Russian fighter tactics were now greatly improved, many Russian pilots showed great reluctance to break off an engagement and return to base when their ammunition was exhausted, and ramming tactics continued to be widely employed. On 8 September 1942, for example, a young pilot of the 520th Fighter Air Regiment, Sergeant B.M. Gomolko, shot down a German bomber and then deliberately rammed another after his ammunition ran out. Gomolko baled out, and as he was descending under his parachute he saw the crew of a shot-down enemy bomber also floating earthwards close by. Gomolko landed, shot one of the Germans who tried to run away, and took the other two prisoner. Gomolko was later commissioned and awarded the Order of Lenin.

One of the highest-scoring Soviet fighter pilots during the battles over the river Volga was Senior Sergeant Vladimir Lavrinenkov, and La-5 pilot with the 287th Air Division, who opened his score by shooting down two Ju 87s in September. A month later, his tally had risen to sixteen. He ended the war with thirty-five victories, having been commissioned and twice awarded the HSU. Another top-scoring La-5 pilot, in the same regiment as Lavrinenkov, was Aleksei V. Alelyukhin, who went on to destroy forty enemy aircraft and who also received the HSU twice.

The Eastern Front battles of 1942 produced one of the greatest epics of individual courage and endurance in history. It involved a fighter pilot named Alexei P. Maresyev, who in April 1942 was flying a Yak-1 fighter on an escort mission with a flight of six Il-2s attacking an airfield near Staraya Russa. The raid took the Germans completely by surprise, the Russian aircraft arriving over the airfield just as two Junkers 52s were taking off. Maresyev shot them both down, but the next instant tracers flickered past his own aircraft as ten Messerschmitt 109s came down on him. In the dogfight that developed, Maresyev found himself out of ammunition. He tried to get away, but cannon shells smashed into his engine and the Yak went out of control. Maresyev's last memory was of a line of pine trees racing up to meet him, a split second before the impact knocked him unconscious.

When he came to, he found that he was lying in deep snow in the middle of a pine forest. He had been flung out of the wrecked aircraft, and both his legs were shattered. He was in agony, but he knew that he had to keep moving at all costs, for the alternative was death from exposure. He had no idea how far he was from the Russian lines. The combat had carried him away from Staraya Russa and he might be anything between 50 and 100 miles inside enemy territory. All he knew was that the front lay somewhere to the east. Summoning all his strength, he began to crawl in that direction.

Alexei Maresyev crawled through the snow for nineteen days, half blind with agony, frequently losing consciousness. His only food consisted of a hedgehog, a few handfuls of berries and some ants, and on one occasion he used his service revolver against a bear that came lumbering towards him out of the forest. Luckily the first shot counted, and the animal fell dead. On the nineteenth day the pilot was picked up by a band of Russian partisans, who made contact with his squadron by radio. His squadron commander, Andrei Degtyarenko, flew a little Po-2 biplane to an improvised landing strip in the forest and picked up the badly injured Maresyev, who was immediately flown to hospital in Moscow. There the doctors found that gangrene had set in, and they were forced to amputate both his legs below the knee.

Despondent, Maresyev became convinced that he would never fly again. Then another hospital patient lent him a book of stories about the First World War, and in it he read how a pilot called Karpovitch had flown with a wooden leg. Maresyev determined to follow the earlier pilot's example, and he got his wish, in the face of strong opposition from many quarters. Fitted with artificial limbs, he not only flew again, but he was back with his squadron in time to participate in the big air battles during the Kursk offensive of 1943.

Another pilot who suffered serious injury on the Russian Front and who returned to combat through sheer determination was a German, Gunther Rall. The commander of 8/JG 52, *Oberleutnant*

Gunther Rall (centre) pictured after scoring his 200th victory.
(Bundesarchiv)

Rall had seen action in the Battles of France and Britain and was operating over the Caucasus at the time of his mishap, which occurred on 28 November 1941. Flying a Messerschmitt Bf 109F, he was on patrol with his wingman between Taganrog and Rostov when they encountered some Russian fighters. Rall shot one down in flames, his thirty-sixth victory; it was dusk, and temporarily blinded by the glare from the burning Russian fighter he failed to see another Russian coming down on him.

With his engine out of action, Rall glided westwards and, seeing a group of German tanks, set himself up for a belly landing near them. The landing was fast and heavy and Rall failed to see a number of obstacles. The wings and engine broke away from the fighter and he was knocked unconscious. Some tank men dragged him from the aircraft and he was taken to a field hospital in Taganrog, where his back was found to be broken in three places. He was out of action for nine months, slowly regaining his mobility, and against all odds he was back in action by August 1942.

On 3 September 1942, following his 65th victory, *Oberleutnant* Rall was awarded the Knight's Cross. During the following month his score reached 100, bringing him the award of the Oak Leaves to the Knight's Cross. From April 1943 to March 1944 he served as Kommandeur of III/JG 52, and on 29 August 1943 he achieved his 200th victory, a feat for which he was decorated with the Swords. In a single month, October 1943, Rall shot down forty enemy aircraft, and on 28 November his score reached 250. He had more than his share of luck, being shot down eight times.

In April 1944 Rall was transferred to the western front as commander of II/JG 11, taking part in the defence of the Reich. On 12 May, in a fight with P-47 Thunderbolts, a bullet severed his left thumb, causing severe loss of blood. The wound became infected and he was hospitalised for six months. In March 1945 he was appointed Kommandeur of JG 300, flying the 'long-nose' Focke-Wulf Fw 190D. At the end of the war his total score stood at 275, making him the third highest-scoring German fighter pilot.

The list of German fighter pilots who gained an impressive list of victories in the first two years of the fighting in Russia is a lengthy one. It begins with Werner Mölders, who took JG 51 to Russia in June 1951. At that time Mölders' score stood at eighty-two, and now, in the space of just four weeks on the killing-ground of the Russian Front, he added thirty-three more, bringing his total to 115. Before long this score would be passed twice and even three times, but in the summer of 1941 it was considered incredible, and was the greatest achievement since Manfred von Richthofen's eighty victories in World War One.

The *Luftwaffe* High Command sensed it was high time that Mölders had a rest. At the end of July he was withdrawn from the front, promoted to full colonel and given the appointment of Inspector of the *Luftwaffe* Fighter Command. He became the first *Luftwaffe* pilot to receive the coveted Oak Leaves with Swords and Diamonds.

In the afternoon of 21 November, 1941, Werner Mölders boarded a Heinkel He 111 at Chaplinka airfield in the Ukraine, bound for Berlin. The next day, in bad weather, it crashed on the approach to Breslau. There were no survivors.

CHAPTER TEN

On the Offensive

The Battle of Britain was over, and now, in the spring of 1941, RAF Fighter Command was going over to the offensive, with fighter wings – each of three squadrons – carrying out offensive 'sweeps' over France with the object of bringing the *Luftwaffe* to battle. This was a different kind of fighting; not the hectic, day-in, day-out warfare of the previous summer, when survival was as much a matter of luck as expertise, and young pilots – many of whom had only a few hours' experience on Hurricanes or Spitfires – were fortunate to come through their first encounters with the *Luftwaffe* in one piece; this was a scientific form of air warfare, cleverly directed by men who were already experienced fighter leaders, who were constantly evolving new tactics, and who nurtured their untried pilots until they could hold their own in action.

Men like Squadron Leader Jamie Rankin, a Scot from Portobello, Edinburgh, who had originally joined the Fleet Air Arm but later transferred to the RAF. When Rankin was appointed to command No. 92 Squadron at RAF Biggin Hill in March 1941 it was already the top-scoring unit in RAF Fighter Command, and its score increased steadily under Rankin's dynamic leadership. Rankin himself opened his score with No. 92 by destroying a Heinkel He 59 floatplane and damaging a Bf 109 on 5 April. This was followed by a confirmed 109 on the 24th, and in June – a month of hectic air fighting over France – he shot down seven more 109s, also claiming one probably destroyed.

159

Air Marshal William Sholto Douglas became C-in-C Fighter Command in November 1940, and oversaw its move to the offensive in the following year. (RAF)

Rankin went to great lengths to give his wingmen – who were usually newcomers to the squadron – a chance to 'have a go' at the enemy. One pilot who flew with him was Pilot Officer Jim Rosser; he was actually a member of No. 72 Squadron, which was also part of the Biggin Hill Wing, but as Rosser explains:

We didn't always fly operationally with our own squadrons. On this occasion Jamie Rankin was leading the wing and I was flying as his number two, which was a considerable privilege. The *Luftwaffe* was up in strength and there was an almighty free-for-all, during which the wing got split up. I clung to Jamie's tail like grim death, and as we were heading for the Channel he suddenly called up over the R/T and said: 'There's a Hun at two o'clock below – have a go!' I looked down ahead and to the right and there, sure enough, was a 109, flying along quite sedately a few thousand feet lower down. I dived after him, levelled out astern and opened fire.

He began to smoke almost at once and fell away in a kind of sideslip. A moment later, flames streamed from him.

A lot of young pilots got their first break that way, while flying with Rankin. And most of them felt the same as Jim Rosser; with Jamie guarding your tail, you didn't have much to worry about except shooting down the Hun in your sights. Rankin later became the leader of the Biggin Hill Wing, completing three tours of operations on Spitfires and destroying twenty-one enemy aircraft.

Group Captain Jamie Rankin, DSO and Bar, DFC and Bar, Belgian Croix de Guerre, retired from the RAF in 1958 but kept an active interest in the Service, becoming Air Commodore for the Air Training Corps in Scotland until 1964. He died on 20 March, 1975, aged sixty-two.

No. 72 Squadron's commanding officer in the spring of 1941 was Squadron leader Desmond Sheen, an Australian who had begun his operational career with the squadron before the war. In April 1940 he had been posted to No. 212 Squadron, and during the next few months had flown photo-reconnaissance sorties all over western Europe in specially-modified Spitfires, returning to No. 72 Squadron just in time to take part in the Battle of Britain. Sheen was to lead No. 72 Squadron on sweeps over occupied France for eight

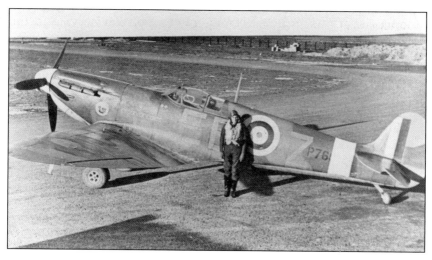

A young pilot of No. 41 Squadron pictured in front of his Spitfire. The aircraft, a Mk IIA, bears the name of the Observer Corps, whose personnel raised the funds to buy it for the RAF. (Source unknown)

months, from March to November 1941. By that time he had flown 260 operational hours and had destroyed six enemy aircraft, probably destroyed two, and damaged five. Sheen surrounded himself with a first-rate fighting team, and the leadership of his subordinate commanders was to emerge in more ways that one during that spring and summer of 1941. Jim Rosser remembers:

> Once, we were on our way back home after a sweep, heading for Manston as usual to refuel, when the weather clamped down. I knew Manston well by this time, and I just managed to scrape in, together with four or five other pilots. Many of the others, however, were relatively new boys and they were in trouble. Then one of our 72 Squadron flight commanders, Ken Campbell, came up over the radio and told everybody to get into a circle and stay put above the murk. One by one he guided them down, wingtip to wingtip, until they were safely on the ground. When he eventually landed, I don't think he had enough fuel left to taxi in. More than one pilot owed his life to Ken that day.

No. 72 Squadron, together with Nos 92 and 609 Squadrons, formed the Biggin Hill Wing, which was led by Wing Commander Adolph Gysbert Malan, a redoubtable South African with eighteen confirmed victories to his credit, a DSO and two DFCs. Known to all and sundry as 'Sailor' because of his pre-war service in the Merchant Navy, he was one of the RAF's foremost air combat tacticians, and his famous 'Ten Rules of Air Fighting' were displayed on crew-room walls throughout Fighter Command. Their message was simple and effective.

1. *Wait until you see the whites of his eyes. Fire short bursts of 1 or 2 seconds and only when your sights are definitely 'ON'.*

2. *Whilst shooting think of nothing else; brace the whole of your body; have both hands on the stick; concentrate on your ring sight.*

3. *Always keep a sharp lookout. Keep your fingers out!*

4. *Height gives you the initiative.*

5. *Always turn and face the attack.*

6. *Make your decisions promptly. It is better to act quickly even though your tactics are not the best.*

7. *Never fly straight and level for more than thirty seconds in the combat area.*

8. *When diving to attack leave a proportion of your formation above to act as top guard.*

9. *Initiative, aggression, air discipline and TEAMWORK are the words that mean something in air fighting.*

10. *Go in quickly – punch hard – get out!*

Sailor Malan was not a talkative man. His business was killing the enemy, and the basic skills of his trade were hammered home hard to those who found themselves under his wing. During the Battle of Britain, when he first rose to fame, the popular Press did its best to surround him with an aura of glamour. War reporters found him uncommunicative, and on the few occasions when he did open up his forthright manner often shocked them. Once, he was asked how he went about shooting down a German bomber. 'I try not to, now,' was his reply. 'I think it's a bad thing. If you shoot them down they don't get back, and no one over there knows what's happening. So I reckon the right thing to do is to let them get back, with a dead rear gunner, a dead navigator, and the pilot coughing up his lungs as he lands. If you do that, it has a better effect on morale. Of course, if you just mean to shoot them down – well, what I generally do is knock out both engines.'

During his time as Biggin Hill Wing Leader, Malan shot down twelve Bf 109s, probably destroyed another Bf 109, shared two more Bf 109s and damaged nine more. On 22 July he was awarded a Bar to his DSO. In August 1941 he was posted to 58 OTU, Grangemouth, as Chief Flying Instructor before travelling to the USA with several other pilots on a lecture tour. By the end of 1941, Malan was back in the UK commanding the Central Gunnery School, where he remained until early 1943

On 1 January 1943, Malan was posted back to Biggin Hill as Station Commander, but although he flew on several more operations he scored no more victories. After taking sick leave, he was given the command of No. 19 Fighter Wing of the Second Tactical Air Force on 1 November 1943. In March 1944 he took command of 145 Wing, which comprised Nos 329, 340 and 341 (Free French) Squadrons. He left the RAF in 1946 with the rank of group captain and returned to South Africa with his family, becoming an active anti-apartheid campaigner.

He died from Parkinson's Disease on 17 September 1963, a few weeks before his fifty-third birthday.

In March 1941 a new Spitfire variant, the Mk V, began to enter service. Converted from Mk I airframes, the Mk V was to be the major Spitfire production version, with 6479 examples completed. The majority of Spitfire Vs were armed with two 20mm cannon and four machine guns, affording a greater chance of success against armour plating. The Mk V was powered by a Rolls-Royce Merlin 45 engine, developing 1415 hp at 19,000ft against the 1150hp of the Merlin XII fitted in the Mk II. Nevertheless, the Mk V was essentially a compromise aircraft, rushed into service to meet an urgent Air Staff requirement for a fighter with a performance superior to that of the latest model of Messerschmitt.

The debut of the Spitfire V came just in time, for in May 1941 the Luftwaffe fighter units began to receive the Messerschmitt Bf 109F. On 11 May, a group of bomb-carrying Bf 109Fs attacked Lympne and Hawkinge, one being shot down by a Spitfire. The Spitfire V, however, failed to provide the overall superiority Fighter

One pilot who distinguished himself during the fighter sweeps of 1941 was a Belgian, Jean Offenberg. Nicknamed 'Pyker' after the Brussels street urchins, he destroyed five enemy aircraft and probably destroyed five more before his death in a mid-air collision in January 1942. (Source unknown)

Command needed so badly. At high altitude, where many combats took place, it was found to be inferior to the Bf 109F on most counts, and several squadrons equipped with the Mk V took a severe mauling during that summer.

Several notable pilots flew their last sorties in a Spitfire V. One of them was the near-legendary Douglas Bader, who flew with artificial legs as the result of a flying accident. Born in St John's Wood, North London, on 21 February 1910, Douglas Robert Stewart Bader was educated at St Edward's school, Oxford, and in September 1928, at the age of 18, he gained a prize cadetship to the Royal Air Force College, Cranwell. On 26 July 1930 he was commissioned and posted to No. 23 Squadron at Kenley, flying Gloster Gamecock fighters. He represented the RAF in various sports, notably Rugby Football, and was a member of the aerobatic team that displayed at the RAF Air Pageant, Hendon. In 1931 No. 23 Squadron converted to Bristol Bulldog fighters, and it was while flying one of these, while giving an impromptu aerobatic display at a flying club, that he crashed and was seriously injured on 14 December 1931, losing both legs. After several months in hospital, often close to death, he recovered and was fitted with artificial legs. He was subsequently invalided from the Service and found employment with the Shell Company, but when WWII broke out in September 1939 he once again volunteered his services and, after many trials and hardships, was again accepted as a pilot by the RAF.

In February 1940, after a refresher course at the Central Flying School, Upavon, he was posted to No. 19 Squadron at Duxford, flying Spitfires. He went to No. 222 Squadron as a flight commander in April, and in the following month he fought in the air battles over Dunkirk. On 1 June he gained his first victory, a Messerschmitt Bf 109. He was then given command of the Hurricane-equipped No. 242 Squadron, which consisted mostly of Canadian personnel and which was in bad shape after the fighting in France. Bader soon instilled a new spirit into the squadron, and showed the Canadians that he intended to lead from in front by destroying a Dornier Do 17 on 11 July. During the Battle of Britain, as a wing commander, he led the Duxford Wing (Nos 19, 242 and 310 Squadrons). This was in the 12 Group area north of the Thames and was not in the thick of the fighting, but by the end of the battle Bader had personally claimed more than a dozen victories and had been awarded the DSO and DFC. Early in 1941 he was given

Douglas Bader seen with his Hurricane at the time of the Battle of Britain. (RAF)

command of the Tangmere Wing, flying Spitfires on 'sweeps' over France. His score continued to rise steadily during this period, reaching a final tally of 22.5 enemy aircraft destroyed.

Handling the large fighter formations which were being pushed across the Channel in the summer of 1941 called for a high degree of skill on the part of the fighter controllers, whose vital role is all too often ignored, or rather eclipsed, in headier tales of air combat. When Douglas Bader came from Duxford to take command of the Tangmere Wing, he was delighted to learn that the new station commander at Tangmere was Group Captain Woodhall, who had been fighter controller at Duxford and who was considered by many to be the finest controller produced by the RAF during the war. Later, Woodhall was to take his skills to Malta, where the pilots he controlled faced more formidable odds than ever before.

Pilot Officer 'Johnnie' Johnson, who flew with the Tangmere Wing in 1941 and who later became the official top-scoring pilot in the RAF, wrote of Woodhall:

Over the radio Woodhall's deep resonant voice seemed to fill our earphones with confidence and assurance. When we were far out over France and he spoke into his microphone it was as if the man was in the air with you, not issuing orders but giving encouragement and advice and always watching the precious minutes, and the headwind which would delay our withdrawal, and the low cloud creeping up from the west which might cover Tangmere when we returned, tired and short of petrol. Then he was always on the ground to meet us after the big shows, to compare notes with Bader and the other leaders. Always he had time for a cheerful word with the novices. And whenever a spontaneous party sprang up in the mess, after a stiff fight or someone collecting a gong or for no valid reason whatsoever, Woodhall was always in the centre of the crowd, leading the jousting with his expensive

'Johnnie' Johnson, who went on to become the RAF's official top-scoring pilot, seen with his Spitfire and Labrador, Sally. (RAF)

accordion, which he played with surprising skill, his monocle still held firmly in place. We were a very happy family at Tangmere in that spring and summer of 1941.

By July 1941 Circus operations, as these missions were called, were very large affairs indeed, with as many as eighteen squadrons of fighters – more than 200 aircraft – covering a small force of bombers. Getting six wings of Spitfires airborne, to the rendezvous at the right time and place, and shepherding them into and out of enemy territory, was something of a nightmare for everyone concerned, and it began on the ground. Three squadrons of Spitfires – thirty-six aircraft – might have made an impressive sight as they taxied round the perimeter of an airfield prior to take-off, but with propellers turning dangerously close to the next aircraft it was all too easy to make a mistake. A late starter would add to the problem as its pilot edged around the outside of the queue, trying to catch up with the rest of his squadron.

Making rendezvous with the bombers – usually over Manston – was another critical factor. A Spitfire's tanks held only eighty-five gallons of petrol, and every minute spent in waiting for the Blenheims to turn up reduced a pilot's chances of getting home safely if he found himself in trouble over France. And over enemy territory the *Luftwaffe* always seemed to have the advantage. No matter how high the Spitfires climbed, the 109s usually managed to climb higher, ready to dive on the 'tail-end Charlies' of the fighter formations and pick them off. There was no dog-fighting in the original sense of the word; the Messerschmitts fought on the climb and dive, avoiding turning combat with the more manoeuvrable Spitfires wherever possible, and the difference between life and death was measured in split seconds. Jim Rosser recalls:

We would cross the Channel in sections, line astern, climbing all the time. We always climbed into the sun, which was absolute hell; your eyes felt as if they were burning down into your head and within a few minutes you were saturated in sweat. It might have been just coincidence, but on every sweep I flew we always seemed to head for Lille, which we hated. It was our deepest penetration at that time, and there was flak all the way.

I will never forget my first operation. Seventy-two Squadron was flying top cover; I was 'Yellow Two', in other words the number two aircraft in Yellow section, and quite honestly I hadn't a clue what was going on. We flew a sort of semi-circle over France, still in sections line astern, and then came out again. I never saw a single enemy aircraft; but we must have been attacked, because when we got home three of our Spits were missing . . .

One of the biggest fighter sweeps of 1941 – code-named Circus 62 – was mounted on 7 August, when eighteen squadrons of Spitfires and two of Hurricanes accompanied six Blenheim bombers in an attack on a power station at Lille. The whole force made rendezvous over Manston, with the North Weald Wing, comprising the Hurricanes of No. 71 (American Eagle) Squadron and the Spitfires of Nos 111 and 222 Squadrons providing close escort for the bombers. Behind and above, as immediate top cover, came the three Spitfire squadrons of the Kenley Wing: Nos 452 (Australia), 485 (New Zealand) and 602. High above this 'beehive' of nearly eighty fighters and bombers came the target support wings, flying at 27,000 feet. There was the Biggin Hill Wing, with Nos 72, 92 and 609 Squadrons; the Hornchurch Wing, with Nos 403 (Canadian), 603 and 611 Squadrons; and Douglas Bader's Tangmere Wing, with Nos 41, 610 and 616. The target support force's task was to assure air superiority over and around Lille while the attack was in progress.

On this occasion, the *Luftwaffe* refused to be drawn into battle in large numbers. Six weeks earlier, the Germans had invaded the Soviet Union, and many fighter groups had been transferred from the Channel area to the eastern front. Those that remained, seriously outnumbered in the face of Fighter Command's growing strength, had been ordered to conserve their resources. The 109s stayed well above the Spitfire formations, shadowing them. From time to time, small numbers of Messerschmitts darted down to fire on the odd straggler, always disengaging when the rest of the Spitfires turned on them.

The bombers, meanwhile, had found Lille obscured by cloud, so had turned back towards the Channel to attack a concentration of barges at Gravelines. A fierce air battle was already in progress over the coast, where two Polish squadrons of the Northolt Wing – Nos 306 and 308 – had been waiting to cover the Blenheims during the final phase of their withdrawal. No 308 Squadron was suddenly attacked by about eighteen Messerschmitts, and in the ensuing engagement two Spitfires were shot down. The Blenheims made their escape unmolested, but the rear support wing, comprising Nos 19, 257 and 401 Squadrons, was also attacked and lost two Spitfires and a Hurricane. The RAF had therefore lost six aircraft, a result which, set against a claim of three Bf 109s destroyed, could hardly be considered favourable, considering the far smaller numbers of enemy aircraft involved.

Another large operation – Circus 63 – was mounted two days later, on Saturday 9 August. This time, the Blenheims' objective was a supply dump in the Béthune area. Once again, Bader's Tangmere Wing formed part of the target support force, but things went wrong right from the start when No. 41 Squadron failed to rendezvous on time. The remainder, unable to wait, carried on across the Channel. For a while, all was peaceful; then, just a few miles short of the target, the 109s hit them hard. For the next few minutes, Bader's pilots were hard put to hold their own, the wing becoming badly dislocated as the Messerschmitts pressed home a series of determined attacks. Bader misjudged an attack on a 109 and suddenly found himself isolated. Six enemy fighters closed in on him and, by superb flying, he destroyed two. The end came soon afterwards, when a third 109 collided with him and severed his Spitfire's fuselage just behind the cockpit. Bader managed to struggle clear of the plunging debris, leaving one of his artificial legs still trapped in the cockpit. His parachute opened, and he floated down to a painful landing and captivity.

After being imprisoned in various PoW camps, Bader ended the war in the notorious Colditz Castle. On his return to the UK he was promoted to group captain and given command of the Fighter Leaders' School at Tangmere and then the Essex Sector of No. 11 Group at North Weald. He retired from the RAF on 21 July 1946 to become a senior executive with Shell Oil. He was knighted in 1976.

Group Captain Sir Douglas Bader died of a heart attack on 5 September 1982, after speaking at a function at the Guildhall. In his post-war years, he was a great inspiration to many seriously injured or handicapped people.

On 12 August, the medium bombers of the RAF's No. 2 Group made their deepest penetration into enemy territory so far when 54 Blenheims bombed two power stations near Cologne. They were escorted by the Westland Whirlwind fighters of No. 263 Squadron, the only fighter aircraft with sufficient range to carry out this task. The Whirlwind was highly manoeuvrable, faster than a Spitfire at

Some of the attacks by the RAF's medium bombers were very effective.
This photograph shows a raid on the Phillips factory at Eindhoven,
Holland. (RAF)

low altitude, and its armament of four closely-grouped 20mm
cannon made it a match for any *Luftwaffe* fighter of the day. As it
was, the Whirlwind experienced a spate of troubles with its twin
Rolls-Royce Peregrine engines, and only two squadrons were ever
equipped with the type. Eventually, it was used in the fighter-
bomber role with considerable success. As August 1941 gave way
to September, some senior Air Staff members began to have serious
doubts about the value of Circus operations. Fighter Command
losses were climbing steadily, and the results achieved hardly
seemed to compensate for them. The only real justification for
continuing the sweeps, apparently, was to ensure that Fighter
Command remained in a state of combat readiness.

The morale of Fighter Command, however, was soon to take a
serious blow. On 21 September 1941, Polish pilots of No. 315
Squadron, on their way home, reported being attacked by 'an
unidentified enemy aircraft with a radial engine'. All sorts of wild

rumours circulated in Fighter Command, the favourite among them being that the strange aircraft were Curtiss Hawks, captured by the Germans and pressed into service. But after all the available information, including gun-cameras shots, was assessed, all speculation was removed. The Focke-Wulf 190 had arrived in France.

The first *Luftwaffe* unit to receive Focke-Wulf 190s on the Channel coast was *Jagdgeschwader* 26, followed by JG 2, and by mid-October 1941 the RAF was encountering the type in growing numbers. Within weeks, the Fw 190 had established a definite measure of air superiority for the Germans. It completely outclassed the Spitfire Vb at all altitudes, and Fighter Command losses rose steadily that autumn. Not until the advent of the Spitfire IX – resulting from the marriage of a Merlin 61 engine to a Mk V airframe – was the balance restored; but the first Mk IXs did not enter service with No. 64 Squadron until June 1942.

As far as Circus operations were concerned, the crunch came on 8 November 1941, when the Blenheims of No. 2 Group and their escorting fighters suffered unusually heavy losses. The whole 'show' went wrong from the start, with poor visibility making it difficult for the bombers and fighters to rendezvous as planned. Combined with a general lack of coordination, this meant that the attacking forces entered enemy territory piecemeal, and the Focke-Wulfs and Messerschmitts were waiting for them. The Intelligence Summary of No. 118 (Spitfire) Squadron gives a typical account.

> It was decided in the afternoon to carry out a most ill-conceived scheme, designated Rodeo 5, in which the Middle Wallop Wing rendezvoused with the Whirlwinds of 263 Squadron over Warmwell and carried out a sweep of the Channel Islands area. The whole sortie seems to have been one long muddle. The Whirlwinds led the Spits much too far south and then returned right over the flak area. 501 Squadron were sent out to deal with the few Huns that put in an appearance when we were on the way back. 118 went back to help, but 501 were not located. The net result was at least three planes damaged by flak and one shot down, and all we could claim was one enemy aircraft damaged . . .

It was the end. Winston Churchill himself decreed that there should be no more large-scale sweeps over the Continent in 1941;

it was now the duty of Fighter Command to gather its strength for the following spring.

But the pattern of the war was about to change dramatically. On the other side of the world, events were moving to a climax that would soon make Pearl Harbor a household name, and bring the unparalleled resources of the United States into the conflict.

CHAPTER ELEVEN

By Daylight to Germany

In the summer of 1942, the RAF Spitfire wings based in southern England were given the task of escorting the four-engined heavy bombers of the US Eighth Air Force, which were beginning to carry out attacks on targets in France and the Low Countries as a preliminary to the planned all-out bombing offensive against Germany. On these relatively short-range operations the Spitfire escort was effective, but when it came to attacks on targets in Germany itself the story was very different, because even with drop tanks the Spitfires did not have sufficient combat radius to escort the bombers further than northern Holland.

Meanwhile, in March 1942 Circus operations had resumed, albeit on a reduced scale. The vulnerable Blenheims of Bomber Command's No. 2 Group were replaced by the faster, more modern Douglas Boston. The number of Bostons taking part in these operations was never more than thirty, but they were often escorted by up to twenty-seven squadrons of Spitfires, nearly half Fighter Command's available strength. On one occasion, on 30 April 1942, no fewer than thirty-eight squadrons of Spitfires were involved in escorting twenty-four Bostons on four separate operations. Only six Bostons were lost in April but Spitfire losses were heavy as the Fw 190s (and, to a lesser extent, the Bf 109Fs) continued to show their superiority over the Spitfire V. For example, eleven Spitfires failed to return on 4 April, fifteen on 12 April, and twelve on 25 April. Spitfire losses for the whole of the month were fifty-nine aircraft.

The sternest test for Fighter Command during this period was the Dieppe operation of 19 August 1942 (Operation Jubilee), one object of which was to bring to battle all the forces of the *Luftwaffe* in northern France and the Low Countries. Control of the RAF part of the operation was given to Air Vice-Marshal Trafford Leigh-Mallory of No 11 Group, and fifty-six squadrons of Spitfires, Hurricanes and Typhoons were placed at his disposal, as well as five Blenheim and Boston squadrons of No. 2 Group and four Mustang squadrons of Army Co-operation Command.

The story of that ill-fated venture, and of the gallantry of the Canadian troops who took appalling casualties in the landing, is well known. Dieppe was a disaster for the RAF, too; in the day's operations the British lost 106 aircraft against the *Luftwaffe*'s forty-eight. Of the RAF losses, eighty-eight were fighters, and the majority of these were Spitfires.

Tuesday, 29 September 1942, was a significant day for the officers and men of Nos 71, 121 and 133 'Eagle' Squadrons at Debden. At a formal parade, they were handed over to VIII Fighter Command, United States Army Air Force, to become the 334th, 335th and 336th Fighter Squadrons of the 4th Fighter Group. From now on, the primary task of the pilots would be bomber escort to the Boeing B-17s that had become operational in the United Kingdom that summer.

The pilots of No. 133 Squadron had already had an unhappy taste of this kind of mission on 4 September, when twelve brand-new Spitfire IXs accompanied a formation of B-17 Fortresses in an attack on Morlaix. A serious navigational error, compounded by bad weather, had resulted in eleven of the twelve Spitfires running out of fuel over the Brest peninsula on the return flight. Four pilots were killed and the rest taken prisoner; only one Spitfire made it home. The physical casualties were bad enough, but a severe blow to the Americans' pride followed when re-equipment arrived in the shape of Spitfire Vs.

The fiasco proved that whatever else the Spitfire might be, it was not an escort fighter, and that was precisely what the American bombers were going to need as they penetrated deeper into enemy territory, even though the first unescorted raid on Germany seemed to indicate that the daylight bombers might just get away with it. The target was the naval base at Wilhelmshaven, on the north German coast.

On the morning of 27 January, 1943, fifty-five B-17s took off from their English bases and set course over the North Sea. The weather was far from ideal for high-level precision bombing, and at altitude the cold was intense. The sub-zero temperatures knifed through the thickest flying clothing; machine guns, turrets and camera mechanisms froze, while windscreens and bomb sights were obscured by opaque layers of frost. One of the navigators described the outward flight:

> At about 1030 the altimeter indicated 25,000 feet. The cloud cover had ended, far below, and we could see the surface of the sea – like a sheet of glass. At 1045 the Captain warned the crew to be extra alert. I looked out to the right and could see the outline of the coast of Germany and the row of islands that lay just off it. At 1057 we were just over the islands and at 1100 the tail gunner reported flak at six o'clock, below. It was from the coastal islands and was the first time we were fired on from German soil. At this time we were beginning to turn and we crossed the island of Baltrum and went into German territory. As we turned, the bombardier elevated the muzzle of his gun and fired a burst so that the tracers arched over into Germany. The first shots from our ship, *Hell's Angel*, but not the last!

A formation of B-17 Flying Fortresses bombing a target in Germany.
(USAF)

The American raid took the German defences by surprise. Fifty-three Fortresses unloaded their bombs on the Wilhelmshaven harbour installations, opposed by only a handful of Focke-Wulf 190s; two more Fortresses bombed Emden. Only three B-17s failed to return, appearing to vindicate the Americans' belief that fears for the success of unescorted long-range daylight operations were unfounded. It would not be long before packs of determined *Luftwaffe* fighter pilots shattered the myth. In the days that followed the Wilhelmshaven mission, however, it was the weather and not the *Luftwaffe* that formed the main obstacle to the daylight bombing programme, with rain, sleet and dense cloud cover extending over the whole area of the North Sea. In seventeen days only one attack was carried out, in conditions of severe icing and sub-zero temperatures. The raid took place on 4 February, and the target was the port of Emden. Because of the freezing conditions dense contrails formed behind the American formation at a much lower altitude than usual, enabling the enemy fighters to concentrate on it without difficulty. Fifty fighters, including eight Bf 110s of a night fighter unit, engaged the bombers over the north coast of Germany and a fierce air battle developed. Six Fortresses were shot down but the Germans also suffered heavily, losing eight fighters. On 16 February eight more bombers were lost during an attack on the locks leading to the basin of the St Nazaire U-boat base on the French coast.

Ten days later another 8th Bomber Command formation battled its way through intense opposition to attack Wilhelmshaven for a second time. Seven bombers were lost. The end of one of them, a B-24 Liberator, was described by *Leutnant* Heinz Knoke, a Messerschmitt 109 pilot with II/JG 2, who was to end the war with a score of fifty-two enemy aircraft destroyed, the majority of them four-engined heavy bombers.

I come in for a second frontal attack, this time from a little below. I keep on firing until I have to swerve to avoid a collision. My salvoes register this time. As I swing round I turn my head. Flames are spreading along the bottom of the fuselage of my Liberator. It sheers away from the formation in a wide sweep to the right.

Twice more I come in to attack, this time diving from above the tail. I am met by heavy defensive fire. My plane shudders from the recoil of the two cannon and the 13-millimetre guns.

I watch my cannon shell-bursts rake along the top of the fuse-lage and right wing, and I hang on to the stick with both hands. The fire spreads along the right wing. The inside engine stops. Suddenly the wing breaks off altogether. The body of the stricken monster plunges vertically, spinning into the depths. A long black trail of smoke marks its descent. One of the crew attempts to bale out, but his parachute is in flames. Poor devil! The body somersaults and falls to the ground like a stone.

At an altitude of 3000 feet there is a tremendous explosion, which causes the spinning fuselage to disintegrate. Fragments of blazing wreckage land on a farm 200 or 300 yards from the Zwischenahn airfield, and the exploding fuel tanks set the farm buildings on fire . . .

In January 1943, the USAAF's 4th and 56th Fighter Groups in England began to receive the first examples of a new fighter, the Republic P-47 Thunderbolt, a big, radial-engined aircraft with an armament of six 0.50-inch machine guns. It was still incapable of escorting the American daylight bombers into Germany, but its range was much better than the Spitfire's and it could extend fighter cover for a considerably greater distance along the bombers' route.

The 4th Fighter Group's first commander was Chesley G. Peterson, a colonel at the age of only twenty-three, who had com-manded No. 71 Eagle Squadron in the RAF. He had six confirmed victories, and gained another before his place as commander of the 4th FG was assumed by Colonel Don Blakeslee. (After the war, Peterson rose to the rank of Major General, serving in various capac-ities around the world He retired from the Air Force on 1 August, 1970, at the age of 49. He lived in Ogden, Utah, and later moved to the Air Force retirement village at March AFB in Riverside, California. He died at the age of 69 on January 28, 1990, and was buried with full military honours at Riverside National Cemetery).

Peterson's successor, Don Blakeslee, like many other American volunteers, had joined the RCAF, and on arriving in England in May 1941, he had been assigned to No. 401 (Canadian) Squadron. After that he flew with No. 133 Eagle Squadron, and by the time he took over the 4th FG he had two confirmed kills, plus a number of probables and damaged. On 15 April 1943 Blakeslee became the first Thunderbolt pilot to destroy an enemy, shooting down a Focke-Wulf 190 over the French coast. Later, he was to increase his total to 15.5.

Chesley G. Peterson, photographed while commanding No. 71 Eagle Squadron. (USAF)

The other Thunderbolt unit in England, the 56th Fighter group, did not receive its full complement of P-47s for several weeks, and it was not until April 1943 that it was declared operational. The 56th FG was commanded by Colenel Hubert 'Hub' Zemke, a remarkably able fighter leader whose personal score was to rise to 17.75 before his combat days ended. Many of the best-known USAAF aces of the European Theatre were to cut their teeth with Zemke's 'Wolfpack', as the 56th became known; men like Major Robert S. Johnson, who went on to become the first American pilot to match the score of the World War One US air ace, Eddie Rickenbacker, with twenty-six enemy aircraft destroyed, and who was go gain two more victories on top of that; Francis Gabreski who would become the third-ranking US ace with a score of thirty-one, and who would add six and a half MiG-15s to it in action over Korea; Walker Mahurin, with twenty-one victories in World War Two and three and a half more in Korea; and David C. Schilling, who gained twenty-two and a half victories, five of them in one action on 23 December 1944.

The Eighth Air Force's first ace, however, belonged to another Thunderbolt unit, the 78th Fighter Group. This had arrived in England late in 1942, equipped with Lockheed P-38 Lightnings, but these had been transferred to North Africa soon afterwards as replacements for the P-38 Groups already there, which had suffered badly in the air battles over Tunisia. The 78th FG re-equipped with Thunderbolts in February 1943, and in May Captain Charles P. London scored his first victory. Two more enemy aircraft fell to his guns in the weeks that followed, and then, on 30 July, he destroyed a Focke-Wulf 190 and a Messerschmitt 109 to raise his score to five.

A superb fighter-leader, Hubert Zemke led his 56th Fighter Group to fame over Europe. (USAF)

Robert S. Johnson, who was to follow Francis Gabreski into fourth place in the table of American aces, did not score his first victory until June 1943. Flying over France with the 61st Squadron, Johnson sighted twelve Fw 190s cruising a few thousand feet below. At that time, American fighter tactics generally involved waiting to be attacked first by the enemy – a policy with which the young pilot heartily disagreed. Exasperated, he broke formation and dived on the Focke-Wulfs, who failed to spot him until it was too late. Passing through their formation at high speed he tore a 190 apart with a short burst from his six machine guns, then climbed hard to rejoin his own formation. The remaining Focke-Wulfs followed him, and in the ensuing battle Colonel Zemke shot down two of them. When he returned to base, Johnson received a severe reprimand for breaking formation, and was told that if he did it again he would be grounded.

A few days later, while sticking rigidly to his station, he was almost shot down when the Thunderbolts were 'bounced' by a squadron of Messerschmitts. It came as a considerable relief when, not long after this incident, the commander of the Eighth Air Force's fighter units, Major-General Anderson, sought and obtained approval for more aggressive tactics.

Bob Johnson's early months in combat were not spectacular; nevertheless, he formulated sound fighting tactics which ultimately were to pay high dividends. Next to Zemke, he became the man most sought by newcomers to the group, eager to gain from his tactical knowledge, and his advice to them was simple:

Never let a Jerry get his sights on you. No matter whether he is 100 yards or 1000 yards away, a 20-mm will carry easily that far and will knock down a plane at 1000 yards. It is better to stay at 20,000 feet with a good speed with a Jerry at 25,000 feet than it is to pull up in his vicinity at a stalling speed. If he comes down on you, pull up into him, and nine times out of ten, if you are nearly head-on with him he'll roll away to his right. Then you have him. Roll on to his tail and go get him.

These tactics saved his life time and again. One day in the summer of 1943, Johnson's squadron was escorting B-17s in a raid

Robert S. Johnson being congratulated by a member of his ground crew after scoring a kill.

on Kiel when the contrails of enemy fighters were sighted to the south. Johnson immediately pulled the lever to jettison his long-range fuel tank, but it was jammed. There was no time to worry about it now; fifteen Focke-Wulfs were diving on the bombers and Johnson's section turned to engage them.

We went at the nearest ones head-on, and they broke for the deck. They kept coming and I kept hitting them head-on, driving them down. I was making my third pass when Hamilton [one of the pilots in Johnson's section] yelled over the R/T 'Get these bastards off my tail!' I still had that belly tank. I kept yanking at the release, and it wouldn't drop.

Down below at 16,000 feet three planes were going round and round – two Fws on Hamilton. One would make a pass at him from the front while the other got on his tail. I put my ship in a dive but I couldn't pull out in time. That belly tank was interfering with the trim. As I pulled up, Hamilton did a turn-over and gave the gun to one of the Huns. He went down on fire, and Hamilton then got on the other's tail.

It was a clear day. We were over the coast, the line of breakers curving white against the shore. People were watching from below. It must have been a good show, but the damned fools might have got hit. Hamilton didn't need any help from me any more, and I sat over and above him and his Hun, watching the fun. Hamilton got his second plane – and then I looked round and saw a Hun on my tail.

As he came in on my tail, shooting, I did a tight climbing turn. The Jerry had the position – and I had that belly tank. He kept inside me, trying for a deflection burst. I held the turn until his nose dropped a bit. Then I slipped down and hit him.

Then he was on me again and we went through the same thing. On this turn my belly tank finally dropped. When his nose dipped I came over and hit him again. We went through this four times, and it took ten minutes, which is a long, long time in a dogfight. Then his cockpit jumped into the air and the plane flew under it. He was coming apart, and I gave him another burst just to make sure of it.

On the ground, Johnson was a quiet man. Apart from flying, his great loves were photography and wood carving – the latter in-herited from an apprenticeship as a cabinet-maker at home in

Lawton, Oklahoma. He spent many hours making carved souvenirs for the other pilots in the group, and in his off-duty hours he was often to be seen in the countryside around Halesworth, where the group was based, photographing the English villages and rural scenes. He spent a lot of time with the local people, and as a result his Oklahoma drawl became mingled with the soft accents of Suffolk. It was a habit of speech that was never to leave him.

While Bob Johnson was carving out a reputation for himself, an RAF namesake – James Edgar Johnson – had taken the first steps on a ladder that would place him high in the ranks of the Allied aces of World War Two. Born at Melton Mowbray, the son of a police inspector, 'Johnnie' Johnson was educated at Loughborough School and joined the RAF Volunteer Reserve pre-war, completing his basic flying training in the spring of 1940 and learning to fly Spitfires with No. 57 Operational Training Unit at Hawarden, Flintshire. Early in September 1940 he was commissioned as a pilot officer and posted to No. 19 Squadron at Duxford, but the Battle of Britain was in full swing and 19 Squadron had no time to train inexperienced pilots. Johnson was therefore switched to No. 616 Squadron, which had been pulled back to Kirton-in-Lindsey for a rest. An old rugby injury reared its head and put him in hospital for a while, and he did not rejoin his squadron until late December.

Johnson's first taste of action came in January 1941, when he claimed a Dornier 17 damaged, but it was not until 616 Squadron moved back into the front line that he really got to grips with the enemy. In February 1941 the squadron moved south to Tangmere to form part of the Tangmere Wing, commanded by Douglas Bader from March. In May, during a sweep over Gravelines, Johnson shot down his first Messerschmitt 109.

During the weeks that followed the Tangmere Wing carried out many sorties over occupied France. Johnson usually flew as Bader's number two, and in those summer months he learned much about the science of air fighting from the more experienced pilot. By the autumn of 1941 – following a spell of hectic combat during which Bader was shot down and taken prisoner – he had flown forty-six sorties over enemy territory and had claimed the destruction of six enemy aircraft, which brought him the award of the DFC.

In the winter of 1941-42 No. 616 Squadron moved north for a rest, after which Johnson was given command of No. 610 Squadron at Ludham in Norfolk. From this airfield the squadron carried out numerous sweeps over Holland before moving to West Malling in August 1942, where No. 610 formed a wing together with the New Zealand 485 Squadron and the Canadian 411 Squadron.

In March 1943 Johnson, newly promoted to wing commander, was posted to Kenley to lead a Canadian fighter wing, equipped with Spitfire IXs, and it was now that he adopted the personal call-sign 'Greycap', another name for the Canada Goose, which he was to use for the rest of the war. He gained his first victory with the wing on 3 April, when the formation he was leading encountered Focke-Wulf 190s while escorting Typhoon fighter-bombers on a strike across the Channel. The Spitfires dived on the enemy formation and Johnson picked on the Focke-Wulf on the extreme left. He missed with his first burst, but the second hit the enemy fighter behind the cockpit and on the wing root. The Focke-Wulf dropped away, burning.

During his tour with the aggressive Canadian wing, Johnson's victories mounted rapidly. On 5 April he damaged three more 109s, shot down another on 11 May, and shared one with other Spitfire pilots on 13 May. During the next two weeks he destroyed another Fw 190 and claimed a share in a Messerschmitt 109. More Focke-Wulfs fell to his guns on 15, 17, 24 and 27 June, followed by a trio of Messerschmitts on 15, 19 and 25 July. On the last day of the month he shared a 109 and on 12 August he shared another, together with one damaged. On 17 August he and three other pilots combined to sheet down a Messerschmitt 110. Another Messerschmitt 109 went down on 23 August, followed by Focke-Wulf 190s on 26 August and 4 September. Johnnie's personal score now stood at twenty-five enemy aircraft destroyed. His decorations included the DSO, DFC and Bar, and the American DFC, awarded for his work in leading the Canadian wing on escort duties with the bombers of the US Eighth Air Force.

The terrible losses suffered by the Eighth Air Force's daylight bombers in August 1943 underpinned the desperate need for an effective long-range escort fighter. By far the worst day was 17 August, the first anniversary of 8th Bomber Command's attack on Rouen in 1942, when the Eighth Air Force mounted a maximum-effort strike on two nerve centres of the German aircraft industry, the Messerschmitt factory at Regensburg and the ball-bearing plants at Schweinfurt. What followed was the biggest air battle seen up to that time. An eye-witness to it was Lieutenant-Colonel

Beirne Lay, Jr., flying as an observer on the Regensburg attack with a crew of the 100th Bombardment Group. Based at Thorpe Abbots in Suffolk, the 100 BG, which had been operational since 23 June 1943, was to suffer such appalling losses during its combat career that it became known as the 'Bloody Hundredth'.

At 1017 hours, near Woensdrecht, I saw the first flak blossom out in our vicinity, light and inaccurate. A few minutes later, two Fw 190s appeared at one o'clock and whizzed through the formation ahead of us in a frontal attack, nicking two B-17s in the wings and breaking away beneath us in half rolls. Smoke immediately trailed from both B-17s, but they held their stations. As the fighters passed us at a high rate of closure, the guns of our Groups went into action. The pungent smell of burnt powder filled our cockpit, and the B-17 trembled with the recoil of nose and ball gun turrets. I saw pieces fly off the wing of one of the fighters before they passed from view.

Here was early action. The members of the crew sensed trouble. There was something desperate about the way those two fighters came in fast right out of their climb without any preliminaries. Three minutes later the gunners reported fighters climbing up from all around the clock, singly and in pairs, both Fw 190s and Me 109s. Every gun from every B-17 in our Group was firing, crisscrossing our patch of sky with tracers. Both sides got hurt in this clash, with two Fortresses from our low squadron and one from the Group ahead falling out of formation on fire with crews baling out, and several fighters heading for the deck in flames with their pilots lingering behind under dirty yellow parachutes. I noticed an Me 110 sitting out of range on our right. He was to stay with us all the way to the target, apparently reporting our position to fresh squadrons waiting for us down the road. At the sight of all these fighters I had the distinct feeling of being trapped. The life expectancy of our Group suddenly seemed very short, since it appeared that the fighters were passing up the preceding Groups in order to take a cut at us.

Swinging their yellow noses round in a wide U-turn, a twelve-ship squadron of Me 109s came in from twelve o'clock in pairs and in fours, and the main event was on. A shining silver object sailed over our right wing. I recognized it as a main exit door. Seconds later, a dark object came hurtling through the formation, barely missing several props. It was a man, clasping his knees to his head, revolving like a diver in a triple somersault. I didn't see his 'chute open.

A B-17 turned gradually out of the formation to the right, maintaining altitude. In a split second, the B-17 completely disappeared in a brilliant explosion, from which the only remains were four small balls of fire, the fuel tanks, which were quickly consumed as they fell earthwards. Our airplane was endangered by falling debris. Emergency hatches, exit doors, prematurely opened parachutes, bodies, and assorted fragments of B-17s and Hun fighters breezed past us in the slipstream.

I watched two fighters explode not far beneath, disappearing in sheets of orange flame, B-17s dropping out on every state of distress, from engines shot out to control surfaces shot away, friendly and enemy parachutes floating down, and, on the green carpet far behind us, numerous funeral pyres of smoke from fallen fighters, marking our trail. The sight was fantastic: it surpassed fiction . . . I watched a B-17 turn slowly out to the right with its cockpit a mass of flames. The co-pilot crawled out of his window, held on with one hand, reached back for his chute, buckled it on, let go, and was whisked back into the horizontal stabilizer. I believe the impact killed him. His 'chute didn't open.

Ten minutes, twenty minutes, thirty minutes, and still no letup in the attacks. The fighters queued up like a bread line and let us have it. Each second of time had a cannon shell in it. Our B-17 shook steadily with the fire of its .50s, and the air inside was heavy with smoke. It was cold in the cockpit, but when I looked across at the pilot I saw that sweat was pouring off his forehead and over his oxygen mask. He turned the controls over to me for a while. It was a blessed relief to concentrate on holding station in formation instead of watching those everlasting fighters boring in. It was possible to forget the fighters. Then the top turret gunner's muzzles would pound away a foot above my head, giving a realistic imitation of cannon shells exploding in the cockpit, while I gave an even better imitation of a man jumping six inches out of his seat.

A B-17 of the Group ahead, with its right Tokyo tanks on

fire, dropped back to about 200 feet above our right wing and stayed there while seven of the crew successively baled out. Four went out the bomb bay and executed delayed jumps, one baled from the nose, opened his 'chute prematurely and nearly fouled the tail. Another went out the left waist gun opening, delaying his 'chute opening for a safe interval. The tail gunner jumped out of his hatch, apparently pulling the ripcord before he was clear of the ship. His 'chute opened instantaneously, barely missing the tail, and jerked him so hard that both his shoes came off. He hung limp in the harness, whereas the others had shown immediate signs of life after their 'chutes opened, shifting around in the harness. The B-17 then dropped back in a medium spiral and I did not see the pilots leave. I saw it just before it passed from view, several thousand feet below us, with its right wing a sheet of yellow flame.

After we had been under constant attack for a solid hour, it appeared certain that our Group was faced with annihilation. Seven of us had been shot down, the sky was still mottled with rising fighters, and it was only 1120 hours, with target-time still thirty-five minutes away. I doubt if a man in the Group visualised the possibility of our getting much further without one hundred per cent loss . . . Our Group firepower was reduced thirty-three per cent; ammunition was running low. Our tail guns had to be replenished from another gun station. Gunners were becoming exhausted. One B-17 dropped out of formation and put its wheels down while the crew baled out. Three Me 109s circled it closely but held their fire, apparently ensuring that no-one stayed in the ship to try for home.

Near the IP, at 1150 hours, one hour and a half after the first of at least 200 individual fighters attacks, the pressure eased off, although hostiles were still in the vicinity. We turned at the IP at 1154 hours with fourteen B-17s left in the Group, two of which were badly crippled. They dropped out soon after bombing the target and headed for Switzerland. Weather over the target, as on the entire trip, was ideal. Flak was negligible. The Group got its bombs away promptly on the leader. As we turned and headed for the Alps, I got a grim satisfaction out of seeing a rectangular column of smoke rising straight up from the Me 109 shops.

The rest of the trip was a marked anticlimax. A few more fighters pecked at us on the way to the Alps. A town in the Brenner Pass tossed up a lone burst of futile flak. We circled over Lake Garda long enough to give the cripples a chance to rejoin the family, and we were on our way towards the Mediterranean in a gradual descent. The prospect of ditching as we approached North Africa, short of fuel, and the sight of other B-17s falling into the drink, seemed trivial matters after the vicious nightmare of the long trip across southern Germany. We felt the reaction of men who had not expected to see another sunset. At 1815 hours, with red lights showing on all the fuel tanks in my ship, the seven B-17s of the Group which were still in formation circled over a North African airdrome and landed. Our crew was unscratched. Sole damage to the airplane: a bit of ventilation around the tail from flak and 20mm shells. We slept on the hard ground under the wings of our B-17, but the good earth felt softer than a silk pillow.

For the 8th Bomber Command the ordeal of 17 August 1943 was not yet over. In the early afternoon 229 Fortresses crossed the Dutch coast en route to bomb the ball-bearing factories at Schweinfurt. On this occasion determined fighter attacks began as soon as the formation reached German territory. The Gruppen attacked in pairs, one engaging the Allied fighter escort and the other the bombers. At times more than 300 German fighters were in the air, and fierce battles raged along the route to the target. In addition to cannon and machine guns, some of the fighters were armed with 21cm rockets. A direct hit by one of these was enough to tear a bomber apart, and several B-17s were lost by this means.

The fighter attacks intensified after the Americans' P-47 escort turned for home; thirty-six Fortresses were shot down, bringing 8th Bomber Command's total loss for the day to sixty bombers. Over 100 more were damaged, many of them so severely that they had to be scrapped.

Early in October, after a five-week lull, it was judged that the Eighth Air Force was ready to resume its deep-penetration attacks; but when they started again, the lessons of August were rammed home even more forcibly. During one week, between 8 and 14 October, when the Americans attacked Bremen, Marienburg, Danzig, Münster and once again Schweinfurt, they lost 148 bombers and nearly 1500 aircrew. On the Schweinfurt raid, on 14 October, which became known as Black Thursday, the *Luftwaffe* flew over 500 sorties and destroyed sixty of the 280 bombers taking part – over twenty per cent. Wing Commander 'Johnnie' Johnson, leading his Canadian Spitfire wing into the Low Countries to escort the returning bombers, described the aftermath of this terrible encounter:

> It was a clear afternoon, and we first saw their contrails many miles away, as well as the thinner darting contrails of the enemy fighters above and on either flank. As we closed the gap we could see that they had taken a terrible mauling, for there were gaping holes in their precise formations. Some Fortresses were gradually losing height, and a few stragglers, lagging well behind, were struggling to get home on three engines.
>
> We swept well behind the stragglers and drove off a few 109s and 110s, but the great air battle was over, and what a fight it must have been, because more than half the bombers we nursed across the North Sea were shot up. One or two ditched in the sea, and many others, carrying dead and badly injured crew members, had to make crash-landings. How we longed for more drop tanks, so that some of the many hundreds of Spitfires based in Britain could play their part in the great battles over Germany . . .

With the Eighth Air Force reeling from this succession of disasters and RAF Bomber Command beginning to suffer increasingly heavy losses at the hands of the German night-fighter force, the prospect for the combined Allied air offensive looked grim. In the RAF's case, a solution would soon come in the shape of the long-range Mosquito night fighter, which would patrol the flanks of the night bomber streams and stalk its enemy counterparts; but for the American daylight bombers, the problem was different. What was needed here was a fighter with sufficient fuel to escort the B-17s and B-24s all the way to the target, engage the enemy fighters in combat, and have enough fuel remaining to escort the bombers home again. Such an aircraft, the North American P-51 Mustang, was already in service with the RAF in the tactical reconnaissance role, and in November 1943 the first USAAF Mustang unit, the 354th Fighter Group, established itself at Boxted, near

The North American P-51 Mustang was first used by RAF Army Cooperation Command. This example belongs to No. 26 Squadron. (Air Marshal Sir Frederick Sowery)

Colchester in Essex, where it came under the operational control of the Eighth Air Force. It was the first of many, and the superb Mustang – eventually fitted with a Packard-built Rolls-Royce Merlin engine – was without doubt the aircraft that went on to win the daylight battle over Europe.

But that was in the future, and in the meantime a single Mustang Group, assisted by a couple of Mustang-equipped RAF squadrons, was not enough to bring about a dramatic reduction in the losses suffered by the heavy bombers, and in the first weeks of 1944 – with the Eighth Air Force committed to the battle on a bigger scale than ever before – these once again assumed alarming proportions. Of the 238 that attacked the fighter production factories at Oschersleben on 11 January, for example, sixty again failed to return. But there was to be no respite. The top priority at the outset of 1944 was the destruction of the *Luftwaffe*, and it had to be achieved within a limited period as an essential prelude to the projected Allied invasion of Europe. The directive that went out to all Commands from General H.H. Arnold, the USAAF Chief of Staff, at the beginning of the New Year was concise.

'Destroy the Enemy Air Force wherever you find them, in the air, on the ground and in the factories.' It was to prove a formidable challenge, for 1944 would find the *Luftwaffe*'s fighter force at the peak of its effectiveness.

CHAPTER TWELVE

Aces of the Night

At the end of 1941 nine squadrons of Beaufighters were assigned to the night defence of Britain, one having formed during the summer and three having converted from Defiants. The squadrons were No. 25 at Wittering (Northamptonshire), 29 at West Malling (Kent), 68 at High Ercall (Shropshire), 141 at Drem (East Lothian), 219 at Tangmere (Sussex), 255 at Coltishall (Norfolk), 307 at Exeter (Devon), 60 at Predannack (Cornwall) and 604 at Middle Wallop (Hampshire). Six Defiant night fighter squadrons were also still on the Order of Battle. They were No. 96 at Wrexham (Denbighshire), 125 at Fairwood Common (Glamorgan), 151 at Coltishall, 153 at Ballyhalbert (Co Down), 256 at Coltishall, and 264 at West Malling. Added to these was No. 85 Squadron at Hunsdon in Hertfordshire, equipped with Douglas Havocs.

The real answer to the prayers of the RAF night fighter squadrons was the de Havilland Mosquito. The first Mosquito fighter squadron, No. 157, formed at Debden in Essex on 13 December 1941, its first aircraft, a dual-control Mk II, arriving at Debden's satellite airfield, Castle Camps, on 26 January 1942. Seventeen Mk IIs were delivered to Maintenance Units for the fitting of AI Mk V, and by mid-April No 157 Squadron had nineteen NF Mk IIs on its inventory, three of them without radar. By this time No. 151 Squadron at Wittering had also begun to rearm with the NF Mk II, with sixteen aircraft on strength at the end of April. As the two squadrons built up their night flying hours,

The de Havilland Mosquito was the RAF's most versatile combat aircraft, and excelled in the night-fighter role. (RAF)

practised interceptions and night gun-firing (which revealed the need for flash eliminators on the nose-mounted .303in Browning guns which when fired blinded the pilot to everything outside the cockpit) the crews became increasingly happy with their new aircraft. Its armament of four 20mm Hispano cannon and four Brownings was formidable, and – unlike the arrangement in the Beaufighter – the radar observer sat facing forwards in the cockpit, on the pilot's right and slightly behind him.

Although the two Mosquito night-fighter squadrons made several contacts with enemy aircraft during the first month of the German offensive, the Beaufighter squadrons remained in the fore-front of the action, and it was not until 29 May that the first successful interception was made by a Mosquito, during a raid on Grimsby. At 0430 Flight Lieutenant Pennington of 151 Squadron was vectored on to a Heinkel 111 and opened fire on it over the North Sea. The Heinkel, with one engine on fire, spiralled down into the haze and Pennington lost it, claiming it as a probable. His own aircraft was damaged by return fire and he flew back to base on one engine. In another incident, Pilot Officer Wain damaged a Do 217E, and on 30 May Squadron Leader Ashfield of 157 Squadron damaged a Dornier 217 off Dover. On 3 May No. 264

Squadron began to rearm with Mosquitoes at Colerne, Wiltshire, the squadron flying its first night combat patrol on the 13th.

It was not until the end of June that the Mosquito night fighters scored their first confirmed victories. On the night of 24/25 June, aircraft of No. 151 Sqn accounted for two Do 217E4s, shooting down a Dornier of 2/KG40 into the North Sea and another into the Wash. The squadron claimed two more enemy aircraft, a Heinkel 111 and a Do 217, before the end of the month, but there is no confirmation of these claims in records of enemy losses. It was a frustrating time for No. 157 Squadron; despite numerous patrols, its crews failed to score a confirmed victory until 22/23 August, when Wing Commander Gordon Slade and Pilot Officer Truscott shot down a Dornier 217 of 2/KG2 at Worlington, Suffolk.

By the beginning of 1943 the RAF's night fighter squadrons were turning increasingly from defence to offence. The Mosquito's long range and heavy armament of four 20mm cannon made it highly suitable for the night intruder role, as well as for local night air-defence. The intruder Mosquitoes (and Beaufighters), although stripped of their AI for operations over enemy territory, were fitted with a device named Serrate which, developed by the Tele-

Serrate Mk II installation in a Mosquito night fighter. (TRE)

communications Research Establishment as a result of information on enemy night-fighting radars brought back by special counter-measures aircraft, enabled the British fighters to home-in to the enemy's airborne radar transmissions. It had a range of about 50 miles, and was first used operationally in June 1943 by No 141 Squadron, which scored 23 kills in three months with its help. No. 141 Squadron's commander was Wing Commander J.R.D. 'Bob' Braham, whose combat report describes a night action off the Dutch island of Ameland on the night of 17/18 August 1943. Braham was flying a Beaufighter Mk VI, and his navigator was Flight Lieutenant H. Jacobs.

> We took off from Coltishall at 2200 hours on intruder patrol to Stade. We flew to a point north of Schiermonnikoog and then turned NE at 2254. We continued on course for about five minutes when we sighted one Me 110 flying east and jinking. We turned and followed him towards the coast, closing in on the aircraft until we were at 300 yards range, 20 degrees star-board astern and a little below. Fire was opened with a two-second burst from all guns and strikes were seen all over the enemy aircraft. Smoke came from the port engine and the Me 110 dived to port. We gave him another two-second burst from 250 yards and he caught fire and dived into the sea, burning on the water. Immediately afterwards we saw a second Me 110 (which had been chasing us) a little above and turning gently to starboard on an easterly course. We gave a one-second burst of cannon and machine gun at 50 yards in a gentle turn. The enemy aircraft appeared to blow up and we had to pull up and turn to port to avoid ramming it. At that point we saw one man bale out and his parachute open, and the enemy aircraft dived vertically into the sea in flames . . . we landed at Wittering at 0145.

Bob Braham, a pre-war regular RAF officer, had been involved in the development of night-fighting techniques since the begin-ning of the war, and he destroyed his first victim – a Dornier 17 – while flying a Blenheim of No. 29 Squadron on 24 August 1940. By July 1941 he had four kills to his credit, all at night, and he increased this score to six by the end of the year. During this period, his observer was Sergeant Gregory, who was later commissioned.

After a rest from operations (during which, incidentally, they destroyed a Dornier 217 in a Beaufighter 'borrowed' while on a visit to their old squadron) they rejoined No. 29 Squadron in July 1942, and in just a few weeks they destroyed three enemy bombers and damaged three more. In October 1942 the Braham-Gregory team shot down a Junkers 88 and a Dornier 217. In the following month, Braham was promoted and given command of No. 141 Squadron, beginning night intruder operations in June 1943. On his first such mission, on 14 June, he shot down a Messerschmitt 110, and by the end of September he had brought his score to twenty enemy aircraft destroyed, nineteen of them at night. He was now level with John Cunningham, but his second operational tour was at an end and it was not until February 1944 that he was again permitted to fly operationally, and then only on a limited basis, as Wing Commander (Night Operations) at HQ No. 2 Group. In the meantime, No 141 Squadron, together with Nos 169 and 239, had been transferred from Fighter Command to No. 100 (Counter-measures) Group, the task of the three squadrons being bomber support.

During their first three months of operations the three squadrons combined claimed only 31 enemy aircraft destroyed or damaged, and six of these were shot down by Bob Braham. In March 1944 No. 100 Group's fighter force was joined by No. 515 Squadron, operating Beaufighters and later Mosquito VIs. This unit, however, was not equipped with Serrate.   During this period, changing his tactics, Braham made six low-level daylight intruder sorties into occupied Europe in March and April 1944, and on five of these trips he destroyed seven enemy aircraft. On the first sortie on 5 March (he was now flying a Mosquito, borrowed from No. 305 Squadron at Lasham) he shot down a Heinkel 177, the biggest aircraft he had so far destroyed.

His run of luck came to an end on 25 June 1944, when, flying a No. 21 Squadron Mosquito, he was hit by flak and had to make a forced landing on a sandbar near Ringkobing, Denmark. He spent the rest of the war in prison camp, as did his Australian navigator, Flight Lieutenant Don Walsh. Braham's score at the time of his capture was twenty-nine confirmed kills, making him the leading RAF night fighter pilot. He was also the first RAF pilot ever to be awarded three DSOs and three DFCs. Later, he was awarded the Air Force Cross for his work at the Central Fighter Establishment in the early post-war years.

In 1952, Braham transferred to the RCAF, where among other appointments he commanded No. 432 All-Weather Squadron, flying Avro Canada CF-100s. He remained in the RCAF until 1968.

Bob Braham died of an inoperable brain tumour in Halifax, Nova Scotia, on 7 February 1974, just two months short of his fifty-fourth birthday.

During the early weeks of 1944 the AOC-in-C Bomber Command, Air Chief Marshal Sir Arthur Harris, had been making determined efforts to persuade the Air Staff to release more night-fighter squadrons for bomber support operations as a matter of priority. In April he wrote a strong letter to the Vice Chief of the Air Staff in which he recommended the transfer of at least ten fighter squadrons to No. 100 Group; in the event, a conference convened at the Air Ministry on the 20th of that month decided to authorize the transfer of only two, Nos 85 and 157, both armed with Mosquitoes. This meagre increase did little to improve the effectiveness of No. 100 Group's night fighter force. One of the problems was that Mosquitoes equipped with the latest Mk VII/VIII AI radar were forbidden to operate over

A Halifax bomber silhouetted against the fires of a German city. As Germany's night-fighter force grew more efficient, the need for bomber support became vital. (RAF)

enemy territory, and the Mk IV that equipped most of the 100 Group night fighters was subjected to increasing interference from enemy countermeasures.

To make matters worse, the usefulness of Serrate was over. The German Lichtenstein AI radar on which it was designed to home onto had been replaced by the more advanced SN-2, which worked outside Serrate's frequency cover. The end result was frustration for the night fighter crews. In June 1944, for example, only one enemy aircraft was destroyed in the course of 140 sorties.

The situation improved somewhat towards the end of 1944, when Mosquitoes equipped with the latest AI radar were cleared to operate over enemy territory, and the old Serrate Mk I was replaced by a new version, the Mk IV. Some aircraft were also equipped with a new device known as Perfectos, which emitted a pulse that triggered the IFF (Identification Friend/Foe) sets of German night fighters and enabled the Mosquitoes to home onto the answering signal.

Nevertheless, No. 100 Group's fighter force never really succeeded in getting to grips with the enemy night fighters. Quite apart from equipment problems, the Mosquito crews were faced with the formidable task of operating deep inside enemy territory as complete free-lancers, with no help from other quarters. Furthermore, enemy fighters had to be intercepted before they entered the bomber stream, because once they were inside it was extremely difficult to make radar contact with them owing to the profusion of other echoes.

The tactics employed by the Mosquitoes usually began with a bombing and cannon attack on enemy night fighter airfields a few minutes before the bomber stream entered the area of German GCI radar coverage. Other Mosquitoes would work on the flanks of the stream, about 40 miles from it and at a higher altitude, in the hope of intercepting enemy fighters before they reached the bombers. As the bombers were on their way home from the target, more Mosquito fighter-bombers loitered in the vicinity of the German airfields, waiting to catch the night fighters as they came in to land.

Few of the RAF's night fighter crews received publicity; in fact, many night fighter pilots achieved notable successes and remained almost entirely unknown outside the Service, at least until long after the war. One of them was Flight Lieutenant George Esmond Jameson, a young New Zealand pilot who, on the night of 29 July

1944, set up an Allied record by destroying four enemy aircraft in one night. He was flying a Mosquito of No. 488 RNZAF Squadron on patrol over Normandy, and his navigator was Flying Officer Norman Crookes. Jameson's combat report tells part of the story.

I was patrolling the Coutance-St Lo area when I saw an unidentified aircraft approaching head-on at 5000 feet height. Against the dawn I saw that it was a Junkers 88 and as I turned hard to port I followed him as he skimmed through the cloud tops. I closed to 300 yards and there was a series of explosions from the ground caused by the Junkers dropping his bombs as he tried to get away. I gave two short bursts as we came to the next clear patch, and after a fire in the port engine and fuselage the Ju 88 went down through the clouds vertically, hitting the ground near Caen.

As Jameson looked down at the debris of the Ju 88, Norman Crookes detected another aircraft on his radar and steered the pilot towards it. As he closed in, the unexpected happened: yet another Junkers suddenly burst out of the cloud, dead ahead of the Mosquito. The German pilot saw the danger and went into a diving turn, trying to regain the shelter of the clouds, but he was too late. Jameson opened fire from a range of 350 yards, and flames were soon streaming back from the Junkers' starboard engine. The aircraft fell through the cloud layer, burning fiercely, and plunged into the ground.

Almost immediately I obtained a brief visual on an aircraft crossing from port to starboard some 5000 feet away and identified as a Ju 88. My navigator confirmed this and took over on his 'box of tricks', keeping me behind the enemy aircraft, which was now taking violent evasive action and at the same time jamming our equipment. When we were down to almost treetop height I regained the visual at only 250 yards, opening fire immediately and causing the Junkers to pull up almost vertically, turning to port with sparks and debris falling away. The Ju eventually stalled and dived into a four-acre field where it exploded. This was near Lisieux and as the time was now 0515 hours I climbed back to 5000 feet and requested control to vector me back to any activity, as I had already observed further anti-aircraft fire through the clouds ahead.

Flight Lieutenant George Jameson, New Zealand night-fighter ace, prowled the Normandy beach-head in search of enemy aircraft .(RNZAF)

The anti-aircraft fire, Jameson soon established, was directed at a Dornier 217, whose pilot spotted the Mosquito as it closed in and began a series of violent evasive manoeuvres. Just as the Dornier was about to plunge into cloud, Jameson opened fire and saw his shells bursting on the enemy's fuselage. The Dornier went down in flames, the rear gunner continuing to fire back almost until the bomber hit the ground.

George Jameson's final score was eleven enemy aircraft destroyed, one probably destroyed and two damaged, all of them at night or in weather conditions so bad that day fighters were unable to operate. Eight of the enemy bombers were shot down while trying to attack Allied forces in Normandy, and the four kills of 29 July were all achieved within twenty minutes. He left the squadron on 15 August 1944 and returned to New Zealand, being awarded the DSO shortly afterwards. He died on 21 May, 1998.

One Mosquito night fighter/intruder team that enjoyed considerable success was Flight Lieutenant James Benson and Squadron Leader Lewis Brandon (navigator) of No. 157 Squadron. Together, they scored seven confirmed kills, with a number of claims for aircraft probably destroyed and damaged, and also destroyed six V-1 flying bombs in the summer of 1944.

On the night of 11/12 September 1944, while flying bomber support operations with No. 100 Group, they were flying over the island of Seeland, off the south-east coast of Denmark, when Brandon picked up a transmission from an enemy night fighter radar A few moments later, he made contact with the suspect aircraft and steered Benson towards it. In the clear moonlight, the enemy was identified as a Junkers 188; it was flying in broad circles, apparently orbiting a German radio beacon. Benson slid in astern of the 188 and fired a burst into it, seeing his 20mm shells strike home on the night-fighter's starboard wing root. The 188 lost speed rapidly, its starboard engine catching fire, and Benson had to pull up sharply to avoid a collision. The 188 was last seen plunging earthwards, streaming flames. At that moment, Brandon picked up another contact. It was a second Ju 188, and it had probably been engaged in a night-fighting exercise with the first. Benson closed in rapidly and gave the Junkers a two-second burst; bright flames streamed back from the enemy's ruptured fuel tanks and it dropped away towards the Danish coast, shedding great chunks of wreckage. The Mosquito sped through the cloud of smoke and debris that the Junkers left in its wake; when Benson and Brandon returned to base they found their aircraft smothered in oil and scarred by pieces of flying metal.

From June 1944, the RAF's night fighters had to contend with a new menace: the V-1 flying bomb. The Mosquito night fighter squadrons opened their score against the V-1s on the night of 15/16 June 1944, when a Mosquito VI of No. 605 Squadron from

Pursued by a Hawker Tempest, a V-1 flying bomb speeds low over the Kent countryside. (Source unknown)

A V-1 explodes under attack by a Hawker Tempest flown by Wing Commander R.P. Beamont. (IWM)

Manston (Flight Lieutenant J.G. Musgrave and Flight Sergeant Sanewell) exploded one over the Channel. Musgrave reported that 'it was like chasing a ball of fire across the sky. It flashed by our starboard side a few thousand feet away at the same height as we were flying. I quickly turned to port and gave chase. It was going pretty fast, but I caught up with it and opened fire from astern. At first, there was no effect so I closed in another hundred yards and gave it another burst. Then I went closer still and pressed the button again. This time, there was a terrific flash and explosion and the whole thing fell down in a vertical dive into the sea. The whole show was over in about three minutes.'

Four Mosquito squadrons – Nos 96, 219, 409 and 418 – were assigned exclusively to anti-V-1 night patrols, and were joined later in June by Nos 85, 157 and 456, the first two temporarily reassigned from their intruder work. Other squadrons operated against the

V-1s on a part-time basis, as priority was given to patrolling the Normandy beachhead. Between them, the seven full-time anti-V-1 Mosquito squadrons claimed 471 flying bombs, while the part-timers claimed 152 to give a combined total of 623, or about one-third of the RAF's total claim against the V-1s. Detachments of the USAAF's 422nd and 425th Squadrons also operated against the V-1s, their Black Widows being temporarily based at Hurn, but the crews were as yet inexperienced and they had little success, destroying nine flying bombs between them.

Although the Mosquito squadrons bore the brunt of night operations against the V-1s, one other squadron played an extraordinary part in the defence against the flying bombs. This was No. 501 (County of Gloucester) Squadron, armed with Hawker Tempest Mk Vs. The story was told to the author by one of the squadron's pilots, Flight Lieutenant A.J. 'Jimmy' Grottick, who took part in these activities from first to last.

On 2 August 1944 No. 501 Squadron moved to Manston. The unit was now fully equipped with Tempests, and the move was preparatory to crossing over to the Continent to join the Second Tactical Air Force. It was at this point that the axe fell. Several of us were seen – mainly those who had more night-flying hours in their log books than the others – and given an option. Either we could be reappointed to another operational unit, or we could go off for a rest period, probably as instructors on an operational training unit. Together with others given the option, I elected to remain operational.

We were transferred from 501 Squadron on to what was known as a Fighter Interception Unit, also at Manston. So great had the V-1 menace become that it was decided to set up a special night-fighter unit under the command of Squadron Leader Joe Berry. This, flying Tempests, would attempt to provide an effective response to V-1s coming in at night. At first, the FIU was just twelve pilots strong, but within about a week the loss rate had become so great – mainly through accidents – that the strength had been almost halved.

At the end of August 1944 the name Fighter Interception Unit was dropped, and the unit assumed the identity of No. 501 Squadron. The day-fighter pilots of the original 501 Squadron were allocated to 2nd TAF units, and so the County of Gloucester Squadron began an entirely new phase, operating solely at night in pursuit of its task. We were left in no doubt about the importance of the job we had to do. Squadron Leader Berry was called to HQ 11 Group and was given specific high-level instructions, which he passed on to us. He had been informed that Winston Churchill had taken a special interest in the new Tempest night fighter set-up, and that the Prime Minister had issued the following directive:

'So great is the threat, espacially at night, of the new V-1 menace, and the possibilities in terms of morale so dire, that No 501 Squadron must consider itself expendable. The Squadron will continue to fly, though there may be little chance of interception, however bad the weather.'

So, night after night, through September and onwards, patrols of 501 Squadron would take off in weather so bad that it sometimes grounded other squadrons during daylight hours. This, together with the fact that our own anti-aircraft gunners now had the benefit of radar gunlaying apparatus and proximity fuzes, made our night operations decidedly hairy. Squadron Leader Joe Berry was one of our early casualties; he had been in the anti-flying-bomb business a long time, and by the time of his death his score stood officially at sixty-one destroyed, plus another which he shared with two more pilots. Berry was lost about the middle of September, at the same time as Flight Lieutenant Snowy Bond, a New Zealand pilot, and another New Zealander whose name I forget. Both had been members of the old 501 Squadron in the pre-Tempest days. [according to records, Squadron Leader Berry was shot down by flak over Veendam, Holland, on 2 October 1944].

The Squadron was taken over by Squadron Leader Parker-Rees, who came to us from No. 96 Squadron and who was an experienced Mosquito night fighter pilot. At this time No 501 Squadron had seventeen pilots on strength, drawn from a wide area of operational experience.

Midway through September 1944 No. 501 Squadron was moved from Manston to Bradwell Bay, sixteen miles north-east of Southend in Essex, and continued its regular anti-V-1 patrols from this new location. By the time of the move to Bradwell Bay our defences had become rather more organized; strong anti-aircraft forces had been mustered in the south-east corner of the country, and with their new equipment were beginning to take a substantial toll of the V-1s. We were all 'zoned', and No. 501 Squadron was responsible for an area over the Thames estuary between Southend and London. Fortunately, our patrol height was somewhat higher than the altitude setting of the anti-aircraft shells. It was also considerably higher than the normal height at which the V-1s flew. As I recall, they flew at between 500 and 1000 feet. As you may well understand, this was not a comfortable height from which to deliver attacks on anything at night, especially something streaming a long, fiery tail and liable to explode in your face. We were equipped with a ground proximity warning device which was supposed to illuminate a red lamp in the cockpit at 500ft above ground level. I don't think it ever worked.

From this point on it was the anti-aircraft defences that got the majority of the V-1 intruders. Our task was to try to intercept those that got through the anti-aircraft net. The period of night-fighting extended from August 1944 to the end of March 1945, and towards the end of this priod No. 501 Squadron was moved from Bradwell Bay to Hunsdon, in Hertfordshire, just north of London. During the whole of this period I managed to down two V-1s. I had attempted numerous interceptions throughout the winter, but I had always been beaten to the kill by the AA guns. My first V-1 kill was on the night of 29 October, the V-1 falling somewhere in the vicinity of Chelmsford. My aircraft was Tempest SD-V.

My second V-1 was shot down on the night of 26 March 1945, when I was operating out of Hunsdon. It was an interesting kill, both for myself and for 501 Squadron. The V-1 crashed and exploded near North Weald, and as far as I can ascertain this was the last success scored against an enemy intruder over Britain. The V-1 offensive ended on 29 March, when a V-1 came down at Datchworth, near Hatfield, but this was not intercepted. At the end of March 1945 No. 501 Squadron's role as a night fighter squadron came to an end.

One point about the Tempest and the flying bomb. As I mentioned earlier, the V-1 was programmed to come across at low level, usually at between 500ft and 1000ft and at high speed, but this was variable. According to official sources, the V-1's average penetration speed was 400mph, but the second one I caught must have been doing close on 500. From 5000 feet plus, my Tempest picked up some 580mph IAS before I was able to catch up with it and destroy it.

Officially, No. 501 Squadron was credited with the destruction of more than 100 V-1s during that dark and freezing winter, but Flt Lt Grottick believes this figure to be exaggerated.

It was the anti-aircraft that got most of the flying bombs penetrating at night. All that was left for us to do was to try to catch the remnant that got through this first line of defence.

Nevertheless, there is no disputing the courage and skill of the pilots who launched themselves into the darkness night after night, in single-engined aircraft that were ill-equipped for the job they had to do, with the knowledge that they were officially expendable. The Mosquito squadrons also began to take losses in the later phases of the campaign against the V-1. In September 1944, with their bases in the Pas de Calais overrun by the Allied advance, the enemy began flying bomb attacks on London and other UK targets,

Personnel of No. 501 Squadron and Hawker Tempest, autumn 1944. Flight Lieutenant Jimmy Grottick is second from the right in the front row. (James Grottick)

such as Portsmouth and Southampton, with V-1s air-launched from Heinkel He 111s of KG53. Later in September air launches were made against east coast targets from positions off the Dutch coast. Catching the Heinkel launchers was very difficult, for they flew slowly at low level, and several Mosquitoes were lost to return fire, or because they stalled at low speed while trying to intercept. In an attempt to improve interception rates, a radar picket ship, the frigate HMS *Caicos*, and a specially-equipped radar Wellington of the Fighter Interception Unit were used to direct the Mosquitoes, which patrolled over the sea at about 4,000 feet between Britain and Holland. These operations continued until 14 January 1945, by which time KG53 had lost seventy-seven aircraft, forty-one of them on operations.

Although investigations into the use of airborne radar had been carried out in the late 1930s, the Germans were much slower than the British to develop AI radar for military use. As early as July 1939 the German communications firm, Telefunken, had shown that it was possible for an intercepting aircraft to be fitted with AI equipment, and had carried out a practical demonstration with a rudimentary set mounted in a Junkers 52. The *Luftwaffe* Technical Office, however, had shown no interest in the device, and so Telefunken had developed it into a radar altimeter. The AI concept was resurrected in the summer of 1940 and development went ahead, but there were a lot of snags to be overcome. One of them was that an internally-mounted antenna produced too weak a signal, so Telefunken had no choice but to opt for an externally-mounted aerial array – a far from satisfactory arrangement, not least because of the drag it produced.

Meanwhile, On 26 June 1940, just after the end of the fighting in France, the commander of *I/Zerstörergeschwader* 1 (I/ZG1) had been summoned to a high-level conference in The Hague. His name was *Hauptmann* Wolfgang Falck, and he had recently completed a lengthy report on attempts by his unit, which was armed with Bf 110s, to intercept British bombers passing over its base at Aalborg, in Denmark. Falck had trained his best crews in instrument flying and had held a battle flight on readiness every night, hoping to catch the elusive bombers with the help of a 'Freya' radar station off the north German coast (an experimental unit that had been operating on the island of Wangerooge since the autumn of 1939). The crews had met with no success, but they were the only fighter aircrew in the *Luftwaffe* with substantial experience of night flying, and the upshot of the meeting was that Falck was appointed to command the first night fighter *Geschwader*, NJG1, to be formed out of a *Gruppe* of ZG1 and one of JG2 (IV/JG2, which had just converted from Bf 109s to Bf 110s.) These were now redesignated I/NJG1, under *Hauptmann* Radusch, and III/NJG1, under Major Blumensaat. In addition, a second *Gruppe*, I/NJG2, was also formed under *Hauptmann* Karl-Heinrich Heyse, primary for intruder operations over Britain.

It was apparent that NJG1's night fighters, lacking any aid to interception other than the eyesight of their crews, would have to co-operate closely with searchlights and sound locators. A belt of these was already in place on an oblique line west of Münster; General Josef Kammhuber, in charge of the German night air defences, now ordered it to be extended to north and south until it stretched for some twenty-five miles along the approach to the Ruhr. Individual fighters were each allocated a sector within this belt, orbiting a radio beacon, their crews hoping to pick up a bomber once the searchlights were illuminated.

It was hardly surprising that the night fighters registered few successes with these tactics, and it was not until October 1940, with the introduction of the first Wurzburg fighter-direction radars, that matters began to improve. The system was somewhat cumbersome, involving a 'Freya' station to provide early warning, and two Wurzburgs, one to track the incoming bomber and the other to direct the night fighter. The biggest snag with the whole system was that only one fighter could be controlled at any one time within each sector, and the fighter could not be handed over from one sector to another. The fighter controller could bring the interceptor to within a mile or so of its target, but it was in that last mile – with the fighter pilot depending on his eyesight alone – that the problems really began. Often, despite the fact that they knew they were within a few hundred yards of the bomber, the night fighters failed to intercept. When they did so, it was with a larger element of luck.

On the night of 16/17 October 1940, for example, *Oberleutnant* Ludwig Becker, commanding 6/NJG2, and his radio operator, *Feldwebel* Staub, made the first successful ground-controlled interception of an enemy aircraft, assisted by information from a Freya set passed to them by the fighter controller, *Oberleutnant* Werner Schulze. They destroyed their target, a Wellington, but it was pure chance that they spotted the bomber's exhaust flames in the night sky. The night fighters' chances of success decreased in the spring of 1941, for the weight of Bomber Command's offensive was concentrated on the French Channel ports over a period of several weeks. When the main offensive again switched to German industrial targets in May the night fighter crews once more had their chance to score, and on the night of 2/3 June 1941 a Bf 110 crew, *Feldwebels* Kalinowski and Zwickl, became the first to destroy an enemy bomber – a Short Stirling – over the German capital, Berlin.

On 27/28 June, when seventy-three Wellingtons and thirty-five Whitleys were despatched to attack Bremen, returning crews reported, for the first time, that they had been subjected to intense night fighter attacks. Encountering bad weather, many crews attacked Hamburg in error, and five Whitleys were shot down by night fighters over the city – four of them by *Oberleutnant* Eckardt of II/NJG1, the biggest success so far by a German night fighter pilot. Night fighters accounted for a further three bombers over Hamburg two nights later. By mid-July 1941 the German night-fighter force had 134 twin-engined fighters deployed in the west, and trained crews were reaching the *Staffeln* in growing numbers.

On 1 August the 1st Night Fighter Division was given Air Corps (*Fliegerkorps*) status, and Kammhuber set up a new HQ at Zeist, near Utrecht. The air defence system underwent a substantial re-organization with the creation of the so-called 'Kammhuber Line.' This comprised a searchlight and flak belt, about 22 miles deep, and an overlapping network of circular air defence zones (known as *Himmelbett* , or 'four poster bed' zones) extending along the North Sea coast from Denmark to Belgium. A further searchlight and flak belt and nine more *Himmelbett* zones protected Berlin, while joint night fighter and flak zones were set up to defend the industrial areas of the Ruhr. The system was as tightly controlled as Kammhuber could make it, but the fact remained that each ground controller could still only direct a single fighter, whose pilot then had to rely on his vision to make contact with the target; but this deficiency was about to be put right.

Meanwhile, In July 1941 a prototype AI set, named Lichtenstein, was installed in a Messerschmitt 110 based at Leeuwarden, Holland. On 9 August this aircraft, crewed by *Oberleutnant* Ludwig Becker and *Feldwebel* Josef Staub, intercepted a Wellington bomber with the aid of Lichtenstein and shot it down. Despite this success, Kammhuber had to maintain constant pressure to have his night fighters fitted with AI radar, and it was not until early in

1942 that Lichtenstein-equipped aircraft began to reach the night-fighter wings (Nachtjagdgeschwader) in any numbers. Once they did, the effectiveness of the German night fighter force increased immeasurably, and some pilots began to achieve quite remarkable scores.

One of them was *Hauptmann* Werner Streib, commanding I/NJG1 at Venlo, who – accompanied by his observer, *Gefreiter* Lingen – had destroyed his first bomber, a Whitley, on the night of 20/21 July 1940 while flying a Bf 110. In August 1941 Streib destroyed three more bombers, and on the night of 1/2 October he intercepted and destroyed three Wellingtons inside forty minutes. Streib went on to gain sixty-six victories, and for a long time he was Germany's top-scoring night-fighter pilot; but close behind him came *Oberst* Helmut Lent, a veteran Bf 110 pilot who had fought over Poland, Norway and in the defence of Germany against the early (and disastrous) daylight raids on the north German ports by RAF Bomber Command.

On 1 November, 1941, Lent formed a new night fighter *Gruppe*, II/NJG2; his *Staffel* commanders were *Hauptmann* Rudolf Schönert, *Hauptmann* Prince Lippe-Weissenfeld, and *Hauptmann*

Ludwig Becker. All of them went on to achieve exceptional night-fighting scores. Helmut Lent destroyed 102 aircraft at night and eight by day before his death in a flying accident on 7 October 1944; Lippe-Weissenfeld got fifty-six before his death in action on 12 March 1944; and Becker had forty-six kills when he too was shot down, in February 1943.

Oberst Helmut Lent, the second-ranking German night-

Only one other German night fighter pilot exceeded Helmut Lent's score of enemy bombers destroyed. (Bundesarchiv)

fighter ace, was awarded the Third Reich's highest decoration, the Oak Leaves with Swords and Diamonds. So was the top-scorer, Major Heinz-Wolfgang Schnaufer, who gained an incredible 1212 victories in the night sky over Germany. Schnaufer scored many multiple kills; on 25 May 1944, for example, he shot down five Lancasters in a quarter of an hour, and on 21 February 1945 he destroyed two Lancasters in the early morning and seven more after nightfall, a total of nine in a single day. Schnaufer was a quite exceptional pilot, and his achievement was all the more noteworthy in that he gained his victories in just 164 combat sorties. Heinz-Wolfgang Schnaufer survived the war, returning to his family's wine business, only to be killed in 1950 when his car was in collision with a French lorry near Bordeaux.

By the spring of 1943, General Josef Kammhuber had five *Geschwader* and 400 twin-engined fighters under his command on bases stretching from Holland to the Mediterranean. However, he was the first to realise that 400 night fighters were not enough to counter the great armadas of four-engined bombers that were beginning to make deeper inroads into Germany night after night, and he consequently proposed a major extension of the Himmelbett air defence system, with eighteen night fighter *Geschwader* covering the whole of Germany. The aircraft would be fitted with improved AI equipment and the ground radar network would also be modernised.

Kammhuber pushed relentlessly for the expansion of his night fighter force and it was his undoing. Nothing could convince Hitler that the *Luftwaffe*'s night fighters were not already destroying enough enemy bombers to cripple the RAF's night offensive. Kammhuber rapidly began to fall from favour, and his cause was not helped when, during a series of heavy attacks on Hamburg in 1943, Bomber Command rendered the Himmelbett system virtually impotent by the use of 'Window', bundles of tinfoil strips cut to the wavelength of the enemy warning radar and dropped from attacking aircraft to confuse the defences. In November 1943, Kammhuber was relieved of his appointment as commander of the German night fighter force and transferred to *Luftflotte* 5 in Norway. He was reappointed as commander of the night fighter force in 1945, but by that time the command had virtually ceased to exist. He joined the post-war *Luftwaffe* and was appointed Inspector of the *Bundesluftwaffe* in 1956, a post he held until 1962. He died on New Year's Day, 1986.

The paralysing of the Himmelbett system led to the evolution of new tactics, stemming from a proposal made by one *Oberst* von Lossberg of the General Staff. He recommended that night fighters be released from the confines of the Himmelbett zones, where their movements were too restricted and susceptible to radar jamming, and instead mix freely with the bomber stream, the fighter pilots making visual attacks. The idea was approved, and it was decided as a first step to increase the strength of *Jagdgeschwader* 300, formed a month earlier under the command of Major Hajo Herrmann, himself a fighter ace. This was the pioneer *Wilde Sau* (Wild Boar) unit; equipped with single-engined fighters, its task was to patrol directly over German targets, the pilots endeavouring to pick out enemy bombers in the glare of searchlights and fires.

The idea was quickly adopted by other night fighter units, including NJG 1, and it achieved considerable success, although at great risk to the attacking fighters, which had to contend with German flak as well as defensive fire from the RAF bombers. The

Hans-Joachim 'Hajo' Herrmann, seen here on the left, was a talented exponent of the dive-bomber before turning his hand to night fighting.
(Bundesarchiv)

following combat report, one of the few to survive the wholesale destruction of *Luftwaffe* records that took place in the final days of the war, was made by *Leutnant* Musset of 5/NJG 1. His observer was *Gefreiter* Hafner and he was flying a Messerschmitt Bf 110.

At 2347 hours on 17.8.43 I took off from Berlin on a *Wilde Sau* operation. From the Berlin area I observed enemy activity to the north. I promptly flew in that direction and positioned myself at a height of 4300 metres over the enemy's target, Peenemünde [Germany's secret rocket weapons research establishment, hit by 597 RAF heavy bombers that night – author]. Against the glow of the burning target I saw from above numerous enemy aircraft flying over it in close formations of seven or eight.

I went down and placed myself at 3400 metres behind one enemy formation. At 0142 I attacked one of the enemy with two burst of fire from directly astern, registering good strikes on the port inboard engine, which at once caught fire. E/A (enemy aircraft) tipped over to its left and went down. Enemy counter-fire from rear gunner was ineffective. Owing to an immediate second engagement I could only follow E/A's descent on fire as far as a layer of mist.

I make four claims, as follows:

1. Attack at 01.45 on a four-engined E/A at 2600 metres from astern and range 30-40 metres. E/A at once burned brightly in both wings and fuselage. I observed it until it crashed in flames at 0147.

2. At 0150 I was in position to attack another E/A from slightly above, starboard astern and range 60-70 metres. Strikes were seen in starboard wing, and E/A blew up. I observed burning fragments hit the ground at 0152.

3. At 0157 I attacked another four-engined E/A at 1830 metres from 100 metres astern. Burning brightly in both wings and fuselage it went into a vertical dive. After its crash I saw the wreckage burning at 0158. Heavy counter-fire from rear gunner scored hits in both wings of our own aircraft.

4. At 0159 I was ready to attack again. E/A took strong evasive action by weaving. While it was in a left-hand turn, however, I got in a burst from port astern and range 40-50 metres,

which set the port wing on fire. E/A plunged to the ground burning brightly, and I observed the crash at 0201. Enemy counter-fire from rear gunner was ineffective.

A few minutes later I attacked another E/A which took violent evasive action by weaving. On the first attack my cannon went out of action owing to burst barrels. I then made three further attacks with MG and observed good strikes on the starboard wing without, however, setting it on fire. Owing to heavy counter-fire from enemy rear gunner I suffered hits in my own port engine. At the same time I came under heavy fire from aircraft on the starboard beam, which wounded radio operator in the left shoulder and set my Me 110's port engine on fire. Thereupon I broke off the action, cut my engine and flew westwards away from the target area. No radio contact with the ground could be established, and ES signals were also unavailing. As I was constantly losing height, at 1800 metres I gave the order to bale out.
As I did so I struck the tail unit with both legs, thereby breaking my right thigh and left shin-bone. After normal landings by parachute my observer and I were taken to the reserve military hospital at Güstrow.

Four heavy bombers, each with a crew of seven, destroyed in fifteen minutes, together with one probably destroyed and one damaged! And such engagements were by no means uncommon during the night battle over Germany. That night, forty RAF bombers failed to return from Peenemünde. The loss would certainly have been higher, had it not been for a diversionary effort by a small force of RAF Mosquitoes, which dropped flares over Berlin and duped the defences into believing that this was the objective. The result was that 148 *Wilde Sau* fighters patrolled over the capital for the best part of an hour without sighting a single enemy aircraft.
While *Wilde Sau* operations continued, Telefunken had been hard at work developing a new AI radar that would not be susceptible to 'Window' jamming. In October 1943 the night fighter units began to receive the new Lichtenstein SN-2 AI radar, which was free from both electronic and 'Window' jamming. It had a maximum range of 4 miles and a minimum range of 450 yards, and it was not long before some night fighter crews began to register a

formidable number of successes with its help. In the autumn of 1943 two more homing devices were also developed for use by night fighters, the Naxos-Z and the Flensburg. The former enabled the fighters to home on to transmissions from the RAF's H2S navigational radar, and the latter was designed to lock on to radiations from the 'Monica' tail warning radar carried by the bombers.

In the summer of 1943 the German night fighters also began to receive a new type of armament, which was to prove horribly effective. Devised by an armourer named Paul Mahle and known as *Schräge Musik* (Slanting Music), it involved the mounting of two 20mm cannon, their muzzles pointing upwards at a fixed angle, on a wooden platform in the upper fuselage of a night fighter. This arrangement enabled the fighter to take advantage of a bomber's blind spot and attack it from directly below with the aid of a reflector sight mounted on the cockpit roof.

Schräge Musik was used for the first time on the night of 17/18 August 1943, when two crews of II/NJG 5 destroyed six RAF bombers in the space of thirty minutes The German airman reported that the Halifaxes and Lancasters were extremely vulnerable to this form of attack. The large area of their wings was impossible to miss, and since the wings contained the fuel tanks a relative short burst was usually enough to set a bomber on fire. Between the night of the Peenemünde raid and 2 October, the crews of II/NJG 5 scored eighteen victories with the aid of *Schräge Musik* for no loss to themselves.

Despite the problems of equipment and organisation that handicapped the German night fighter force, its success rate reached an unprecedented peak in the spring of 1944. In the course of three big air battles over darkened Germany Bomber Command suffered crippling losses. On the night of 19/20 February, seventy-eight out of a force of 823 bombers despatched to attack Leipzig failed to return; seventy-two more were destroyed during an assault on Berlin on 24/25 March, and then, five nights later, came the most catastrophic loss of all, and the greatest triumph for the German night fighters.

At nightfall on 30 March, 1944, 795 heavy bombers set out from their English bases to attack the vital industrial centre and railway junction of Nuremberg. The night was cloudless and calm, and across a great arc of Europe stretching across Holland, Belgium, northern France and north-west Germany the *Luftwaffe* night-fighter crews were at cockpit readiness. At 2200 reports began to come in of small-scale attacks by Mosquitoes on several airfields in Holland and of minelaying operations over the North Sea, but the GOC I Fighter Corps, *Generalmajor* Josef Schmid, realised thast these were simply diversions and kept his fighters on the ground. Then, at 2230, the German coastal radar-stations detected a major raid building up on the other side of the Channel, and a few minutes later the bomber stream was reported to be heading south-eastwards towards Belgium. At 2330 Schmid finally ordered his fighters into the air.

This time, instead of carrying out the usual procedure and making several abrupt changes of course to confuse the enemy defences, the bomber stream steered due east for 150 miles after making landfall on the enemy coast, and the night fighters had no difficulty in locating their targets. The route to Nuremberg was marked by a series of fiery beacons as one heavy bomber after another fell burning from the sky. From all over Germany the night fighter *Gruppen* converged on the bomber stream, and several pilots scored multiple kills in the running battle that developed. The greatest success was achieved by *Oberleutnant* Martin Becker of I/NJG 6, who destroyed six Halifax bombers in half an hour, between 0020 and 0050. Nor was that all; after landing to refuel and rearm, Becker took off again in his Bf 110 and shot down a seventh Halifax as it was on its homeward flight.

Other pilots who achieved notable successes that night were *Oberleutnant* Helmut Schulte of II/NJG 5, who destroyed four heavy bombers; *Leutnant* Wilhelm Seuss of IV/NJG 5, who also shot down four; and *Oberleutnant* Martin Drewes of II/NJG 1, who destroyed three.

Martin Becker's skill as a night-fighter pilot caused Bomber Command grievous losses.(Bundesarchiv)

For RAF Bomber Command, the cost of the Nuremberg raid was stupendous. Ninety-five bombers failed to return and seventy-one were damaged. The loss – 11.8 per cent of the attacking force – was the highest ever sustained by the Command. It was the greatest victory achieved by the German night-fighter force during the war, but it was also its last. One by one, the leading German night fighter pilots were swallowed up in the cauldron of the air war as 1944 wore on; the *Luftwaffe*'s night-fighter resources dwindled steadily through attrition in combat and through Allied bombing. For example, 465 Bf 110s, earmarked for night fighting, were destroyed by bombing in February 1944 alone.

In the first half of 1943, General Kammhuber had pressed strongly for the production of new twin-engined types designed specifically for night fighting. At the forefront of these was the Heinkel He 219 Uhu (Owl), the prototype of which had flown in November 1942 after months of delay caused by lack of interest by the German Air Ministry. By April 1943 300 examples had been ordered; kammhuber wanted 2000, but in the event only 294 were built before the end of the war. Formidably armed with six 20mm cannon and equipped with the latest AI radar, the He 219 would undoubtedly have torn great gaps in Bomber Command's ranks had it been available in quantity. It also had a performance comparable to that of the Mosquito, which other German night fighters did not, and therefore could have engaged the RAF's intruders on equal terms.

Admittedly, the He 219 suffered froma series of technical troubles in its early development career, but what it might have achieved in action was ably demonstrated on the night of 11/12 June 1943 by Major Werner Streib of I/NJG 1. Flying a pre-productioon He 219 on operational trials from Venlo, he infiltrated an RAF bomber stream heading for Berlin and shot down five Lancasters in half an hour. The only sour note for Strein sounded when the flaps of the He 219 refused to function and the aircraft over-ran the runway on landing, breaking into three pieces. Streib and his observer escaped without injury.

Werner Streib was one of thirty *Luftwaffe* night fighter pilots to score forty or more victories. Between them, they destroyed 1800 aircraft – the equivalent of 120 RAF bomber squadrons. The two top-scorers have already been mentioned; in third place was Major Sayn-Wittgenstein with eighty-three victories, who was killed on 21 January 1944.

Their exploits were largely eclipsed by those of the German day fighters, who received the lion's share of publicity. But it should never be forgotten that, in the early months of 1944, the German night-fighter force came close to bringing the RAF's night offensive to a standstill.

CHAPTER THIRTEEN

Aces of the Eastern Front, 1943–45

The winter of 1942-43 showed that Russian fighter pilots could match, and often outfight, their German counterparts. The days when *Luftwaffe* aces could notch up fantastic scores against inexperienced, poorly-trained enemies were gone forever, and now, in the early weeks of 1943, Russian fighter squadrons everywhere along the 1200-mile front were beginning to receive equipment that was more than a match for the Bf 109, and which was capable of meeting the latest Focke-Wulf 190s on equal terms. As well as the La-5, there was the Yakovlev Yak-9, which was a progressive development of the Yak-1. A heavy fighter, the Yak-9 – which was to be built in greater numbers than any other Russian fighter – could also be used in the fighter-bomber and reconnaissance roles, and one version armed with a 37mm cannon was effective against armour.

By the middle of November 1942, one-quarter of the Soviet Air Force's fighting strength had been assembled on the Stalingrad front in preparation for the massive Soviet counter-offensive, which began on 20 November 1942, and ended with the utter destruction of the German Sixth Army at the end of January 1943. During this period some Russian fighter pilots joined the ranks of the aces with unexpected ease, wreaking fearful slaughter on the lumbering transport aircraft that were making desperate attempts to supply the tens of thousands of German troops trapped in the

The Junkers Ju 52 transports suffered dreadful casualties at Stalingrad. Romanian aircraft, like this one, also took part in the airlift. (Source unknown)

Stalingrad pocket. On 9 January 1943, for example, eighteen pilots of the 235th Fighter Air Division attacked sixteen Ju 52 transports flying into Stalingrad. Nine Junkers went down on the first firing pass; five crashed in flames and the other four made forced landings. The remaining seven Ju 52s tried to turn back, but the fighters pursued them and destroyed six more.

The battle for Stalingrad was a major turning point in the war on the Eastern Front, but the greatest was the Battle of Kursk, which took place in the summer of 1943. The German offensive at Kursk was to be their last, and it was broken in eight days. Overhead, massive formations of aircraft, as many as 500 at a time, were locked in combat. In seventy-six major air battles which took place during the first day, the Russians shot down 106 enemy aircraft and lost ninety-eight of their own.

It was during the Kursk battle that the man who was to become the top-scoring Allied fighter pilot of World War Two scored his first victories. His name was Ivan Nikitovich Kozhedub, who flew his first combat mission on 26 March 1943, when he was posted as a senior sergeant to the 240th Fighter Regiment, flying La-5s on the Voronezh Front. His first combat successes came in July 1943, when, now a lieutenant, he destroyed two Ju 87s and a Bf 109. His tally grew at an astonishing pace. In August 1943, now a squadron commander, he destroyed three Bf 109s, an Fw 190 and another Ju 87. He continued to enjoy success into October, when his regiment became involved in furious air battles over the Dnieper River; in ten days of action he accounted for eleven enemy aircraft. After that, he was rested from combat for a while.

In the fierce air fighting over Kursk, one exploit stood out above all others. On 6 July, Guards Lieutenant Aleksei K. Gorovets, flying a Yak-9, was returning alone from a mission when he sighted a formation of twenty Ju 87 Stukas heading for the Russian lines. Using cloud cover to good advantage, Gorovets stalked the enemy formation until he was right on top of it, then he dived on the rear-most flight of dive-bombers. Three Stukas fell in flames before the startled Germans knew what was happening, and in the next few minutes the Russian pilot pressed home attack after attack, destroying six more bombers before he was fatally wounded by return fire. He was made a posthumous HSU.

The successful Soviet counter-attack at Kursk, followed by the recapture of Orel and Kharkov, created favourable conditions for the development of a general offensive on the southern wing of the Soviet-German front. The Soviet Supreme Command decided to free the entire left bank of the Dnieper, subsequently pushing on across the river and establishing a firm bridgehead on the oppo-site bank. The Russian offensive opened on 26 August 1943, supported by some 600 aircraft of the 16th Air Army, and the

ensuing air battle produced some noteworthy exploits. On 24 September, for example, Colonel Nikolai Varchuk, com-mander of the 737th Fighter air regiment and already a Hero of the Soviet Union, was leading a group of Yak-9s on a ground attack escort mission when he sighted forty German bombers,

Ivan Kozhedub went on to become the top-scoring Allied fighter pilot, with 62 victories. (Via J.R. Cavanagh)

escorted by fifteen Fw 190s, heading for the German lines. Ordering the rest of his group to continue with the escort mission, Varchuk broke away with his wingman and attacked the bombers, shooting one down. As he pulled away from his attack, Varchuk was engaged by two Focke-Wulfs; he out-manoeuvred them and destroyed both in a series of head-on passes.

One Russian pilot who began his rise to fame in October 1943, as the Germans strove to dislodge the Russians from their bridgehead on the right bank of the Dnieper, was Lieutenant Kirill A. Yevstigneyev, a flight commander with the 240th Fighter Air Regiment. In the course of nine dogfights he destroyed twelve enemy aircraft, and his score continued to rise steadily during the months that followed. He was twice made a Hero of the Soviet Union, and by the end of the war he had flown 300 combat sorties, taken part in 120 air battles and shot down fifty-six enemy aircraft.

But it was a German fighter pilot who began to capture the headlines on the Eastern Front in 1943. His name was Erich 'Bubi' Hartmann, who had joined JG 52 at Soldatskaya, north of the Caucasus Mountains, in October 1942. Hartmann quickly became convinced that the key to success in air fighting lay in getting as close as possible to his opponent and opening fire at point-blank range. The tactics were simple, and they worked. By the end of March 1943 Hartmann had destroyed five enemy aircraft, and two months later his score had risen to seventeen.

The fight in which he claimed his seventeenth victim, on 25 May, was very nearly his last. He was climbing away after shooting down an La-5 fighter when, blinded by the sun, he collided with another enemy aircraft and only just managed to nurse his crippled fighter over the lines before making a forced landing. After that he was sent back to Germany for a brief rest, returning to the front in July. His return to combat was marked by a series of incredible leaps in his score; on the 5th he shot down four more Russian aircraft, and two days later he destroyed seven in a series of hectic air fights.

By 3 August, 1943, Hartmann had fifty confirmed victories. He was now flying up to four sorties a day, and with the Russians on the offensive on most sectors of the front action was not hard to find. On 5 August his score stood at sixty, ten more Russian aircraft having gone down before his guns, and two weeks later he had equalled the score of World War One ace Manfred von Richthofen, with eighty kills. By the end of October his tally stood at 148, an achievement that won him the award of the Knight's Cross of the Iron Cross. Two years earlier, fifty victories would have been sufficient to bring him a similar honour; but times had changed, and now decorations came harder to Germany's fighting men.

His victories during the long summer of 1943 were accompanied by their share of close shaves. The closest of all came on 19 August, when the squadron – now stationed in the Donets Basis – was ordered to take off in support of the German ground forces, threatened with encirclement following a major Russian breakthrough. Over the front line the Messerschmitts encountered forty Ilyushin Il-2s, escorted by as many fighters, and a fierce battle developed. Hartmann shot down a pair of Il-2s, but then his own aircraft was hit and he was compelled to make a forced landing. As he was climbing from the cockpit, he was relieved to see a German truck approaching. The relief, however, was short-lived, for the soldiers that jumped from the vehicle were Russians.

Hartmann, clutching his stomach and pretending to be injured, was taken to the Russian HQ in a nearby village. Some time later, after nightfall, he was placed on a truck which set off eastwards, deeper into Russian territory. The German was accompanied by two Russian soldiers, one driving, the other sitting in the back with him. Suddenly, a flight of German aircraft swept overhead and the pilot braked sharply, ready to jump from the vehicle and take cover.Hartmann seized his chance. Bounding to his feet he struck his Russian guard a crippling blow in the stomach and leaped over the tailboard, running for his life through a field of tall sunflowers. After five minutes he stumbled into a small valley and threw himself full length on the grass, gasping for breath.

After a while he got up and started to walk westwards, but the whole area was crawling with Russians and he returned to his valley, resolving to wait until nightfall before attempting to reach the German lines. As soon as darkness descended he set off. After a few minutes he sighted a Russian patrol and followed it, reasoning that it was probably heading for the German lines. Eventually, the Russians came to a hill and began to climb the slope. As they reached the summit they were greeting by intense small-arms fire and scattered.

As the enemy disappeared Hartmann ran up the hill towards the enemy positions, shouting in his own language. As he topped the rise, a bitter disappointment awaited him: the German troops had melted away into the night. He started walking westwards again, and for two hours he stumbled across country. Suddenly, a challenge rang out through the darkness, accompanied by a shot. A bullet snicked through his trouser leg. A moment later he was seized and bundled roughly into a dugout, where a suspicious German officer interrogated him. He had only just established his identity when the Russians attacked. Hartmann found himself with a rifle in his hand, firing into the darkness until the enemy assault melted away. It was the most terrifying experience of his career. The next day he returned to his squadron, much chastened by what he had undergone. One of his colleagues recalled later:

> He had lived through an experience very few of our men survived. It seemed to me that in these few harrowing hours he had grown much older.

By the time Hartmann scored his 150th victory in the autumn of 1943 he had become a celebrity on both sides of the front line. His name was mentioned frequently in German propaganda broadcasts and his photograph appeared in the newspapers alongside those of other top-scoring pilots of JG 52. To the Russians he was 'Karaya One', his radio callsign with which they had become familiar; later they nicknamed him *Cherniye Chort* (Black Devil), and offered a reward of 10,000 roubles to any pilot who shot him down.

To support their offensive across the Dnieper, the Russians threw almost the whole of their fighter forces into ground attack

Erich Hartmann (standing) was the top-scoring fighter pilot of all time, with 352 victories. Captured by the Russians at the war's end, he endured a brutal ten-year captivity before his release in 1955. He served in the Federal German *Luftwaffe* and died on 19 September, 1993. (Bundesarchiv)

operations, at the same time reserving some fighter regiments to escort the transport squadrons which, when the spring thaw rendered the roads impassable, air-lifted supplies of food, ammunition and fuel to the advancing troops. In seventeen days, Li-2 transport aircraft (the Russian equivalent of the Douglas DC-3 airliner) flew 4817 sorties, carrying 670 tons of fuel and supplies and over 5000 men, reinforcements on the way out and wounded on the way back. It was a vital task, and one which could not have succeeded without strong fighter escort, for the *Luftwaffe* was still very active on the Dnieper Front.

One unit tasked with fighter escort was the 866th Fighter Air Regiment, which was equipped with La-5s and was commanded by Captain Aleksandr I. Koldunov. Early in April 1944, a mechanised cavalry group broke through deep into the enemy's rear and found itself surrounded. Six Li-2s were detailed to ferry in supplies so that the group could hold on until the main body of troops arrived, and six La-5s of the 866th, led by Koldunov, were detailed to escort them. Over the front line, the Russian formation was engaged by twelve Fw 190s. Koldunov took on the German leader in a head-on attack; at the last moment, when a collision seemed inevitable, the German lost his nerve and broke away, exposing his belly to Koldunov's fire. The 190 went down in flames. Koldunov immediately engaged a second 190 and shot that down too. It was his twenty-second victory. The La-5s escorted the transports until the latter had made their drops, then escorted them safely back to base.

Koldunov was made a Hero of the Soviet Union in August 1944; by the end of the war he had been awarded a second gold star and his score had risen to forty-six. (His victories in the air were actually thirty-six; the Russians, like the Germans, included aircraft destroyed on the ground in their total of kills.)

During the summer and autumn offensives of 1943, one Yak-9 fighter regiment had achieved considerable success. Although they bore the same camouflage and red star markings as any other Soviet fighter unit, the aircraft carried distinctive squadron emblems: a white Cross of Lorraine, symbol of the fighting French, stamped on their tail-fins, and blue, white and red bands painted around their spinners. The unit was known as the 'Regiment Normadie', and most of its pilots were Frenchmen. Its official designation was Groupe de Chasse 3, and it had been formed at Rayak in the Lebanon on 1 September 1942, with British aid. Two

French and Russian pilots of the Regiment Normandie. (ECP Armées)

months later, the entire complement of seventy-two officers and men had been transferred to Russia, where the unit was initially armed with Yak-1 fighters.

The Regiment Normandie went into action on the Orel Front on 22 February, 1943, under the leadership of Commandant Jean Tulasne, and on 5 April Capitaine Albert Preziosi destroyed its first enemy aircraft. The regiment was stationed less than fifteen miles from the front line, which enabled the pilots to fly a large number of tactical support missions. By the end of the Kursk battle, the regiment's score had risen to forty enemy aircraft destroyed, and the French pilots subsequently took part in the bitter air fighting over Smolensk, Yelnya and Vitebsk. During the last months of 1943, they accounted for a further seventy-seven German aircraft for the loss of twenty-five of their own number.

In January 1944, after a short rest from operations, Ivan Kozhedub returned to combat. By the end of March his score had risen to thirty-four; he had already been awarded the gold star of a Hero of the Soviet Union when his score stood at twenty, and now he received a second. During this period Kozhedub was engaged in a neck-and-neck race with Kirill Yevstigneyev, who in June 1944 had a total of forty-four kills, one more than Kozhedub.

In that month, with Soviet forces advancing westward from the Dnieper and the Crimea liberated, the Russians went on the offensive on the Northwestern Front, pressing hard against German and Finnish forces south and west of Leningrad. In this area, which was densely forested and studded with lakes, there were few forward airstrips suitable for fighter operation, and so the advancing ground forces had only limited fighter support. The fighter regiments that were crammed into the few available forward strips flew intensively, the pilots making five or six sorties daily.

Many fighter pilots distinguished themselves during this campaign. They included Major Andrei V. Chirkov, commander of the 196th Fighter Regiment, who on 28 June engaged three Bf 109s, shot one down and forced the others to flee. He ended the war with a score of twenty-six. Then there was 2nd Lieutenant Dmitri Yermakov of the 159th Fighter Regiment, who shot down eight enemy aircraft in as many days; Lieutenant Vladimir Serov, who also destroyed eight aircraft and who was to end the war with a score of twenty-six; and Major Piotr A. Pokryshev of the 275th Fighter Air Division, whose score in the Karelian campaign against

One of the Regiment Normandie's fighter pilots, Lieutenant Roger Sauvage. (ECP Armées)

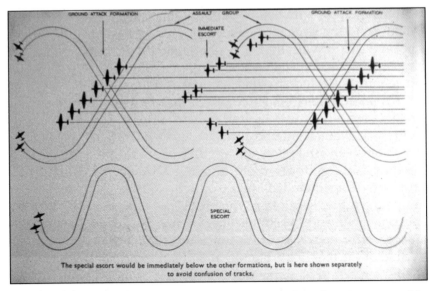

The special escort would be immediately below the other formations, but is here shown separately to avoid confusion of tracks.

Diagrams showing how Soviet fighter pilots developed tactics to provide the best protection for the assault aircraft they were escorting (Author)

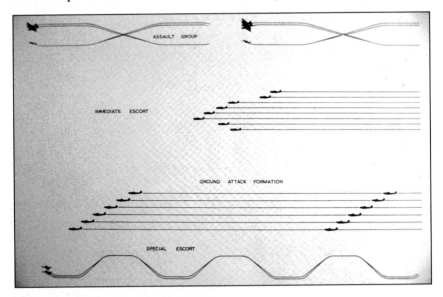

the Finns rose to twenty. In all, twenty-six pilots of the 275th Air Division became Heroes of the Soviet Union in June 1944.

The main Soviet objective, in the summer of 1944, was the destruction of the German Army Group Centre. Centred on Minsk, this army group, which was under the command of Field Marshal Walter Model, comprised the 2nd, 4th and 9th Armies and the 3rd Panzer Army: a total of fifty divisions, with 1000 tanks and some 1400 combat aircraft. The destruction of Army Group Centre would not only result in the expulsion of German forces from Russian soil; the army group was defending what amounted to a broad highway that led into the heart of central Europe, and if Model's forces were smashed that highway would be left wide open. In readiness for the offensive, the Russians assembled over two and a half million men on four fronts, stretching in a great arc from the Baltic to the Dnieper.

The great Russian offensive opened on 22 June, 1944 – three years to the day after the Wehrmacht smashed into the Soviet Union – and the weeks that followed were marked by some of the fiercest air fighting of the war.

In the northern Ukraine, the main Soviet thrust was directed towards Lvov, which was held by a mixture of German and Hungarian forces. In this sector, fighter support was provided by the 7th Fighter Air Corps; one of its formations, the 9th Guards Fighter Air Division, was commanded by Aleksandr Pokryshkin and was equipped with American-built Bell P-39 Airacobras, aircraft which had been no match for the Japanese Zero fighters in the Pacific Theatre. The Russians, on the other hand, took to the American fighter and had considerable success with it.

On 13 July 1944, Pokryshkin and two of his flight commanders, Captain Grigorii Rechkalov and Lieutenant Andrei Trud, were each leading a flight of four Airacobras when they encountered a formation of forty

Aleksandr Pokryshin was Russia's second top-scoring fighter pilot. Like Ivan Kozhedub, he became a Hero of the Soviet Union three times. (Via J.R. Cavanagh)

Stukas and Henschel Hs 129 assault aircraft, escorted by eight Fw 190s. While Trud's flight took on the fighters, Pokryshkin and Rechkalov attacked the bombers, which immediately formed a defensive circle. Together with his two wingmen, Lieutenants Golubev and Zherdev, Pokryshkin gained height and then dived into the middle of the circle, turning with the Stukas and opening fire when the opportunity presented itself. He quickly shot down one Ju 87, then found himself in trouble when a Focke-Wulf dropped into the melée and got on his tail. Golubev shouted a warning over the radio and tried to get into position to open fire, but dared not do so for fear of hitting his leader. The German's cannon punched a hole in Pokryshkin's starboard wing, and the ace's career might have ended there and then if Zherdev had not managed to shoot down the German with an excellent deflection shot. Despite the damage to his aircraft, Pokryshkin went on to shoot down two more Stukas; his pilots destroyed six more.

Soon afterwards, Aleksandr Pokryshkin received the third of his gold stars. Of the other pilots engaged in this action, Rechkalov rose to be third-ranking Soviet ace with fifty-eight victories; Golubev's score was thirty-nine and Trud's twenty-four. There is no record of what became of Zherdev.

Another Soviet ace who increased his score in the summer of 1944 was Captain Aleksandr Klubov, who had first seen combat in Pokryshkin's regiment in the summer of 1942. Klubov had a reputation for remaining extremely calm, even under the most hectic conditions. On one occasion, he set off on a lone reconnaissance mission and became overdue. Pokryshkin, who had stayed behind at base, called him repeatedly over the radio and eventually made contact, wanting to know what was happening. 'I'm in the middle of a scrap,' was the laconic reply.

As dusk was falling, Klubov's aircraft appeared over the airfield, behaving very eratically. It was pitching violently, as though on a switchback. Klubov made his approach, gunning the engine from time to time, and brought the fighter down on its belly. He climbed from the cockpit, unhurt, as the other pilots came running up. The aircraft was a complete wreck, riddled from end to end with cannon shell and machine gun bullet holes. Klubov explained that he had been attacked by six Bf 109s and that he had shot down two of them before a third had shot away his elevator controls. Nevertheless, he had managed to make his escape and had kept the aircraft flying by careful use of the throttle, cramming on power to bring the nose up when the fighter showed signs of going into a dive. A lesser pilot would have baled out.

During a five-day period in August 1944, while flying in support of German forces that were pushing into Romania, Aleksandr Klubov destroyed nine enemy aircraft. During his combat career, which lasted until his death in action in November 1944, he flew 457 sorties and gained thirty-one victories. He was posthumously awarded a second gold star.

While the Russians advanced to the Vistula and established a series of bridgeheads on the west bank of the river, Soviet forces were pushing the Germans steadily back through Latvia and Estonia. By the end of the year, Estonia had been liberated completely and the German forces that remained in Latvia were penned up in the north-west corner of the country. They were still there when the Germans surrendered in 1945. Ivan Kozhedub, already the leading scorer among the Russian fighter pilots, operated on this front during the autumn of 1944. His regiment was a special unit, and was liable to be sent anywhere on the front where the fighting was toughest. It was equipped with the new Lavochkin La-7, basically similar to the La-5 but with aerodynamic improvements that gave it a better combat performance.

Another new aircraft that made its appearance on the Eastern Front in late 1944 was the light and very manoeuvrable Yak-3. One of the units to receive the new type was the Regiment Normandie, which was now operating on the Third Byelorussian Front as part of the 2nd Air Army. Between 22 June and the end of August, while still flying their Yak-9s, the French pilots destroyed a further thirty German aircraft. In September and October, they were engaged in a bitter period of air fighting over the Niemen and East Prussia. Their main opponents were Focke-Wulf Fw 190 fighter-bombers, mostly flown by inexperienced pilots who had hurriedly converted from Junkers 87s and who were incapable of getting the best out of the faster and more agile Focke-Wulfs. One one memorable day in October, the Frenchmen, led by Lieutenant-Colonel Pierre Pouyade, destroyed twenty-six enemy aircraft for no loss to themselves. The exploit earned them the honorary title of the 'Normandie-Niemen Regiment'.

In September, the Russians occupied Romania and Bulgaria. The following month, they captured Belgrade and moved north-westwards into Hungray to begin a winter offensive against the German and Hungarian armies which were still putting up a stiff

Yakovlev Yak-3s of the Normandie-Niemen Regiment seen at le Bourget, Paris, on their homecoming in 1945. (ECP Armées)

resistance. By mid-December, 180,000 German and Hungarian troops were besieged in Budapest. At the turn of the year, the front ran from Yugoslavia to the Baltic, cutting across Poland and Czechoslovakia and running along the border of East Prussia. The stage was now set for the great offensive of 1945. For the final thrust that would take them into Germany the Russians had assembled nearly five million men, twice as many as the opposing Germans, divided among forty-five field armies, eleven Guards armies, five shock armies and six tank armies. A vast air umbrella over the offensive would be provided by the 17,000 combat aircraft of thirteen air armies, outnumbering the *Luftwaffe* on the Eastern Front by ten to one.

The *Luftwaffe* suffered terrible losses during those last weeks of the war in the east. Groups of bomb-carrying Focke-Wulfs and Messerschmitts were thrown against the advancing Russians in what amounted to suicide missions. Weighed down by their bombs, they were easy prey for the Russian fighters. On 18 January, six La-5s of the 9th Guards Fighter Air Regiment, commanded by Captain Pavel Golovachev, attacked a formation of twenty-five Fw 190s and shot down five of them; the remainder jettisoned their bombs and fled. Golovachev, twice a Hero of the Soviet Union, had a score of thirty-one enemy aircraft destroyed when the war ended.

At the beginning of February 1945, with the Russians pushing towards Berlin, the Germans scraped together their last reserves of aircraft in a desperate attempt to gain air superiority over the Eastern Front. The German High Command still entertained hopes of concluding a separate armistice with the western Allies; the goal now was to hold up the Soviet advance for as long as possible, in order to buy time. During the first two weeks of February the initiative sometimes passed to the Germans, as most of the Russian fighter airfields were unusable because of mud, but matters improved during the second half of the month and the *Luftwaffe's* losses began to mount once more.

One of the last major air battles of the eastern war took place on 18 April, when twenty-four Yak-9s of the 43rd Fighter Air Regiment, led by Senior Lieutenant Ivan G. Kuznetsov, sighted thirty-five Fw 190s and Bf 109s, all carrying bombs and heading for the front line. Using cloud cover to good advantage, the Russian pilots stalked the enemy for some distance and then pounced on them, scattering them and forcing them to jettison their bombs on their own ground forces. In the ensuing air battle Kuznetsov shot down four enemy aircraft, as did two other pilots, Ivan Chernenkov and Nikolai Gribkov.

During the final phases of the battle for Berlin, there were outbreaks of bitter fighting over the shattered German capital. On 28 April, seven La-5 pilots of the 263rd Fighter Air Regiment attacked twenty-five Focke-Wulfs which were attempting to strike at Soviet troops. Second Lieutenant Nikolai Brodsky sliced through the enemy formation and shot down a 190, and was immediately attacked himself by six more. He escaped by pulling up into the clouds, then turned and dived clear to find another 190 in his sights, which he shot down. Captain Andrei Chetvertkov also destroyed two enemy aircraft in this battle, and altogether the Russians accounted for seven.

On that same day, Yak-9s of the 515th Fighter Air Regiment landed at Tempelhof airfield, within the perimeter of Berlin. Forty-eight hours later, Adolf Hitler committed suicide and the battle for Berlin entered its final hours.

Ironically, neither of Russia's top-scoring air aces was there to witness the final German surrender. Ivan Kozhedub had flown to Moscow a couple of days earlier to represent the air units of the First Byelorussian Front at the traditional May Day parade, while Aleksandr Pokryshkin's division had moved south to an airfield near Prague. The Czech capital was the last pocket of German resistance in the east, the garrison holding out for a week after the fall of Berlin.

On 9 May 1945, the day of the final German surrender in Prague, Major Viktor Golubev – one of Pokryshkin's pilots, and the sixteenth-ranking Sovietr air ace – shot down a Messerschmitt 109 over the city. It was the last aircraft to be destroyed in air combat in the European war, and Golubev's thirty-eighth kill. He was one of 203 Soviet pilots to destroy twenty or more enemy aircraft since June 1941 – a cumulative total of 5324. It was no mean contribution to the Allied victory in the air.

CHAPTER FOURTEEN

From Normandy
to the Baltic

In the late summer of 1943, the only fighter in operational service in the European Theatre in the late summer of 1943 that was capable of escorting the Fortresses and Liberators all the way to Berlin and back was the Lockheed P-38 Lightning. Four fighter groups were equipped with the P-38 in England, starting with the 55th FG in September 1943, but although the Lightnings managed to hold their own in combat, they were generally inferior to *Luftwaffe* fighters at altitudes of over 20,000 feet, which was where most of the air battles took place. The Lightning was not the answer.

The answer was the North American P-51 Mustang. Designed in 1940 to meet an RAF requirement for a fast, heavily-armed fighter capable of operating effectively at heights of over 20,000 feet, the early Mustangs were fitted with an Allison engine, whose performance proved disappointing at altitude, so the RAF used the Mustang as a high-speed ground attack and tactical reconnaissance fighter from July 1942. It did not enter service with the USAAF until 1943, and the first Mustang unit arrived in Britain in November that year. This was the 354th Fighter Group, equipped with P-51Bs powered by Packard-built Rolls-Royce Merlin engines, which made all the difference to the fighter's performance.

Based at Boxted, near Colchester, the 354th FG initially came under the command of the US Ninth Air Force. On 1 December the

North American P-51D Mustangs escorting Flying Fortresses on a
mission into Germany. (Jack Brannon)

group's Mustangs took off on their first operational mission, a
sweep over Belgium and the Pas de Calais. The twenty-three pilots
who took part were led by Colonel Don Blakeslee of the Debden-
based 4th Fighter group, flying a P-47 Thunderbolt. On 5
December the 354th FG – now under the operational control of the
Eighth Air Force – flew the first P-51 mission to Amiens, but
the *Luftwaffe* failed to appear and the Mustang pilots returned to
base without having fired their guns in anger.

On 13 December the 354th flew the longest fighter mission of the
war up to that date when the Mustangs, together with P-38
Lightnings of the 55th Fighter Group, escorted B-17s to Kiel and
back, a round trip of 1000 miles. Three days later, the Mustangs
once again penetrated deep into Germany on an escort mission to
Bremen, and it was on this raid that the group's first enemy
aircraft, a Bf 110, was destroyed by Lieutenant Charles F. Gumm of
the 355th Squadron. Charles Gumm went on to become the 354th
Fighter Group's first ace, destroying six enemy aircraft. He was
tragically killed on 1 March 1944, when he suffered engine failure
during a training sortie not far from his base. While turning steeply
at low altitude in an attempt to avoid the little village of Nayland,
his wing struck a tree and the Mustang crashed, killing its pilot.

By the end of the year the 354th FG had shot down eight enemy aircraft for the loss of eight Mustangs. It was not an encouraging result, and the pilots entered the New Year determined to increase their success. Their chance came on 5 January 1944. They were once again escorting B-17s to Kiel when the American formation was attacked by large numbers of enemy fighters and a fierce battle developed. When it ended, the Mustang pilots had claimed the destruction of eighteen enemy aircraft for no loss.

The *Luftwaffe* was up in strength again on 11 January, when the 354th escorted the Fortresses to Oschersleben. The bomber formation was repeatedly attacked by enemy fighters from the moment it crossed the coast; by the time the target was reached the bomber groups had become dislocated and the escorting Mustangs scattered all over the sky.

One of the Mustang pilots on this mission was Major James H. Howard. He was already an ace and a highly experienced fighter pilot, having shot down six Japanese aircraft while flying P-40s with the American Volunteer Group in Burma. Now, high over Germany, Howard found himself alone, the only Mustang accompanying a group of Fortresses which was about to be attacked by over thirty Messerschmitt 110s.

Howard went straight for the enemy fighters in a head-on attack, destroying one Bf 110 immediately. Disconcerted, the rest broke in all directions as the Mustang sped through them. The Germans formed up for a second attempt and once again Howard broke them up, sending another fighter down in flames. It was only the beginning. Three more times the enemy attacked, and three more times Howard fought them off single-handed. During the two final attacks, only one of the Mustang's guns was working, but Howard managed to shoot down a third enemy fighter and damaged at least three more. At last, probably short of fuel or ammunition, the Germans broke off the action and dived away.

For his exploit, Major Howard later received the Medal of Honor. He was the only British-based fighter pilot to win the highest US decoration for valour during the Second World War. He later increased his score to twelve. He remained in the USAF after the war, reaching the rank of brigadier-general. He then became a successful businessman, eventually retiring to Florida.

On 11 February the 354th's Mustangs again fought their way through strong *Luftwaffe* opposition to Frankfurt, claiming

One of the leading Mustang aces was Major Don Gentile of the 4th Fighter Group, who destroyed twenty-seven enemy aircraft. He is pictured here with his P-51D, Shangri-La. Gentile was killed in a Lockheed T-33 jet trainer accident on 28 January 1951. (USAF)

fourteen enemy aircraft destroyed for the loss of two of their own number. One of the latter was Colonel Kenneth R. Martin, the group's commander. Himself an ace with five victories, Martin was forced to bale out when he collided with a Bf 110; he survived the experience and spent the rest of the war in prison camp. Command of the 354th was assumed by James Howard, and during the last week of February he led the group in its longest penetration so far, a 1100-mile round trip to Leipzig. During this raid, the Mustang pilots claimed another sixteen enemy aircraft destroyed.

While the American fighter pilots were tussling with the *Luftwaffe* at high altitude, Jack Rose, now a squadron leader and commanding No. 184 Squadron, had been fighting a very different war. The squadron was armed with rocket-carrying Hurricane Mk IVs, as was No. 164 Squadron, commanded by Squadron Leader 'Humph' Russell, an old friend of Rose's. As Jack Rose points out, operations with the Hurricane IVs against heavily-defended targets brought their share of problems.

The Hurricane IV's low speed in comparison with contemporary fighter aircraft, and its poor armament after the rockets had been released (one .303 Browning in each wing) meant that operations could only be carried out in selected circumstances: Spitfire fighter cover, when this could be arranged, good low cloud cover or the use of semi-darkness. Spitfire escorts were unpopular with the Spitfire pilots as all our operations were at low level, and to maintain effective contact with us this meant flying lower, slower and longer than they would have liked.

Cloud cover was useless unless we could escape into it quickly, so this ruled out medium and higher cloud. My log book records a number of instances (usually entered in the log book as Operation Twitch) when we started out, mostly from Manston, but were recalled before reaching the enemy coast as cloud cover was reported by the Met people to have lifted. Firing the rockets at low level in the dark was not on, as a regular practice, so we made use of darkness to approach the enemy coast, timing our arrival for abnout first light so that, with eyes by them accustomed to the gloom, we could attack and make a quick getaway while their was still half an hour or so to dawn.

In June 1943 a couple of such attacks were made on shipping off the Dutch coast. The first of these, on 17 June, consisted of four aircraft (we normally flew four aircraft on such operations) piloted by myself, Flight Lieutenant Ruffhead, Flying Officer Kilpatrick (Australian) and Flying Officer Gross (Canadian). We each fired our 60 lb rockets in ripples at ships anchored close inshore and we all returned with nothing worse than a few bullet holes. Soon afterwards we had a visit from someone at Boscombe Down, who was rather put out that a special PR flight had not been laid on to record the damage inflicted by the rockets. This was, I believe, the first use in western Europe of rockets fired from fighter-type aircraft, and the 'boffins' were keen to assess their effect. Later, of the four of us on that operation, Ruffhead, Kilpatrick and Doug Gross were all killed.

The next such attack, a few days later, was carried out by myself, Warrant Officer Starmer (missing on this sortie), Flight Lieutenant 'Dutch' Holland, and Flight Sergeant Wallace, who was later killed. 'Dutch' Holland later had a miraculous escape when he was shot down in a Typhoon attack on a concentration of enemy armoured vehicles well to the south of the Allied beachhead on D-Day Plus One; he had a series of hair-raising adventures before he managed to link up with friendly troops. 'Humph' Russell of 164 Squadron was shot down during one of the anti-shipping operations and was a PoW for the rest of the war.

Later, in the winter months of 1943-44, just before we re-equipped with Typhoons, we carried out a series of attacks on so-called 'No-ball' (V-1 flying bomb) targets in northern France. We were then operating from Woodchurch, one of the airfields scattered over Romney Marsh and speedily constructed of wire mesh on grass. My log book records attacks on numbered No-ball sites 40, 88, 28, 46, 81 etc and also on named sites at Montorquet, Bois Nigle, La Longueville and so on. We usually flew, again in fours, when the cloud conditions gave the maximum cover if needed. Photographs were always used for the final approach.

The damage inflicted by the Hurricanes of the two ground-attack squadrons was achieved only at considerable cost. On one occasion, during an attack on a No-ball site that cost Flight Lieutenant Ruffhead his life, three out of the four Hurricanes he

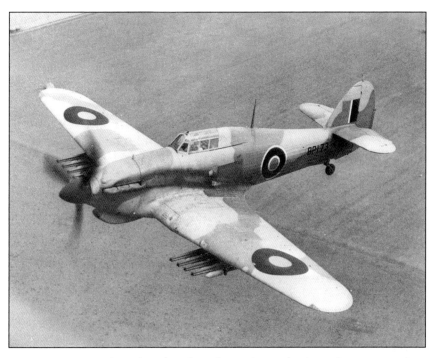

A Hurricane Mk IV fitted with eight rocket rails. (British Aerospace)

was leading failed to return. The incident was witnessed by Free French pilot Pierre Clostermann, who was flying one of the escorting Spitfires and who would go on to become France's top-scoring pilot with 33 victories.

> Powerless, I watched the tragedy. Flight Lieutenant Ruffhead, just as he let go his salvo of rockets, was killed instantly. His disabled Hurricane recovered with incredible violence and zoomed vertically upwards, its propeller stationary. At the top of the trajectory one wing tilted, the aircraft hung as on a thread suspended in space, motionless, then went into a spin.
>
> As in a nightmare I saw Warrant Officer Pearce's Hurricane literally mown down with a burst of 37mm. The tail came off, the machine crashed into a wood, scything down the trees, scattering jets of burning petrol.
>
> The other two Hurricanes attacked simultaneously. Struck by a direct hit, Sergeant Clive's machine exploded and was soon nothing but an inchoate mass of flame, dragging a long

trail of black smoke. By a miracle, Bush the Australian was luckier; he succeeded not only in placing his eight rockets in the control room but even in extricating himself from the barrage of flak, in spite of an enormous gash in his fuselage, not to mention two bullets in the thigh and one in the side.

Early in 1944 No. 184 Squadron re-equipped with Typhoons, which Jack Rose flew during the D-Day landings and their aftermath until August, when he was posted to India to take command of No. 113 Squadron, flying Hurricane fighter-bombers.

Meanwhile, in February 1944, three more USAAF fighter groups had become operational with Mustangs in England. In the Ninth Air Force, the 354th Fighter Group was joined by the 363rd FG on 22 February, while on 11 February the first Mustang group to form within the Eighth Air Force, the 357th, flew its first operational mission, a fighter sweep over Rouen. The Eighth Air Force's second Mustang group was Don Blakeslee's 4th, which exchanged its P-47s for P-51s on 27 February. Less than twenty-four hours later, Blakeslee was leading the group into action on an escort mission over France; his pilots had less than an hour's flying time on the Mustang!

There was considerable rivalry between the Mustang and Thunderbolt groups, and the fact that on more than one occasion Mustangs returned to base badly shot up after being mistaken for Messerschmitt 109s by Thunderbolt pilots served to intensify it. The rivalry was particularly keen between the 354th and Hub Zemke's 56th 'Wolfpack' Fighter Group. In the summer of 1943, Zemke's pilots hasd claimed the destruction of 100 German aircraft in 86 days. Early in 1944 the 354th went all out to better this score, and on 21 February, their eighty-third day of operations, the tally of the Mustang pilots stood at ninety-two enemy aircraft destroyed. By night fall that day the 354th's score had risen to 103, and the next day twelve more enemy aircraft were claimed during a mission to Oschersleben.

On 6 March 1944 Allied fighters appeared over Berlin for the first time when Don Blakeslee's 4th Figher Group escorted B-17s to the German capital. What followed was one of the most bitterly contested air battles of the war. When it ended the Americans had lost sixty-nine bombers and eleven fighters, but the *Luftwaffe* lost eighty aircraft, almost half the defending force. During March alone, 'Blakeslee's Bachelors' claimed 156 German aircraft confirmed, together with eight probables; of these, 100 were claimed from 18 March to 1 April inclusive.

Although these claims were undoubtedly greatly exaggerated in the whirl of combat, there were sure signs that the *Luftwaffe* was beginning to weaken. As one American pilot put it, 'The German pilots could no longer retreat to safety. The Mustangs had them with their backs against the wall.'

What was particularly serious for the *Luftwaffe* was that the great air battles over German soil were costing the lives of their most experienced fighter leaders. One of them was *Oberstleutnant* Wolf-Dietrich Wilcke, *Kommandeur* of JG 3 'Udet', which had recently been moved to Germany from the southerh sector of the Eastern Front. Wilcke already had 137 Russian aircraft to his credit when he arrived back in Germany, and he subsequently destroyed a further twenty-five American fighters and bombers to bring his score to 162. He was killed in action on 23 March 1944. JG 3 had already lost another leading ace in November 1943, not long after it was redeployed to Germany; he was Major Kurt Brändle, who had gained 170 kills on the Eastern Front and a further ten in the west before he was shot down and killed.

Then there was *Oberst* Hans Philip, *Kommandeur* of JG 1, who destroyed 206 enemy aircraft – twenty-eight of them American – before his death in action in October 1943; *Hauptmann* Joachim Kirschner of JG 27, whose score at the time of his death over Germany on 17 December 1943 was 188, twenty claimed in the west; *Oberst* Egon Mayer, *Kommandeur* of JG 2 'Richthofen', all of whose 102 victories were claimed on the Western Front and who was shot down by Mustangs on 2 March 1944; and finally Walter 'Gulle' Oesau of Battle of Britain fame, shot down after claiming his 125th victory on 11 May 1944. As a tribute, JG 1 was named after him.

Others survived, among them famous names such as Adolf Galland, who continued to fly and fight even though he was theoretically bound to a desk in his post of general in charge of fighters. In the spring of 1944, Galland found out what it was like to meet the Mustang in combat. On 8 March, together with Johannes Trautloft, another fighter ace, he took off to intercept a huge force of American bombers on its way to Berlin. The two pilots came upon a straggling B-17 and Galland shot it down, Trautloft having turned for home with jammed guns. Then a flight of Mustangs pounced, and Galland found himself fleeing for his life. He extracted every last ounce of power from his Fw 190, but he was unable to shake off his pursuers and bullets streamed past his aircraft, unpleasantly close. In desperation, he employed an old trick that had saved his life once before, during the Battle of Britain; he fired off everything he had into the open air ahead of him. Grey smoke trails from his guns streamed back towards the Mustangs, whose pilots broke away hard in surprise. Galland, making full use of the precious seconds he had gained, managed to get away.

Another fighter leader who survived was *Oberst* Josef 'Pips' Priller, *Kommandeur* of JG 26 'Schlageter'. JG 26 had served on the Channel coast for a long time, and its pilots had built up enormous combat experience against the RAF and, more recently, the USAAF. Priller scored 101 victories, all of them in the west, and later became Inspector of Fighters in the west in place of Galland after the latter fell out with Hermann Göring. Priller died on 20 May 1961 at Bobing in Upper Bavaria, aged only forty-five.

Apart from the nucleus of surviving German aces, who were very, very good, the majority of *Luftwaffe* pilots in 1944 showed none of the skill and flair of two years earlier, although they continued to fight bravely and often suicidally.

As the year wore on, some of the men who flew the American escort fighters began to register formidable successes. One of them was Major George E. Preddy, who had arrived in England with the 352nd Fighter Group, flying P-47s, in July 1943. It was not until 1 December that he scored his first kill, but in the early months of 1944 his score began to mount rapidly. Later, the 352nd FG converted to Mustangs.

On 6 August, 1944, Preddy was to lead the 352nd on a bomber

Josef 'Pips' Priller led his fighters into action against overwhelming Allied air superiority over Normandy in June 1944. (Bundesarchiv)

escort mission to Germany. This came as bad news, because he and several other pilots had held a party of considerable proportions the night before, the Met men having indicated that the weather would be too bad for operations. Preddy was still under the influence when he delivered his briefing, and at 32,000 feet on the outward leg he was sick all over the cockpit and himself. Then, as they approached the target, the B-17s were attacked by enemy fighters. Preddy's combat report describes what happened next.

We were escorting the lead combat wings of B-17s when thirty-plus Me 109s in formation came into the third box from the south. We were 1000 feet above them so I led White Flight, consisting of Lieutenant Heyer, Lieutenant Doleac and myself, in astern of them. I opened fire on one near the rear of the formation from 300 yards dead astern and got many hits round the cockpit. The enemy aircraft went down inverted and in flames.

At this point Lieutenant Doleac became lost while shooting down an Me 109 that had gotten on Lieutenant Heyer's tail. Lieutenant Heyer and I continued our Attack and I drove up behind another enemy aircraft, getting hits around the wing roots, setting him on fire after a short burst. He went spinning down and the pilot baled out at 20,000 feet. I then saw Lieutenant Heyer on my right shooting down another enemy aircraft.

The enemy formation stayed together taking practically no evasive action and tried to get back for an attack on the bombers who were off to the right. We continued with our attack on the rear end and I fired on another from close range. He went down smoking badly and I saw him begin to fall apart below us.

At this time four other P-51s came in to help us with the attack. I fired at another 109, causing him to burn after a short burst. He spiralled down to the right in flames. The formation headed down in a left turn, keeping themselves together in rather close formation. I got a good burst into another one causing him to burn and spin down. The enemy aircraft were down to 5000 feet now and one pulled off to the left. I was all alone with them now, so went after this single 109 before he could get on my tail. I got in an ineffective burst causing him to smoke a little. I pulled up into a steep climb to the left above him and he climbed after me. I pulled it in as tight as possible and climbed at about 150 miles an hour. The Hun opened fire on me but could not get enough deflection to do any damage. With my initial speed I slightly outclimbed him. He fell off to the left and I dropped down astern of him. He jettisoned his canopy as I fired a short burst getting many hits. As I pulled past, the pilot baled out at 7000 feet.

I lost contact with all friendly and enemy aircraft so headed home alone. CLAIM: Six (6) Me 109s.

After this remarkable action Preddy went home on leave, returning to the 352nd FG in November. On Christmas Day, he was flying south-west of Coblenz when he sighted two Bf 109s, which he chased and shot down; they were his 25th and 26th victims.

Soon afterwards, near Liège, he saw a low-flying Focke-Wulf 190 and went after it. The two aircraft ran into a storm of American anti-aircraft fire. Preddy tried to break away, but he was too late. Moments later, he was killed when his Mustang plunged into the ground. His brother, Lieutenant William R. Preddy, was also killed while carrying out a strafing attack in Czechoslovakia on 17 April, 1945.

In the late summer of 1944, Allied fighter pilots began to encounter increasing numbers of Messerschmitt Me 262 jet fighters. With a top speed of 540 mph, the Me 262 was a good 100mph faster than any Allied fighter in service at the time. It was armed with a battery of four 30mm cannon, and although it suffered from a number of technical problems – unreliable engines with a life of only twenty-five hours being one of them – it could have inflicted unacceptable losses on the USAAF's daylight bombers had it gone into full production as a fighter in the latter half of 1944. Hitler, however, became obsessed with the notion of using the Me 262 as a high-speed bomber, and it was in that role that the Me 262 entered full *Luftwaffe* service in October 1944, having undergone operational evaluation since July.

Jim Rosser, now a flight lieutenant and flying Spitfire XIVs with No. 66 Squadron, was on patrol at 15,000 feet over Venlo in Holland one day in September 1944 when he sighted a 262 a few thousand feet lower down.

I don't think anyone had actually managed to shoot down a 262 at that time, and I thought this was my big chance. I went down after him, flat out, but he saw me coming and opened the taps. Smoke trails streamed from his turbines and off he went; I hadn't a hope in hell of catching him, so I gave up and rejoined the formation.

The incident had an interesting sequel. Years after the war, when I was stationed in Germany, I met a colonel in the Federal German *Luftwaffe*. We had a few drinks and got talking. We compared dates, places and times, and by one of those extraordinary coincidences it turned out that he had almost certainly been the pilot of 'my' 262. He said that if I had kept after him, it was on the cards I would have got him. His fuel was very low, and he couldn't have maintained full throttle for more than half a minute. But there it was; I got shot down near Arnhem a few days later, so never did get another chance to have a crack at a jet.

Meanwhile, in August 1944, sufficient numbers of a new German jet aircraft type, the Arado Ar 234 bomber, had become available to permit the release of some Me 262s to form a jet-fighter trials unit at Lechfeld, near Augsburg. It was originally commanded by Oberst Tierfelder, who was killed when his aircraft crashed in flames on one of the unit's first operational missions. His successor was Major Walter Nowotny, who, at the age of twenty-three, was one of the *Luftwaffe*'s top fighter pilots with 258 kills, 255 of them achieved on the Eastern Front. By the end of October the *Kommando Nowotny*, as the unit had come to be known, was transferred to the airfields of Achmer and Hesepe near

Walter Nowotny (right) pictured with Hannes Trautloft, commander of the famous JG 54 'Green Hearts' *Geschwader*. (Bundesarchiv)

Osnabrück, astride the main American daylight bomber approach route into Germany.

Because of a shortage of adequately trained pilots, coupled with technical problems, the *Kommando Nowotny* was usually able to fly only three or four sorties a day against the enemy formations, yet in November 1944 the pilots destroyed twenty-two aircraft. By the end of the month, however, the unit had only three serviceable 262s out of a total of thirty on strength, a rate of attrition accounted for mainly by accidents rather than enemy action.

On 8 November, 1944, Walter Nowotny was the pilot of one of five Me 262s which took off to attack an American bomber formation. Operating from the 262 bases was now a very hazardous undertaking since the Allies had pinpointed their positions, and for several days they had been subjected to heavy attacks by fighter-bombers. Additional 20mm flak batteries were brought up and organised into flak lanes, extending for two miles outwards from the ends of the main runways to provide a curtain of fire during the jet fighters' critical take-off and landing phases. For additional protection, a group of Focke-Wulf 190s was assigned to the air defence of Achmer and Hesepe.

On this November morning, in the operations room at Achmer, the German controllers followed the course of the air battle that developed at 30,000 feet over Germany. They heard Nowotny claim a victory, and also heard one of the other 262 pilots state that he was being shot down by Mustangs. A few minutes later, Nowotny came on the air again to report that his port engine had failed and that he was coming in to make an emergency landing. Some time later, his 262 was sighted on the approach about four miles away from Achmer with wheels and flaps down and at least six Mustangs behind it. The observers on the ground saw Nowotny's undercarriage come up and the 262 go into a steep climbing turn on one engine. He had obviously decided to try to fight it out rather than land, which would have been suicide. A few seconds passed, then the watchers saw the 262 and its pursuers disappear behind a low hill. There was a dull explosion followed by a column of black smoke. The Mustangs climbed away pursued by scattered bursts of flak, leaving the wreckage of Nowotny's 262 scattered over a field near the village of Bremsche.

Soon after Nowotny's death, the jet fighter *Kommando* returned to Lechfeld for further training. Most of the pilots had only ten hours' experience on the 262, and the air battles of November had shown that not even the jet fighter's superior speed would compensate for the lack of experience when confronted with veteran Allied fighter pilots.

One of the latter was Captain Charles Yeager of the 357th Fighter Group, who on 6 November 1944 was leading a flight of Mustangs north of Osnabrück when three Me 262s were sighted, flying on an opposite course to the Mustangs and at two o'clock low. The Mustangs dived down from 10,000 feet and Yeager attacked the last jet in the trio, scoring some hits before the jets pulled away. A few moments later he sighted the 262s again, flying under the cloud base, and fired a high deflection burst at the leader. Again he scored hits, and again the 262s used their superior speed to get away. Then, a few more minutes into his patrol, Yeager spotted another 262 approaching to land at an airfield. Braving intense flak, he dived down at 500mph and fired a short burst into the 262's wing. The jet crash-landed just short of the airfield, its wing shearing off.

A couple of weeks earlier, 'Chuck' Yeager had destroyed five Bf 109s in a single sortie. He ended the war with eleven and a half confirmed victories, and later became famous for his flights in the Bell X-1 series of rocket-powered research aircraft, becoming the first man to fly faster than sound.

The fighter unit assigned to protect the Me 262 bases at Achmer and Hesepe was III/JG 54, which was equipped with the 'long-nose' Focke-Wulf 190D-9, the latest and most powerful version of that famous fighter aircraft. III/JG 54 came under the operational command of JG 26, still commanded by 'Pips' Priller. The leader of III/JG 54 itself was another ace, *Hauptmann* Robert 'Bazi' Weiss, an Austrian from Vienna. On 29 December, 1944, Weiss and three other pilots were shot down and killed in a fight with Spitfires near their base.

Although the later versions of the Spitfire were a match for the Fw 190D-9, only one RAF fighter type stood a reasonable chance of catching the elusive Me 262. This was the Hawker Tempest, the most powerful Allied fighter to see action in World War Two. The first Tempest squadrons had been sent into combat in the summer of 1944, their task to protect London against the V-1 flying bombs, and fifty-two Tempest pilots had destroyed five or more of these pilotless jet-propelled aircraft. The top-scoring pilot of the V-1 offensive was Squadron Leader J. Berry, who destroyed sixty-one flying bombs; he was followed by Squadron Leader R. van Lierde,

Wing Commander Roland Beamont, seen during his time as Chief Test Pilot with English Electric. (British Aerospace)

a Belgian pilot, who shot down forty, and Wing Commander Roland Beamont – who commanded the Tempest Wing, and who was to achieve fame after the war as a test pilot with English Electric – with a score of thirty-two.

In September 1944 five Tempest squadrons – Nos 3, 56, 80 and 274 RAF, and No. 486 RNZAF – deployed to northwest Europe in support of the Allied forces advancing through Belgium and Holland. From Brussels, the Tempests moved up to Volkel, in Holland, where they formed No. 122 Wing. This was commanded by Wing Commander P.G. Jameson, DSO – the same officer who had taken the Hurricanes of No. 46 Squadron to Norway in May 1940 and who had narrowly escaped with his life when the carrier HMS *Glorious* was sunk. For Jameson, the wheel had turned full circle.

Several of the Tempest pilots were already aces. Squadron Leader Bob Spurdle, a New Zealander who commanded No. 80 Squadron, had destroyed eight enemy aircraft, probably destroyed four more, and damaged at least fifteen; another New Zealander, Squadron Leader Evan 'Rosie' Mackie, who assumed command of No. 80 Squadron in December, already had fifteen enemy aircraft to his credit, and celebrated his arrival by shooting down an Fw 190 on 24 December. His final score was to rise to twenty-one.

The most successful Tempest pilot of all, however, was an American. Squadron Leader D.C. Fairbanks had joined the RCAF in the summer of 1941, and had completed a tour of operations flying Spitfires with No. 501 Squadron early in 1944 before joining No 274 Squadron as a flight commander in time to take part in the V-1 battle. Fairbanks, who had one victory to his credit during his Spitfire days, destroyed at least eleven enemy aircraft while flying Tempests. His outstanding period came during the early weeks of

The immensely powerful Hawker Tempest Mk V made a considerable
impact on the air war over northwest Europe in its latter stages.
(British Aerospace)

1945. On 4 January he shot down an Fw 190, after which he was
awarded a DFC, and on the 14th he claimed another Fw 190 and a
Bf 109. On the 23rd he destroyed a Ju 52 transport, together with
one Ju 88 destroyed and one damaged on the ground. On 11
February he shot down an Me 262, damaging another on the 14th,
and two days later he claimed a pair of Me 109s. On 22 February he
shot down a pair of Fw 190D-9s, followed by a third on the 24th.
His luck ran out over Rheine on the following day, when his
section of six Tempests was bounced by Focke-Wulfs; he was shot
down and taken prisoner. After the war, David Fairbanks became
a test pilot with de Havilland Canada. He died of natural causes at
the early age of fifty-two.

Close behind Fairbanks came Squadron Leader Warren
Schrader, a New Zealander who was posted to command No. 486
Squadron early in 1945. Schrader had two and a half earlier vic-
tories to his credit, and since arriving in No. 122 Wing he had
destroyed four Fw 190s and a Bf 109. During fierce fighting on 29
April, 1945, Schrader destroyed three Bf 109s and shared a fourth.

Soon afterwards, he was promoted to wing commander and took command of No. 616 Squadron, which had just arrived at Fassberg with Gloster Meteor F.3 fighters. Schrader rounded off his fighting career on 3 May by destroying a Bf 109 and an He 111 on the ground and damaging a Ju 87, also on the ground. In air combat he had a total of eleven and a half kills, nine of them while flying Tempests.

The *Luftwaffe*, meanwhile, had continued to fight hard, with ever-dwindling resources, during those tumultuous weeks of 1945. Out of the *Kommando Nowotny* the nucleus of a new jet fighter unit had been born: JG 7 'Hindenburg', commanded by *Oberst* Johannes 'Macki' Steinhoff. Although JG 7 comprised three groups, only one of these, III/JG 7, made real and continual contact with the enemy, hopping from one base to another, always under threat of air attack. During the last week of February 1945, using a combination of 30mm cannon and R4M air-to-air rockets, the pilots of III/JG 7 destroyed no fewer than forty-five Allied four-engined bombers and fifteen of their escorting fighters for the loss of only four 262s. There were further successes during March, although the 262s' loss rate continued to climb. On one occasion on 24 March, five 262s were shot down by Mustangs and Thunderbolts escorting bombers to Berlin. Despite what was rapidly becoming a serious rate of attrition, on 4 April JG 7 launched forty-nine Me 262s against a formation of American bombers over Nordhausen, destroying ten and claiming fifteen probably destroyed.

Meanwhile, in January 1945, permission had at last been granted for the formation of a new Me 262 fighter unit commanded by *Generalleutnant* Adolf Galland. By the beginning of March Galland had recruited forty-five pilots, all of them highly experienced. They included Macki Steinhoff, who turned over command of JG 7 to Major Theodor Weissenberger – an ace with 208 victories, 175 of them scored in the east – and walked out to join Galland without waiting for any authorioty from his superiors.

Steinhoff was without doubt one of the *Luftwaffe*'s most experienced fighter pilots, having amassed 176 confirmed victories since shooting down his first enemy aircraft – the RAF Wellington near Heligoland on 18 December 1939. As Galland's second-in-command of *Jagdverband* 44, as the Me 262 unit was known, he fought on until almost the last day of the war, when his jet fighter crashed in flames. He survived, despite appalling burns, and in the 1960s rose to be Inspector-General of the Federal German

Luftwaffe ace Gordon Gollob beside his Bf 109, which had collected some damage from a 20mm shell during an air battle. (Bundesarchiv)

Luftwaffe. He later chaired NATO's Military Committee, retiring in 1974. 'Macki' Steinhoff died in February 1994.

Another talented and much-decorated pilot who flew Me 262s alongside Galland and Steinhoff was *Oberst* Gordon Gollob, who had gained 160 victories since the day, four and a half years earlier, when he had fought in his Bf 110 against RAF Spitfires over the Farne Islands during the disastrous raid of 15 August 1940. An Austrian, Vienna-born, Gollob died on 7 September 1987.

Then there was *Oberst* Heinz Bär, who had fought alongside Werner Mölders in the Battles of France and Britain. He had fought in Russia, and over Malta and North Africa, and by April 1944 his score had reached 200. He gained a further four victories before joining JV 44, and scored a record sixteen kills while flying Me 262s, making him the top-scoring German jet pilot. He survived those last hectic air battles over Europe, only to die in a crash while demonstrating a light aircraft in April 1957.

On 7 April 1945, Theodor Weissenberger's JG 7 destroyed twenty-eight Mustangs and Thunderbolts which were escorting American bombers over Germany. On that same day, other Allied

Captain John Voll was the leading ace of the Fifteenth Air Force in the Mediterranean Theatre. (USAF)

fighters sent 183 piston-engined Focke-Wulfs and Messerschmitts to destruction in what was the last series of major air battles in the European war.

Three days later, over 1000 American bombers shattered the Me 262 bases with a rain of high explosive. The 262s shot down ten of the bombers, but with their bases devastated the jet units were broken up. In the last days of April the remnants of Jagdverband 44 moved south to Salzburg, where the jets were grounded through lack of fuel. On 3 May, the surviving Messerschmitts were destroyed by the German ground crews.

In the Italian theatre, the P-51D Mustangs of the Fifteenth Air Force's 31st, 52nd, 325th and 332nd Fighter Groups (the latter composed of all-black personnel, the famous Tuskegee Airmen) ranged far and wide across southern Europe on their bomber escort missions. The top-scoring Mustang pilot of the Fifteenth Air Force was Lieutenant John J. Voll of the 31st Fighter Group, with twenty-one victories. According to Voll, one of the most formidable enemy aircraft he encountered was a Macchi C.202, flown by a pilot of the Fascist *Aeronautica Nazionale Repubblicana* (ANR), which became his thirteenth victory on 23 September 1944. This is his combat report of the encounter:

On our way home I saw a Macchi 202 through a break in the clouds and went after him. Going in and out of the cloud I was chasing his vapour trail rather than actually seeing him all the time and when I finally got into position to fire I glanced behind me and there was another Macchi on my tail. I started firing and although I only used up twenty rounds per gun on the Macchi in front of me, it seemed as though I had used a hundred before my hits blew the cockpit apart and the pilot baled out. I started to attack the other plane, but by this time another had joined the fight. Since the Macchi can turn a shade sharper than the Mustang, they soon had me boxed. I got into a cloud and headed home.

John Voll ended the war with the Distinguished Service Cross, the Silver Star with Cluster, the Distinguished Flying Cross with Cluster, and the Air Medal with twenty-six Clusters. He retired from the USAF in 1969 as a colonel. He died on 12 September, 1987.

CHAPTER FIFTEEN

The Road to Tokyo Bay

The first of the new American combat aircraft to reach the squadrons in the Pacific was the heavy, powerful Chance Vought F4U Corsair, which entered service withy Marine Fighter Squadron VMF-124 (The Checkerboards) at Camp Kearney, California, in September 1942. On 2 February 1943 the unit was declared combat-ready, and on 12 February twelve of its twenty-two Corsairs arrived at Henderson Field, Guadalcanal, to relieve the battle-weary Wildcats. On the following day they flew their first combat mission, escorting B-24 Liberators in a raid on Bougainville in the Solomon Islands. The mission was uneventful and no enemy fighters were sighted, but on a similar mission on 14 February the American fighters, which also included USAAF P-38s and P-40s, was attacked by about fifty Japanese fighters. The Corsair pilots, who were still inexperienced in handling their new aircraft – some had barely twenty hours' flying time on the type – were overwhelmed by superior numbers. In a matter of minutes the Zeros shot down two Liberators, two Corsairs, two P-40s and four P-38s for the loss of four of their own number.

This disaster, which became known as the St Valentine's Day Massacre, was a humiliating start for VMF-124, but it made the pilots determined fully to master their new aircraft, and before long their successes began to mount. In the weeks that followed, VMF-124 destroyed sixty-eight enemy aircraft for the loss of eleven Corsairs and three pilots, an outstanding result by any standards.

One of VMF-124's best pilots during this period was Lieutenant

A flight of Corsairs returning to its carrier. (Chance Vought)

A Corsair landing-on. The aircraft's wing configuration and long nose made carrier operations difficult. (Chance Vought)

Ken Walsh, who destroyed three Zeros on 1 April 1943 and three more on 13 May. A few days later, he added a seventh Zero and two Val dive-bombers to his score over Vella Lavella Island. Walsh eventually went on to attain a score of twenty-one enemy aircraft destroyed, and to be awarded the Medal of Honor. He served a full career in the USMC, retiring as a colonel in the early 1960s.

The leading exponent of the Corsair – which by the autumn of 1943 equipped all the USMC's fighter squadrons – was Major Gregory 'Pappy' Boyington, who had flown for a short time with VMF-122 on Guadalcanal in April 1943. After this, he was given command of VMF-214, which was nicknamed the 'Black Sheep' because it was made up of a group of casual, replacement and green pilots. Boyington soon welded the Black Sheep into shape, and took them into action in the Russell Islands in September 1943. On 16 September, the squadron fought a major air battle over Ballale. It was intercepting a formation of Japanese bombers when it was itself attacked by fifty Zeros, and in the dogfight that

Gregory 'Pappy' Boyington in the cockpit of his F4U Corsair. (USMC)

followed the Black Sheep destroyed twelve enemy aircraft, Boyington himself claiming five. This brought his score so far to eleven, for he had already gained six victories while flying with the American Volunteer Group in China during 1941-42.

On 17 December, 1943, Boyington led the first Allied fighter sweep over the Japanese-held island of Rabaul, which was very heavily defended, and it was over this location, on 27 December, that he scored his twenty-fifth victory, his kills having mounted steadily in the interim. On 3 January 1944 he led his pilots over Rabaul again, and encountered twelve Zeros. Boyington shot down one of them, then dived down through broken cloud with his wingman, Lieutenant Ashmun, to attack another enemy formation. Boyington destroyed two more Zeros, but the odds were too great and both he and Ashmun were shot down in turn. Boyington managed to bale out and spent the rest of the war as a Japanese prisoner, surviving to be liberated in 1945. With twenty-eight victories, he was to remain the top-scoring USMC ace. He, too, was awarded the Medal of Honor. 'Pappy' Boyington died of cancer on 11 January, 1988, aged seventy-five.

The third-ranking Marine Corps ace, behind Boyington and Joe Foss, was First Lieutenant Robert M. Hanson. Unlike the other two, he gained all his twenty-five victories while flying the Corsair, and he was unique in that he destroyed twenty enemy aircraft in just six combat missions, an achievement that was not to be equalled by any other pilot in World War Two. He went into combat late in 1943 with VMF-215, which was one of the Corsair units given the task of providing air support for amphibious landings by US Marines on the south coast of Bougainville.

On 1 November, while flying top cover with the rest of the squadron, Hanson spotted a formation of six Val dive-bombers about to attack the American landing ships. He broke away solo and went after them, shooting one down and forcing the rest to jettison their bombs. He claimed three more aircraft on 3 November, being forced to ditch his aircraft near the US task force when his Corsair's engine was hit, and another on 17 December, by which time VMF-215 had moved to a forward airstrip on Bougainville itself.

On 14 January, 1944, VMF-215 was detailed to escort a force of B-25 medium bombers in a raid on Rabaul. The Americans were attacked by an estimated seventy enemy fighters, and in the wild dogfight that ensued Hanson was credited with the destruction of five of them, doubling his score. He claimed a further four Japanese aircraft over Rabaul in the next two days, and on 24 January, while escorting a formation of Grumman Avenger torpedo-bombers on a shipping strike, he shot down four more Zeros and possibly destroyed a fifth. The Japanese pilots had been stalking the American bomber formation with the aid of cloud cover, and such was the fury of Hanson's attack that the enemy's intentions were completely disrupted.

Two days later, Hanson destroyed three more Zeros on his fifth mission to Rabaul. His score now stood at twenty-one. On 30 January, again while escorting an Avenger shipping strike, he claimed a further three Zeros. With Boyington and Foss now gone – the former to a PoW camp and the latter back to the United States – bets were laid as to whether Hanson would beat both their scores on his next mission to Rabaul, and so become the top Marine Corps ace.

The next trip to Rabaul was laid on for 3 February. Hanson, with three other Corsairs, set out on a fighter sweep over the island, eager for action, but found that Rabaul was covered by dense cloud. Disappointed, the Corsair pilots turned for home. On the way back, Hanson called his leader and asked for permission to

Robert Hanson was the third-ranking US Marine Corps fighter ace, after 'Pappy' Boyington and Joe Foss. (US Navy)

strafe a lighthouse on the southern tip of New Ireland; it was known to be used as an observation post and flak tower by the enemy. He received permission, and his colleagues watched as he dived down to make his strafing attack. Then, to their horror, they saw a puff of smoke as a shell struck his aircraft. A piece flew off the Corsair's wing. Hanson struggled to retain control and tried to ditch the stricken fighter, but at the last moment it cartwheeled across the waves and vanished below the surface. The others circled over the spot for a few minutes, but there was no sign of the pilot.

On 1 August, 1944, seven months after his death, Robert Hanson was awarded a posthumous Medal of Honor.

If the Corsair was a vital instrument in the success of the US Marine Corps' Pacific island assaults, the fighter that eventually took the US Navy's air war to Japan was the Grumman F6F Hellcat, a logical development of the Wildcat with a much better per- formance. The Hellcat first flew in June 1942, and the first operational aircraft were delivered to VF-9 on the USS *Essex* in January 1943. The Hellcat's first operational sorties were flown on 31 August 1943, when aircraft of VF-5 (USS *Yorktown*) strafed Japanese positions on Marcus Island in the western Pacific.

It was a combination of the sturdy little Hellcat and exceptional flying skill that was to produce the US Navy's leading ace of World War Two, Commander David S. McCampbell. His road to the cockpit of a front-line fighter had been long and arduous; in fact, he had almost not made it. A graduate of the Annapolis Naval Academy, he had applied for flying training with the US Navy in 1936, only to be rejected on the grounds of defective eyesight. Determined not to be beaten, he went to a civilian doctor, who submitted him to searching tests and assured him that there was nothing wrong with his eyes at all. McCampbell went back to the Navy doctors, and six months later he was accepted for flight training. He was awarded his pilot's wings on 23 April 1938, but found to his dismay that – because the US Navy was over- subscribed with pilots at that time, and because his medical record still dogged him – he was confined to the role of deck landing officer.

McCampbell's big chance did not come until the spring of 1944, when he was promoted to command Air Group 15 on board the *Essex*, flying Hellcats. His first action came on 19 May, when, flying his 'personal' Hellcat, which he had named Monsoon Maiden, he

Top-scorer Richard Bong (right) chats with fellow Pacific ace Tommy McGuire. (USAF)

led his group on a dawn fighter sweep over Marcus Island. This remote spot in the Pacific, about 1000 miles from Japan, was used more or less as a training ground for air groups about to go into action among the islands to the south and was not very heavily defended, but on this occasion a Japanese anti-aircraft shell struck Monsoon Maiden, setting her belly fuel tank on fire and damaging the rear fuselage. McCampbell jettisoned the tank just in time, and despite the damage to his aircraft he remained over the island, directing the other fighters in attacks on Japanese positions. He got back to the carrier by the skin of his teeth, his main fuel tanks almost dry. Monsoon Maiden was judged to be beyond repair and was dumped over the side.

This mission earned McCampbell a Distinguished Flying Cross and the unqualified respect of his men. Shortly afterwards, flying a new Hellcat named The Minsi, McCampbell led Air Group 15 into action as part of US Navy Task Force 58's offensive against the Marianas, and on 11 June he scored his first victory as aircraft from TF 58's four fast-carrier task groups were pounding Japanese airfields and coastal defensive positions in preparation for the US landings on the islands. Sighting a lone Zero over Pagan Island, McCampbell overhauled it and shot it down in flames.

It had been an easy victory, for the Japanese pilot had taken no evasive action. But there was to be nothing easy about McCampbell's air combats that took place on 19 June 1944, when carrier fighters of TF 58 took part in the greatest and most concentrated air battle of all time. In a day-long action that was to go down in history as the 'Great Marianas Turkey Shoot', American fighters and anti-aircraft fire destroyed no fewer than 400 Japanese aircraft as the enemy made desperate attempts to attack the US invasion fleet in the Philippine Sea.

That morning, David McCampbell led eight Hellcats from the USS *Essex* to intercept a formation of forty bombers, escorted by twenty Zeros. Leaving five of the Hellcats to tackle the fighters, McCampbell dived on the bombers with his wingman and another pilot, personally shooting down four of them while trying to get at the leader. He finally worked his way through to the front of the enemy formation and shot down the Japanese leader too, despite the fact that his guns kept jamming. The air battle lasted just fifteen minutes, and when it ended the Japanese formation was scattered all over the sky. Altogether, the eight Hellcat pilots had claimed twenty-one victories for the loss of one of their own number. That afternoon, McCampbell shot down two more Zeros which were attempting to attack a pair of air-sea rescue seaplanes in the act of picking up some Navy pilots who had been forced to ditch. This brought his score for the day to seven, and the overall tally for the pilots of Air Group 15 was sixty-eight.

Five days later, this score was equalled by a single fighter squadron, VF-2, operating from the USS *Hornet*. At 0600 hours on 24 June, two days after the Battle of the Philippine Sea ended, Task Group 58.1 launched a long-range fighter sweep against the island of Iwo Jima. It comprised forty-eight Hellcats, including fifteen from VF-2. South-east of the island, the Americans encountered about 100 Zeros, and in the air battle that followed the Hellcats of VF-2 destroyed thirty-three enemy fighters. Three Zeros were shot down by Lieutenant Robert R. Butler, who was leading the squadron, while Lieutenants (jg) R.H. Davis, R.W. Shackford, M.W. Vineyard and E.C. Hargreaves shot down four each. The total for the fighter sweep as a whole was sixty-eight Zeros destroyed for the loss of four Hellcats, one of them belonging to VF-2.

While the Hellcats were on their way back from Iwo Jima, the Japanese launched a torpedo attack against the carrier task group.

Eight Hellcats were flying combat air patrol (CAP) over the *Hornet*, and they intercepted the torpedo-bombers while the latter were still several miles short of their objectives. In less than five minutes the American pilots shot down eighteen of the enemy, Ensigns Paul A. Doherty and John W. Dear claiming three and the other pilots two apiece. The Japanese tried later that day, this time with a strong fighter escort, but they fared no better. VF-2 tackled them again and sent sixteen flaming into the sea, several of the pilots who had been in action over, Iwo Jima that morning adding to their scores. That brought VF-2's total number of victories in the day's fighting to sixty-seven, a record for a Navy fighter squadron in a single day. The squadron lost only one Hellcat.

Of the pilots mentioned above, Hargreaves became an ace on 24 June, with five kills before the day's end. He later increased his score to eight and a half. Ralph Davis went on to claim seven and a half kills, Shackford six, and Dear seven, some at night.

The battle for the Philippines saw the combat debut of the man who was to rise to second place in the US Navy's list of aces: Lieutenant Cecil E. Harris, who flew Hellcats with VF-18 on the USS *Intrepid*. He opened a spectacular combat career on 13 September 1944 by shooting down four aircraft in a Japanese formation trying to attack American ships. On 12 October he got four more while taking part in the early series of strikes on Formosa, and on 29 October he repearted the exploit. On this occasion, VF-18's Hellcats were escorting the *Intrepid's* torpedo- and dove-bombers in an attack on Clark Field, in the Philippines. The Japanese contested the raid fiercely, sending up a large number of fighters. Harris caught the first two flights of Zeros on the climb and shot one enemy fighter out of each flight, and in the course of the battle he shot two more Zeros off the tails of Hellcats. His eventual score was twenty-four aircraft.

But it was David McCampbell who retained the top place, and on 24 October 1944 he achieved the most extraordinary combat feat of his career. On that day, the USS *Essex* was one of seventeen US carriers providing air support for the American landings at Leyte, in the Philippines. McCampbell, whose score now stood at twenty-one, was launched from the *Essex* with his wingman, Lieutenant Roy Rushing, and five more Hellcats in response to an incoming bomber alert. The seven fighters headed for Luzon, and before long sighted twenty Japanese dive-bombers heading towards the American fleet. There was as yet no sign of enemy fighters, but

McCampbell shrewdly guessed that they must be around some-where, so he ordered the other five Hellcats to engage the bombers while he and Rushing flew top cover.

Suddenly, a formation of forty Zeros came into view, several thousand feet higher up. McCampbell and Rushing climbed hard towards them. Amazingly, the Japanese pilots made no attempt to break formation and swarm on the heavily outnumbered Americans, but continued to hold their course. The two Hellcat pilots, still climbing, each selected a target and opened fire, sending two Zeros spinning down in flames. Still the Zeros made no attempt to attack, but instead formed a defensive circle. McCampbell and Rushing climbed above them and waited, aware that sooner or later ther Zeros would have to break away for lack of fuel.

They waited for ten minutes, then all at once the enemy circle split up and the Zeros straggled away towards Manila in ones and twos. The two Hellcats went after them, and what followed was one of the strangest and most one-sided combats in the history of air warfare. In a running fight lasting just over an hour, McCampbell shot down nine of the enemy fighters, while Rushing destroyed four and another Hellcat pilot who joined in got two.

David McCampbell, who was awarded the Medal of Honor for this exploit, went on to score four more victories in November, bringing his final score to thirty-four. Roy Rushing's final score was thirteen. Both men returned to the United States when Air Group 15's tour of operations in the Pacific came to an end on 14 November 1944. David McCampbell died in Florida after a lengthy illness on 30 June, 1996.

The drive towards aerial victory in the Pacific was by means all attributable to the United States Navy and Marine Corps. Squadrons of the United States Air Force, the Royal Australian Air Force, the Royal Air Force, the Royal New Zealand Air Force and the Fleet Air Arm also played their part.

At the beginning of 1943 there were nine American and two Australian fighter squadrons in New Guinea. Most were equipped with the Curtiss P-40 Tomahawk, but the American units were beginning to receive the twin-engined Lockheed P-38 Lightning. The first to do so was the 39th Fighter Squadron, 35th Fighter Group, at Port Moresby. Technical problems delayed the Lightning's combat debut, but in its first major engagement with Japanese aircraft on 27 December 1942, the 35th FG claimed fifteen destroyed without loss.

The Lightning's main asset was its long range, which made it very useful as a bomber escort. It could also be useful in other ways, too, as was ably demonstrated on 18 April 1943, when P-38s of the 339th Fighter Squadron, operating at extreme range from Guadalcanal, intercepted and destroyed the aircraft carrying Japan's Admiral Isoroku Yamamoto on a visit to Japanese bases in the Bougainville area. In addition to the Betty bomber carrying Yamamoto, the Lightnings also destroyed two more Bettys and a Zero for the loss of one of their own number.

Two months later, on 16 June 1943, the 339th FS intercepted a large force of Aichi D3A Val dive-bombers and Zeros. One of the squadron's pilots, Lieutenant Murray J. Shubin, destroyed five of them to become the only P-38 'instant ace' of the Pacific war. Shubin went on to gain a total of eleven victories; he survived the war only to be killed in a road accident in 1956.

The top-scoring USAAF ace – and, indeed, the leading scorer of any American pilot – gained all his forty victories while flying the P-38 Lightning. He was Major Richard I. Bong, who became an ace on 5 January 1943 when he shot down his fifth enemy aircraft. He was then flying with the 39th Fighter Squadron of the 35th Fighter Group, but three days later he transferred to the 9th FS of the 49th FG, and it was with this unit that he was to do most of his combat flying. By November 1943 Bong had twenty-one victories, gained in the bitter air fighting over Milne bay and Rabaul, and by the following April his score had risen to twenty-eight. In that month he was sent back

Eugene Valencia's Hellcat fighting team scored major successes in Pacific skies. (US Navy)

to the United States for a long gunnery and instruction course, and on his return to combat later in the year he destroyed a further twelve Japanese aircraft over the Philippines. He got his fortieth victim, a Nakajima Ki.43 Oscar, on 17 December 1944.

In May 1944, Dick Bong was once again sent home. On 6 August, 1945 – the day the atomic bomb fell on Hiroshima – he was killed while flying a Lockheed P-80 Shooting Star, America's first operational jet fighter, at Burbank, California.

The second top-scoring American pilot, Major Thomas P. McGuire, also flew P-38s, rising to fame in the Pacific with the 475th Fighter Group. On 26 December, 1944, McGuire destroyed four Zeros over Los Negros in the Philippines to bring his score to thirty-eight, only two short of Dick Bong's total. On 7 January 1945, he was leading a patrol of four Lightnings on an offensive mission against an enemy airfield at Los Negros when a lone Zero was sighted. The Lightnings dived on the enemy aircraft, which was painted a glossy black. The Zero pilot waited until the Americans were almost in range, then flung his aircraft into a tight left-handed turn that brought him on to the tail of McGuire's wingman, Lieutenant Rittmeyer. A short burst, and Rittmeyer's P-38 went down in flames. The Zero turned easily inside the other three Lightnings, and in an effort to get at him McGuire committed one of flying's deadly sins: he attempted a tight turn at low speed. His P-38 stalled and plunged into the jungle, killing its pilot.

Had he lived, McGuire might have gone on to better Dick Bong's score; but in the battles over the Philippines during those closing months of 1944, two other Lightning pilots were climbing rapidly up the aces' ladder. They were Colonel Gerald R. Johnson and Colonel Charles H. MacDonald, respectively commanding officers of the 49th and 475th Fighter Groups. In October 1944 both groups were operating from Leyte, and there was keen rivalry between the two commanders. On 7 December 1944, MacDonald destroyed three enemy aircraft: Mitsubishi J2M Raiden fighters, known by the Allied code-name of Jack. Still congratulating himself, he took off on a second mission later in the day. Suddenly, Gerry Johnson's voice came over the radio. Probing inland, Johnson had spotted three Nakajima Ki.43 Oscars below him.

'There are three Oscars down below,' Johnson told his wingman. 'Count them – one, two, three.' Almost before the wingman had finished counting, the third Oscar was blazing among the trees.

Gerry Johnson scored twenty-two kills before returning to the United States early in 1945. In October that year, he was flying a B-25 when the aircraft and its crew disappeared without trace in a typhoon. Charles MacDonald finished the war with a score of twenty-seven, fifth among the USAAF aces.

The Supermarine Spitfire also played its part in the Pacific air war, forming a component of the air defences of northern Australia. In 1942, after Japanese carrier aircraft had first attacked Darwin, three squadrons of Spitfires had been shipped to Australia at the urgent request of the Australian government. The three squadrons – Nos 452 and 457 RAAF and No 54 RAF – were formed into No. 1 Fighter Wing, RAAF, under the command of Squadron Leader Clive Caldwell, a highly skilled and experienced fighter pilot who had already gained twenty victories in the Middle East.

The Spitfire variant that was sent to Australia was the 'tropicalised' Mk Vc. In a turning fight, and in the climb, it was outclassed by the Zero fighter, as the pilots of No. 1 Fighter Wing were soon to learn. In February 1943 the Japanese re-opened their bombing offensive against northern Australia, and on the 6th of that month Flight Lieutenant R.W. Foster opened the Spifire's scoreboard in the theatre by shooting down a Mitsubishi Ki.46 Dinah reconnaissance aircraft thirty-five miles off Cape van Diemen. On 2 March Caldwell, now a wing commander, destroyed a Zero and a Nakajima B5N Kate torpedo-bomber, while Squadron Leader A. Thorold-Smith, commanding No. 452 Squadron, also shot down a Zero. The latter pilot was killed on 15 March, when the wing intercepted fourteen Japanese aircraft over Darwin and claimed seven of the enemy for the loss of four Spitfires.

The first major battle occurred on 2 May, when the Japanese sent in a force of eighteen bombers and twenty-seven Zeros from Timor. The Japanese were detected by radar while they were still a long way out to sea – forty-nine minutes' flying time from the coast, in fact – and the wing's thirty-three Spitfires were all airborne within fifteen minutes, climbing hard to meet the raiders. When the Spitfires reached 26,000 feet, however, Caldwell saw that the Japanese formation was still about 4000 feet higher up. To attack it on the climb would have been foolhardy, for the nimble Zeros would have held all the advantages, so Caldwell delayed while his Spitfires got into position above the enemy, with the glare of the sunbehind them. This meant that the Japanese were able to bomb Darwin without meeting any fighter opposition, a fact that later caused a big outcry in the popular press, but Caldwell was quite right in his decision.

Caldwell's Spitfires, unseen against the sun, shadowed the Japanese until they were out over the Timor Sea, then he ordered No 54 Squadron to attack the Zeros while the other two squadrons took on the bombers. The Spitfires went into the attack almost vertically and a furious air battle developed as the Zero pilots, recovering from their surprise, turned to meet the attackers. When the battle was over, five Zeros had been destroyed, but on the debit side five Spitfires had been shot down, two of the pilots being killed, and five more had been compelled to make forced landings after running out of fuel.

In the weeks that followed, however, Caldwell continued to develop the wing's tactics, ignoring the growing storm of criticism about the celebrated Spitfire's lack of success, and one day in July 1943 his efforts paid dividends. On that day, No 54 Squadron was scrambled to intercept a raid on Darwin by forty-seven bombers and their fighter escorts. Only seven Spitfires reached the attackers, but they shot down seven bombers and two Zeros for no loss. Then, on 20 August, three Japanese reconnaissance aircraft appeared over Darwin, heralding another raid; the Spitfires shot down all three of them. The Japanese sent another; it was shot down by Clive Caldwell, his twenty-eighth and last victory. The Japanese sent yet another, this time under strong fighter escort.No 54 Squadron was scrambled to intercept, and the Zeros fell on the Spitfires as they climbed, shooting down three of them. But the Spitfires in turn destroyed one Zero and damaged two more so badly that it is almost certain they came down somewhere in the Timor Sea.

Soon afterwards, the Japanese daylight raids on Darwin ceased and the enemy switched to sporadic night attacks which were to continue, with little effect, until early in 1944. Caldwell's Spitfires had achieved their objective. After the war, Clive Caldwell, who retired as a group captain, became a partner in a cloth importing business in Sydney. He died on 5 August, 1994.

The Spitfire made its appearance in the Burma-India Theatre late in 1943, and played its part in assuring Allied air superiority in the battles that would end with the destruction of the Japanese forces in Burma. Before that, though, it was the Hawker Hurricane that held the line, as Gordon Conway recalled:

On 24 March 1943 we flew our war-weary Hurricane IIBs to Allahabad and returned with new Mk IICs. At last we had Hurricanes with four 20mm cannon and VHF radio! The last few days of March 1943 brought a raid a day, during which 135 and 79 Squadrons intercepted thirty-three bombers at 125,000 feet without fighter escort. The escort had lost their bombers under a cloud layer, and while we had a series of inconclusive scraps at 30,000 feet over base with the fighters, the squadrons down south destroyed eleven of the unescorted bombers.

The fighting in April followed this pattern, starting with more raids against our airfields. Our squadron was involved each time. On the first raid we had visual contact with the fighters and bombers, but we were still climbing when they bombed from 27,000 feet. In the afternoon, on a second scramble, my aircraft was still having its guns checked and was not ready in time for the scramble . . . I later got off alone and joined up with a flight of 67 Squadron at 21,000 feet, just as half a dozen Oscars jumped them. I saw a big red spinner coming up fast behind, called the break and was peppered in my starboard wing and aileron; I can still recall the sur-prisingly loud bang as he hit me. I flicked to starboard as the Oscar dived underneath, hit my attacker in the fuselage and tail and claimed my first 'damaged'.

Our armourers used to clean our cannon throughout the day, taking one aircraft at a time. Mine were being worked on when the wing scrambled against an incoming raid. Despite hasty replacement of covers and panels I was again left behind and climbed up alone under control without making contact with the wing. As I reached 28,000 feet by myself I saw twenty-one enemy fighters coming from my left; they were sweeping at the same height over their bombers, which were in the act of bombing base. The fighters were in two groups, twelve in front and another nine slightly behind and above. I intended a head-on attack as the most suitable under the circumstances, but because of the high closing speed it developed into a classic opposite quarter attack, ending with me in the middle of the two formations, astern of some but with other aircraft visible in my rear-view mirror. I believe that discretion is the better part of valour, so I half-rolled into a tight aileron turn right down to the sea, going so fast that my

bullet-proof windscreen cracked. The Japs must have been as startled as I was, for within a few minutes they were bounced by several of our chaps and hit. We lost one pilot, but in this two-day period claimed six probables and a further eleven damaged. Our new cannons were clearly paying dividends . .
.

The Japanese Air Force was very quiet at the beginning of May 1943, but then launched a series of heavy daylight attacks on the RAF airfields. Gordon Conway, with 136 and 67 Squadrons, was in the thick of the fighting.

On the 22nd they hit us with twenty-five bombers at 20,000 feet, escorted by fifteen plus Oscars. Both 67 and ourselves intercepted; 67 claimed two destroyed, two probables and and one damaged, while we claimed five destroyed, four prob-ables and three damaged . . . I got into the fighter screen and claimed one destroyed and another probable. A week later the Japs repeated this raid, using fifteen plus bombers at 18,000 feet, with twenty plus fighters at 22,000 feet. Joe Edwards was leading, and as he dived on the top fighters, another fighter from a different flight turned on to his tail in front of my sight. I gave this Oscar a long burst of cannon, closing from astern, and he literally fell apart. He seemed to stop in mid-air, his port wheel came down followed by his flaps, and with pieces flying off all around he flicked and spun vertically into the sea, just by the airfield. We claimed five, one and two, while 67 claimed three probables and one damaged. So ended a good month in which our only casualties were two pilots, both of whom escaped with slight injuries . . . In six months we (Nos 136 and 67 Squadrons) had destroyed fourteen enemy aircraft, probably destroyed ten and damaged eighteen for the loss of four pilots. Down south, 79 Squadron had destroyed seventeen enemy aircraft; 135 Squadron had claimed over twenty, but at the great cost of thirteen of their own pilots . . .

Later in the year, Nos 136, 607 and 615 Squadrons converted to Spitfires, and while flying these aircraft Gordon Conway increased his score to seven Japanese aircraft destroyed. Of the twenty-seven pilots who had left England in 1941, fourteen had been killed, six wounded in action and four injured in flying accidents. The latter included Conway himself, injured when he had to bale out of a damaged Hurricane in August 1943. Gordon Conway ended the war as a wing commander and died in January, 2005. His tally of kills placed him among the top-scoring Commonwealth fighter pilots in the Far East; at the head of the list was a New Zealander, Flying Officer Geoffrey Bryson Fisken, who fought over Malaya and Guadalcanal and who claimed eleven victories before being invalided out of the service in December 1943.

In the Pacific, early in 1945, the Allies marshalled their air and naval forces for the final drive towards the Japanese home islands. An essential preliminary was the capture of the island of Okinawa, and it was during this bitter campaign, when the US Navy suffered some of its most grievous losses from Japanese kamikaze suicide attacks, that the Navy's third-ranking fighter ace, Lieutenant Eugene A. Valencia, scored his greatest success. Valencia had already flown one combat tour, destroying seven enemy aircraft, and when he returned to the combat arena with Fighting Squadron VF-9 in the spring of 1945 he had a thorough grasp of Japanese fighting tactics. He found three other pilots who were willing to practise his own tactics to perfection, and turned them into a formidable fighting team. Their names were James E. French, Clinton L. Smith and Harris Mitchell. The team went into action for

Grumman Avengers carrying out a dummy torpedo attack on the aircraft carrier HMS *Formidable* as she passes through the Indian Ocean en route to join the British Pacific Fleet in 1945. She replaced HMS *Illustrious*. (Royal Navy)

the first time over Tokyo in February 1945, and immediately proved its efficiency by shooting down six Japanese aircraft.

On the morning of 17 April, the four pilots set out to strafe Japanese kamikaze bases on Kyushu, but en route they encountered between twenty and thirty Japanese fighters. The Americans had the height advantage, and Valencia put his combat tactics into practice with dramatic results. The four Hellcats dived on the enemy in pairs, in line astern, making one brief firing pass and then climbing to repeat the process. In a matter of minutes, they sent fourteen Japanese aircraft burning into the sea. Valencia himself claimed six, French four, Mitchell three and Smith one. On 4 May, off Okinawa, the team claimed eleven more victories, followed by a further ten on 11 May. When the four pilots ended their combat tour, Valencia had a total of twenty-three kills, French eleven, Mitchell ten and Smith six.

The British Pacific Fleet, designated Task Force 57, with the aircraft carriers HMS *Victorious*, HMS *Implacable*, HMS *Indefatigable* and HMS *Indomitable*, was also present for the final assault on Japan. Its fighter squadrons were equipped with Corsairs, Hellcats, Fireflies and Seafires, and on 1 April 1945, flying a Seafire of No. 894 Squadron, Sub-Lieutenant R. Reynolds – who had already destroyed two German aircraft during operations in the North Atlantic – shot down three Zeros to become an ace. The first Fleet Air Arm pilot to reach the ranks of the aces in the Pacific Theatre alone was Lieutenant D.J. Sheppard, a Corsair pilot with No. 1836 Squadron, who claimed his fifth victim – a Yokosuka D4Y Judy – on 4 May. In July, Lieutenant W.H.I. Atkinson, flying a Hellcat of No. 1844 Squadron, was one of a group of pilots who intercepted a formation of Aichi B7A Grace torpedo-bombers, Japan's newest combat type. He destroyed two confirmed and possibly a third, adding them to at least two aircraft destroyed earlier in the year, and so became the second Fleet Air Arm ace of the Pacific with at least five to his credit.

On 15 August 1945, a week after the dropping of the second atomic bomb on Japan, Admiral Halsey, commanding the US Third Fleet, ordered the cessation of all offensive air operations. When the order reached the task forces off Japan, the first strike of the day was already hitting air bases near Tokyo. The rearmost wave, consisting of the Grumman Avengers of No. 820 Squadron, Fleet Air Arm, from the British carrier HMS *Indefatigable*, was attacked by about fifteen Zeros in the target area. The Japanese

Deadly in an F6F Hellcat, David McCampbell ended the war as the US Navy's top ace. (US Navy)

fighters were immediately overwhelmed by the Avengers' escort, the Seafires of Nos 887 and 894 Squadrons, who shot down eight of the enemy for the loss of one of their own number.

As far as it may be ascertained, this was the last time that fighters met in combat in World War Two.

Select Bibliography

Bekker, Cajus. *The Luftwaffe War Diaries*. Macdonald, 1966
Clostermann, Pierre. *The Big Show*. Chatto & Windus, 1951.
Clostermann, Pierre. *Flames in the Sky*. Chattor & Windus, 1952.
Franks, Norman. *Aircraft versus Aircraft*. Bantam Press, 1986
Galland, Adolf. *The First and the Last*. Methuen, 1955.

The following works by Robert Jackson:
    Aerial Combat: The World's Great Air Battles. Weidenfeld, 1976
    Air Aces of World War II. Crowood press, 2003.
    Air Heroes of World War Two. Arhur Barker, 1980
    Air War at Night: The Battle for the Night Sky Since 1915. Airlife, 2000
    Air War over France, 1939-40. Ian Allan, 1974.
    De Havilland Mosquito. Airlife, 2003.
    Guinness Book of Air Warfare. Guinness Publishing, 1993.
    Hawker Hurricane. Blandford, 1987.
    Hawker Tempest and Sea Fury. Blandford, 1989
    Junkers Ju 87 Stuka. Crowood Press, 2004.
    Mitsubishi Zero. Crowood Press, 2003.
    Mustang: The Operational Record. Airlife, 1992
    Spitfire: The Combat History. Airlife, 1995.
    The RAF in Action from Flanders to the Falklands. Blandford, 1985
    The Red Falcons: the Soviet Air Force in Action, 1919-1969. Clifton Books, 1970
    The World's Great Fighters. Greenwich Editions, 2001

Johnson, Gp Capt J.E. *Wing Leader*. Chatto & Windus, 1952
Knoke, Heinz. *I flew for the Führer*. Evans Brothers, 1953
Mason, Francis K. *The Gloster Gladiator*. Macdonald, 1964
Morgan, Hugh. *Me 262: Stormbird Rising*. Osprey, 1994.
O'Leary, Michael. *United States Naval Fighters of World War II in Action*. Blandford Press, 1980
Toliver, Raymond F and Constable, Trevor J. *Fighter Aces of the Luftwaffe*. Schiffer, 1996
Williamson, Gordon. *Aces of the Reich*. Arms and Armour Press, 1989.

Index

AIR BASES

AIR UNITS

American

Australian